THE
LANGUAGE
OF
FAITH

THE
LANGUAGE
OF
FAITH

**An Introduction to the Semantic Dilemma
of the Early Church**

Samuel Laeuchli

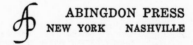

ABINGDON PRESS
NEW YORK   NASHVILLE

THE LANGUAGE OF FAITH

Copyright © 1962 by Abingdon Press

Library of Congress Catalog Card Number: 62-8107

SET UP, PRINTED, AND BOUND BY THE
PARTHENON   PRESS,   AT   NASHVILLE,
TENNESSEE, UNITED STATES OF AMERICA

To

JOHN CLARK JORDAN

In Gratitude

IN MEMORIAM PATRIS MEI

————

Preface

To write history is to write a dialogue. When we lose courage to debate with the scanty evidence of the past, this very evidence dies. As there is no present without the past, there can be no description of the past apart from the joy and despair of the present. But in such a dialogue one partner is the historian himself, embedded in the thought patterns of his age. The past becomes alive when the present lives; but by bringing the evidence to life, history ceases to deal merely with evidence.

The following essay on the problems of Christian language in the second century is such a dialogue. It arose out of fascinating discussions between the biblical, historical, and systematic fields here at Garrett Institute. There has been such a receptivity for patristic contributions that I would hope that this presentation might be of some significance to the contemporary discussion concerning "Christian language."

The inquirer into the early centuries of Christian history is grateful for all stimulation he receives from his colleagues. Professor Reginald Fuller of Seabury Western Episcopal Seminary has gone carefully through the manuscript and taken out as many German idioms as he could find. For this, I am deeply indebted to him. I am equally grateful to my wife, who has helped me faithfully during the writing of this manuscript. And a final word of thanks is due the graduate students of our institution who, by their intensive

7

participation in seminars, have contributed many an insight into the formulation of difficult problems.

SAMUEL LAEUCHLI

Evanston
on the day of the
Creator Spiritus
1961

Contents

CONTENTS

CONTENTS

Introduction

In contemporary theology as well as in philosophy, the problems of language are widely discussed. The novice in either field is sometimes given the impression that this is a completely modern issue, and that, for the first time in history, language is "really" analyzed. As for the method by which this is done, especially in philosophy, such a claim may be correct; but actually the problem of Christian language is as old as the Christian church itself. It was phrased differently. The tools in the struggle were not those of today. And the people who fought on the different sides cannot be identified, of course, with this or that modern position, such as Wittgenstein or Rudolf Bultmann. But the problem existed.

For example, in an attack against the Gnostic use of biblical language, Irenaeus of Lyons compared the Gnostic's use of words to the mosaic of a skillful artist which is disassembled by someone else and then rearranged; thus the gems that made the first image now represent something quite different although they are the same gems (*Adversus Haereses* I.8.1). This is nothing more than a recognition of the cardinal problem in Christian language; Irenaeus realizes that there can be two different languages with the same words. The conflict between him and the Gnostics deals with the question of how one can, or must, set these words in relation to one another in order to have Christian speech. The struggle between Irenaeus and Gnosticism is the fight for a correct mosaic of Christian language. The mosaic is the whole.

What makes the whole? We are at once no longer watching a contest about words but rather a contest about the essence of Christian faith, about the place of ethics and knowledge, about tradition and hierarchy, about the church and the world. The search for the whole is the search for the basic tenor in communication since the whole, the Christ, is constantly preached and received. The problem of Christian language is the first question of Christian faith: "What do you think about Christ?"

The second century provides us with an excellent field in which to study the problems because of the fermenting atmosphere within and without Christian faith and because of the sharp fronts established by the Gnostic and the anti-Pauline types of Christianity. This does not mean that we find Hegelian dialectic here, since one often finds Gnostics where one does not expect them and Christian substance where there should be heresy. This very fact that we have yet no neat border between church and heresy makes a study of this century in turmoil so fruitful. In the disturbing antitheses between conflicting movements, the Christians of this post-Apostolic period seek to understand what it means to believe in Christ. Looking into the second century, we try to understand the forces that arranged the gems of Christian speech and the products of these forces, the mosaics of language as they appear in early Christian documents.

Chapter 1

Gnostic Language

   In front of me lies the *Gospel of Thomas,* that strange mixture of canonical, semicanonical, and apocryphal sayings of Jesus. The baffling document demonstrates vividly the entangled situation of Christianity in the second century. Some of these sayings of Jesus are close paraphrases from the Synoptic Gospels (26). Some are quotations with additions which twist or augment the Synoptic meaning: "Give the things of Caesar to Caesar, give the things of God to God, and give me what is mine" (100). In others, however, strange Gnostic sayings take their turn with the Synoptic allusions: "Whoever has known the world has found a corpse, and whoever has found a corpse, of him the world is not worthy" (56). Side by side with parables of the Kingdom (57, 76) stand startling pantheistic (77) and dualistic (114) expressions.

What makes a statement Gnostic and what prevents it from being Gnostic? Can it be a question of a word used? There are some striking concepts like the Valentinian emanation (προβολή) and "the non-being God" in the negative theology of Basilides which point immediately toward a Gnostic system. Yet not only is the number of such instances exceedingly limited or applicable only to a small sector of Gnostic literature, but this approach may be quite misleading. "Emanation" like "consubstantial" (ὁμοούσιος) will appear in the orthodox camp of the fourth century. Furthermore, the Gnostic terminology, such as "gnosis," "cosmos," "aeon," "pleroma," can be found in various books of the New Testament. The terminology of the *Gospel of Thomas* does not differ radically from the terminology of the Synoptic Gospels. If terminology alone had to

15

furnish the criterion between Gnostic and biblical material, we would be confronted with a most chaotic situation.

It is not the concept itself which can furnish the answer but only the relation in which it stands to other concepts. A chain of pivotal words determines the core of thought. Which chain makes a certain type of language Gnostic? This is the topic of our first chapter. We try to give the answer by a theological investigation of the concepts,[1] examining not only of what the chain consists but, even more, what it lacks. Because, however, we are dealing with linguistic combinations and not merely with isolated terms and phrases, there will always be borderline cases, inside and outside the church, which defy classification. Systematic analysis is no more than an introductory tool by which we approach the complex forces of history.

"Gnosticism" has become one of the chameleonlike terms which are so dear to historical scholarship. The scholar can mold it to his liking. The vagueness and lack of precision in the present use of this concept has a double root. First, the complex nature of the movement in its manifold interlacement with the syncretistic world of the Near East asks for ambiguity in retrospect; to elucidate a syncretistic movement is one of the most difficult historical undertakings. The viewer's approach determines in advance the outcome of his research. Second, because every historical generalization is prone to break down at the borders of the period in question, the margins can be narrowed or stretched *ad libitum*. It is a natural tendency to expand constantly the meaning of a term, precisely because one must—or can—always include one more border case and then another. However, the wider the span is drawn, the more blurred will the actual content of the concept become. "Middle Ages" and "Renaissance" are two sad examples of ultimately meaningless generalizations.[2]

Since the same trend toward all-embracing generalization has affected the use of the term "Gnosticism," we try to counterbalance

[1] Christian syntax often does not differ from non-Christian syntax (Betty I. Knott, *Christian "Special Language" in the Inscriptions*, Vigiliae Christianae, 10 [1956] p. 79), although the content obviously does.

[2] Compare, for instance, among the definitions of "Hellenism" that of Edwyn Bevan (*Hellenism and Christianity* [London: G. Allen & Unwin Ltd., 1921], p. 15), who sees in it the age of "rationalism," and that of Arnold J. Toynbee (*Greek Civilization and Character* [London and Toronto: J. M. Dent & Sons Ltd.,

the trend by limiting it here to the *second-century movement* within, at the borders of, and outside the church. "Gnosticism" is thus the structure of thought of which the church becomes seriously aware in the first half of the second century and by which Christianity is profoundly influenced, positively or negatively, in its formulation of church, canon, and theology. We do not at all deny pre-Christian and outer-Christian existence of either the movement or its thought forms, from the Dead Sea Scrolls to the Mandaeans.[3] However, we want to examine the field at the moment of the greatest conflict. In the controversy between "Church" and "Gnosis," therefore, such

---

1924 and New York: E. P. Dutton & Co., 1924], pp. xi-xiv), who designates with "Hellenism" the whole of Hellenic civilization. Concerning the term "Middle Ages," see the polemic of Karl Heussi (*Kompendium der Kirchengeschichte* [Tübingen, 1937], p. 129).

[3] R. P. Casey ("Gnosis, Gnosticism, and the New Testament" in *The Background of the New Testament and Its Eschatology,* ed. by William D. Davies and David Daube [Cambridge University Press, 1956], p. 79) is quite right, the terminology about Gnosticism is about "to lose any precise meaning." The most limited definition of Gnosticism is given by Henry Longueville Mansel (*The Gnostic Heresies of the First and Second Centuries,* ed. by J. B. Lightfoot [London; J. Murray, 1875]), and again by H. J. Schoeps (*Urkiche, Judenchristentum, Gnosis* [Tübingen, 1956]) who lists his opponents on page 1. The broadest concept is that of Hans Jonas (*Gnosis und spätantiker Geist,* Göttingen, Vol. I, 2nd ed., 1954; Vol. II, 1954) who sees Gnosis in the large scope of late antiquity, comprising, in his definition, Philo as well as Mandaean and Manichaean worlds. The conflict exhibits the breakdown of all periodic systematization. Cullmann is correct in stating that we are often confronted with "a fight about words" (*Die Christologie des Neuen Testamentes* [Tübingen, 1958], p. 38). A creative distinction is made by R. McL. Wilson (*The Gnostic Problem* [London: A. R. Mowbray & Co. Ltd., 1958], p. 261) when he distinguishes a wide and a limited sense of "Gnosticism" or even better ("Gnostic Origins," *Vig. Christ.,* 9 [1955]) "Gnosis" and "Pre-Gnosis." Since we are interested in the "point of contact" between Christian and Gnostic forces rather than in a historical account we cannot deal with the historical question as to whether originally there is in Gnosticism Jewish apocalypticism which has gone bankrupt (Robert M. Grant, *Gnosticism and Early Christianity* [New York: Columbia University Press, 1959]) or Diaspora Judaism in syncretistic excess (Wilson, *op. cit.,* pp. 172 ff.), whether one should stress originally the intellectual elements (Harnack, *Dogmengeschichte* [Tübingen, 1931], Vol. I, p. 259), or the concerns of the "little folks" (Carl H. Kraeling, *Anthropos and Son of Man* [New York: Columbia University Press, 1927], p. 4), and whether or not we are confronted with a pre-Christian "World Religion" (Gilles Quispel, *Gnosis als Weltreligion* [Zürich, 1951]). That we have pre-Christian "Gnostic elements" in the Qumran community is clear (Oscar Cullmann, "Die neuentdeckten Qumrantexte und das

a limitation focuses the discussion on the dynamics behind the formation of Christian theology.

In our first step we seek for the constructive contributions of Gnostic speech. Before we distinguish we inquire into its merit. Then we shall proceed to sift the theological esssence of Gnostic language and to differentiate it from biblical speech. Finally, we have to deal with the most crucial item raised by the Gnostic shakeup: the canon.

THE CHALLENGE OF GNOSTIC LANGUAGE

The Necessity of the Exegetical Encounter

Every epoch speaks a language of its own. This is not only true of the obvious differentiations, such as Middle English, Elizabethan English, Modern English, but also of relatively short historical periods. The German of Luther, of Goethe, of the Romantic Age, of the turn of the century, of today, reveals a constant fluctuation. The same is true even of different groups and individuals within one era. The theologians of contemporary France write a different language from that of the scientists in the Institut Pasteur, and they in turn a different one from the existentialists around Boulevard St. Germain; and all of these use a language quite different from the Parisian underworld with its mysterious idiom. From epoch to epoch, and from one group to another, the frame of speech alters, sometimes so delicately that only retrospective analysis becomes aware of it.

Gnosticism speaks its own language. So does the Apostolic church. So will the Cappadocian theologian. It is less than probable that an average believer of the second century would have any idea of what Gregory of Nazianzus is talking in his anti-Arian orations, not only from the standpoint of issues involved but even from the aspect of idiomatic expression. Moreover, there is not merely *one* type of Gnostic language. The complexity of Gnosticism lies partly in the chaotic diversity of its speech. To read consecutively *Basilides,* the

Judenchristentum der Pseudoklementinen," in *Theologische Studien für Rudolf Bultmann* [Berlin, 1954], pp. 35 ff.). Instead of trying desperately to find one or another cause for the rise of Gnosticism it may seem wisest to speak simply about "spheres of influences" which contributed to the rise of this syncretistic movement (W. C. Van Unnik, *Newly Discovered Gnostic Writings* [Naperville: Allenson, 1960], p. 35).

Evangelium Veritatis, the *Epistle to Flora* and the *Naassene Fragments* is like entering four different worlds. Perhaps it would be altogether wiser to speak of "Gnostic movements" instead of "Gnosticism." Only in its distinction from biblical speech shall we try to establish something like a "Gnostic speech" in general.

Because every epoch speaks its own idiom, there can never be a harmonious confluence of two languages. Yet such a confluence takes place whenever Christian faith touches any culture. Without the presence of biblical speech, there is no Christian faith. When, therefore, biblical language in any form infiltrates an epoch, even only at the periphery, there is a conflict. The moment that a word ("the Savior"), a statement ("we believe in God"), or a quotation ("in the beginning was the Word") is repeated, there is a tension between the meaning in its original frame and the new frame into which it is inserted. This conflict lies at the heart of Christian exegesis. An interpreter can never speak exactly the language of the Bible because he also speaks the language of his environment, his epoch. Even when we maintain the urgent necessity to take the biblical word as seriously as possible, there has never been—and never will be—a moment when the conflict between the word of the Christ and the word about the Christ ceases to exist.

Gnosticism demonstrates that this exegetical conflict is not merely a matter of translation or of philology. A colloquium in Cambridge does not—or at least, no longer in every case—take place in Latin or Greek; any confrontation with the ancient world will therefore be handicapped by a process of translation. That certain terms are often left in the original only emphasizes the difficulties. Yet we are confronted with much more than a linguistic dilemma. Many Gnostics spoke Greek that was no more than a century older than the Greek used in the oldest parts of the New Testament. But it was a Greek with other relations, a language full of different idioms. The same words have other implications; phrases stand in another light. That we have to deal with Latin, Greek, and Coptic texts is not the greatest problem. The meanings of the concepts have shifted, beginning with the most important one— God the Father.

The Gnostics did not escape this conflict, but entered into it. This is their great contribution to Christian exegesis. Here is a

New Testament term: ἁμαρτάνω, "to sin." In the Pauline and
Johannine epistles it maintains a vital place concerning the relation of man to salvation.[4] The second-century Basilides speaks
to people who are concerned with the question of suffering and
who believe in a just God, because martyrdom and justice are live
issues among the Christians of the Roman Empire. How can a
righteous God let an innocent man suffer? Are we not giving up
his justice by assuming that he does so? Basilides "will say anything rather than call Providence evil" (Clement of Alexandria
Stromateis IV.82.2); suffering therefore must be the result of sin.
But how about martyrdom? Because the goodness of God must be
maintained, Basilides postulates unconscious or hidden transgres-
sions (λανθάνοντες πταίσμασιν) as reasons for what appears only
to us as innocent suffering (*Ibid.* IV.81.1). Sin, suffering, and
justice belong together. What we are facing here is a crucial process
into which Basilides dares to enter. He attempts to explain a
difficult biblical term to his time. The biblical concept is put between two flaming words of the present; it is no academic play
with ideas to demand an answer concerning the righteousness of
a "good God" in the torments of persecution! This willingness to
approach the exegetical task even under the most difficult cir-
cumstances, the daring encounter of idioms and languages, makes
the Gnostic quest of vital importance. In the striking formulation
of a Coptic text, Gnosticism "discusses the words" of Christ.[5]
The Naassene fragment explains the Pauline phrases of I Cor. 2:
13-14 and II Cor. 12:24 by bringing them into contact with its
cosmological frame (Hippolytus *Refutatio omnium haeresium*
VII.25-26). *Megale Apophasis* struggles with passages from Isaiah
(Hipp. *Ref.* VI.10.1-2). The *Evangelium Veritatis* is one extensive
commentary on the gospel. The *Epistle to Flora* is a continuous at-

[4] Matt. 18:15; Luke 15:18; Rom. 5:12; John 15:22. Although the synoptics
do not use the term frequently, the issue is vital for the proclamation of Jesus
cf. Rengsdorff in *ThWNT* (*Theologisches Wörterbuch zum Neuen Testament*
[Stuttgart: 1933], I, 305).
[5] *Evangelium Mariae* 9.23 (together with *Apocryphon Johannis* and *Sophia
Jesu Christi* in the edition of Walter C. Till, *Die Gnostischen Schriften des
Koptischen Papyrus Beroliniensis 8502*, TU 60 [Berlin: 1955]). In all Coptic
quotations I quote only the first line of the translation which, in practically
every case, pertains to several lines of the Coptic original.

tempt to grapple with the Old Testament. The Gnostic knows quite well that the exegetical discussion must be conducted in the language of the period and against the background of other thought forms. Biblical words and sentences cannot simply be repeated; they must be understood and explained. To understand and to explain, theology needs the terms of its time if it is to speak at all to its contemporaries. But by using these terms the conflict is here.

Indeed, the conflict is there in the Gnostic texts. The questionable results of this mixture of languages need not occupy us at this moment—that "sin" in the biblical sense and "sins" in the Basilidian sense are actually two different words. The process has gotten under way. We shall have to inquire later at what stages the mixture annuls Christian faith. The conflict lies wide open, and the church should be extremely grateful for such an awakening demonstration of its dilemma.

The Language of Revelation

Even in their wildest speculations the Gnostics seek some sort of continuity of language with the biblical texts. Out of the clear blue falls a quotation from the Old or New Testament. In the midst of a syncretistic comparison, the Ophite Justin throws in some verses of Genesis (Hipp. *Ref.* V.26.36-37). The *Excerpts from Theodotus* bring in biblical phrases in their presentation of Gnostic secrets (for instance *Excerpta ex Theodoto* 31.3; 35.1; 41.3). In the *Evangelium Veritatis* New Testament allusions are frequent: the shepherd with the ninety-nine sheep, the two-edged sword, "the Father is in them, and they are in the Father" (31.35; 26.2; 42.26). The modern observer may feel that the Gnostic theosophist would have been better off by presenting an idea without a biblical "proof text," often painfully forced. However, this desire to establish a certain relation of speech to the world of the New Testament is by no means a peripheral concern. The Gnostic aims at a continuity which points from the outset to the problem of the canon. There is no better documentation for the fact that the quest for a canon was lurking behind the second-century Christian faith than the extreme documents of Gnosticism where eccentric syncretistic material is knotted—if at all possible—to some biblical text.

The urgency of this quest for continuity can be illuminated from another angle. The Gnostics feel the lack of continuity to such a degree that they work with all their poetic capacities to establish esoteric ties.[6] What else is this esoteric desire than the admission of a void? What the Gnostics lack is the linguistic tie to the epoch of revelation, a revelation which means so much in their systems. Hence their arduous quest for unique traditions. If indeed the apocryphal sayings and tales concerning the apostolic period are authentic secret transmissions, then they represent part of the authentic language of faith, and the apparent lack of such a language in the Gnostic books is covered. When Gnosticism fights for its construct of an esoteric tradition, it fights at the same time for a validation of its language. And in doing so it admits the necessity of a continuity of Christian speech with the speech of the Bible. The endeavor to establish an esoteric tradition is an early and powerful witness to the awareness that Christian faith cannot express itself as Christian faith unless it makes use of the language of the gospel.

The Gnostics know even more than this. The claim of an esoteric language is the claim of a *given language*. The Gnostics understand this "given quality" in Christian speech considerably more clearly than many non-Gnostic writers of their age. Because of their emphasis on revelation and redemption, certain Gnostics realize the pertinent fact that Christian language is always a language understood only in faith. The *Evangelium Veritatis* is an exceptional witness for this realization. Because "the Gospel is a Revelation of Hope" (17.2-3), the speech of this gospel is speech which only one who stands within this revelation actually grasps. If to be a Christian is "to have received the grace of knowing . . . through the power of the Word," as the opening of the gospel declares, then words of revelation are not merely what they appear to be. The speech of a Christian is seen in analogy to the perfect book with its "characters belonging to Truth, pronounced only as they are known" (23.9-10). In this analogy, Valentinian Gnosticism has profoundly understood one aspect of the problem of Christian language. This language of faith has a reference all its own. One can only grasp its real meaning in faith. Christian language

---

[6] A revival of the Gnostic esoteric claim from a modern Gnostic viewpoint in R. Spörri, *Vom Geiste des Urchistentums* (Basel: 1941).

exists within these two: revelation and the individual's existence in faith. "How should a person hearken if his name has not been called?" [7]

The Creative Element in Gnostic Language

One of the striking features which astonishes the beginner in reading a Gnostic text is the richness of its language. There streams forth a wealth of concepts, idioms, and phrases, frustratingly confusing at first sight. The Gnostic seeks for the largest possible range of expression. Few periods in Christian theology have exhibited a similar scope of speech.

One of the cardinal concerns in Gnostic communication is the continuous expression of a negative theology, the negative pronouncement of God's essence in a dualistic world. So the Gnostic avails himself of as large a negative vocabulary as he can grasp—"unpronounceable," "non-existent," "infinite," with countless other synonyms—always applying the negative particle to new words.[8] In his attempt to reformulate that which can only be expressed by negation he produces striking formulations: the "unpronounceable mystery," the "unborn spirit," the "unshapen logos." [9] One feels how every author strives to contribute his own metaphor to the already abundant language pointing toward the mystery.

[7] *Apocryphon Johannis* 64.17. Only with great difficulty can the great things of Gnostic faith be revealed to others unless they belong to the special pneumatic genus. Also 75.19 and 76.10 in which *Apocr. Joh.* expresses the concern that only the Gnostic may understand Gnostic language lest it be defiled.

[8] ἄρρητος *Pistis Sophia* 95.221; *Myst. Log.* 45.107; *Unknown Coptic Work* 12.250. (All three works in the edition of Walter C. Till, *Koptisch-Gnostische Schriften* [Berlin: 1955] GCS, Vol. 45, Hipp. *Ref.* VII, 25.4, V. 8.5; ἀνούσιος Hipp. *Ref.* VII.21.1; ἀπέραντος *Sophia Jesu Christi* 85.9; *Pist. Soph.* 95.220; *Myst. Log.* 46.111); *Unknown Coptic Work* 6.233; Hipp. *Ref.* VI.12.3. The "unknown God" of Marcion (Tertullian *Adversus Marcionem* V.16); the symptomatic sets of negative attributes in "Simon" (ἀγέννητος, ἀπαράλλακτος, ἀπέραντος, Hipp. *Ref.* VI.12.3), Basilides (ἀναισθήτως, ἀβούλως, ἀπροαιρέτως, ἀπέραντος, ἀνεπιθυμήτως, VII.21.1 ff.) and *Hermes Trismegistus* (ἀπέραντος, ἀτελής, ἄναρχος IV.8.6). The negation in Hermetic literature is discussed best in R. P. Festugière, "Le dieu inconnu," *La Révélation d' Hermès Trismégiste* (Paris: 1950-1954), IV, 1-78, 303. For the relation between Hermetic and Gnostic literature see Jean Doresse, *Les livres secrets des Gnostiques d' Égypte* (Paris: 1958), quoted henceforth in the augmented English edition, *The Secret Books of the Egyptian Gnostics* (New York: Viking Press, 1960), pp. 275 ff.

[9] Hipp. *Ref.* V.8.7; 7.33; *Exc. ex Theod.* 45.1; *Paraphrase of Shem* (Doresse, *op. cit.,* p. 147).

23

THE LANGUAGE OF FAITH

The central language evolving around the specific redemptive movement in Gnostic religion is one of its attractive qualities. The famous formulation of the Gnostic theme for instance

> Who we were and what we have become,
> where we were and where we were thrown,
> whither we hasten, from what we are redeemed,
> what birth is, what rebirth.
> —*Exc. ex Theod.* 78.2

shows a capacity to address man in a mixture of mystery and intellect which will speak to him. The same can be said about the manifold pattern by which the Gnostic can express this vertical dimension, γνῶσις, ἐπίγνωσις, θεωγνωμία,[10] all meaning one and the same thing, the salvatory knowledge. With captivating flair, this religious terminology describes emanation (προβάλλειν, συζυγία, καταβολή) and its counterparts, ascent and purification ("noetic apprehension").[11]

The attraction of this refined Gnostic terminology lies partly in its subtlety when manifested in philosophic dimension. This especially holds true for Basilides, who designs an intriguing cos-

---

[10] One of the most famous passages on γνῶσις is in the Naassene Hymn (Hipp. *Ref.* V.10). A typical reference from now on in *Evang. Ver.* 23.21. Interesting are the passages in *Evangelium Matthiae* (in Clem. Alex. *Strom.* II.45.4 and III.26.3; Hennecke-Schneemelcher, *Neutestamentliche Apokryphen* [Tübingen: 1959], I, 224). ἐπίγνωσις in Iren. *Adv. Haer.* I.21.4; πρόγνωσις in *Apocr. Joh.* 28.19; θεωγνωμία in *Acts of Thomas* 2; and παναγνῶσις in *Unknown Copt. Work* 1.228.

[11] προβολή *Exc. ex Theod.* 67.1, 21.1, Iren. *Adv. Haer.* I.1.2 ff.; *Pist. Soph.* 2.2; *Log. Myst.* 5.47. προβάλλω *Adv. Haer.* I.1 ff.; *Unknown Copt. Work* 21.265; *Pist. Soph.* 29.43. συμπροβάλλομαι *Adv. Haer.* I.2.6 ἀποβάλλω *Exc. ex Theod.* 61.7. ἐπιπροβάλλω Hipp. *Ref.* VI.31.5. μεταβάλλω-μεταβολή *Adv. Haer.* I.4.5; Hipp. *Ref.* V.8.24 *Pist. Soph.* 128.326, Heracleon *Fragment* 5 (Heracleon's fragments are numbered according to Walter Völker, *Quellen zur Geschichte der christlichen Gnosis* [Tübingen: 1932], pp. 63 ff.) προήλατο designates the movement of Sophia, Iren. *Adv. Haer.* I.2.2; *Pist. Soph.* 10.17. The parallel term is καταβολή *Evang. Ver.* 20.1; Hipp. *Ref.* VII.22.8 (Basilides); τὸ καταβληθέν 21.5. Another group is represented by συζυγία Iren. *Adv. Haer.* I.1.1; σύζυγος Hipp. *Ref.* V.26.14; *Pist. Soph.* 93.214; and ἰσόζυγος Hipp. *Ref.* VI.36.4. Typical in this respect is also the language about σπέρμα *Apocr. Joh.* 76.4; *Evang. Ver.* 43.14; *Pist. Soph.* 70.154; σπορά Stobaeus *Herm.* XXIII.64; and σπείρω Herm. Trism. I.29; *Evang. Evae* in Epiphanius *Panarion* XXVI.3.1. Cf. also κατάληψις νοητική Clem. Alex *Strom.* II.3.10; and ἀποκάθαρσις Hipp. *Ref.* VII.22.7; *Evang. Ver.* 24.6; and the terminology of "ascending" in *Evang. Ver.* 41.27; 42.2; 21.11.

mogony second only to a few philosophical systems in the whole history of the human quest. According to the Hippolytan account, this thinker creates a specific vocabulary as he unveils his thought. At the beginning there is absolute nothingness, the "non-being God" (οὐκ ὢν θεός). Creation unfolds (καταβάλλω) from "non-being sperma" out of a "non-being cosmos." What unfolds are sonships (υἱότης), a first, a second, and a third, and the two celestial cosmoi: the Ogdoad and the sublunary Hebdomad. Let me give one example of the subtle linguistic ability in this religious philosophy:

Once there was nothing; yet this "nothing" was in no way part of that which was; but to say it undisguisedly and candidly, without any quibbling, there was not one single thing at all; when I say: there "was" [once nothing], I do not say that it "was"; I only want to point toward what I want to show, namely that there was really nothing.[12]

For any thinking and searching mind of antiquity this language, a refined tool in the service of a keen mind, will have some fascination.

An authentic fragment of a letter by Valentinus himself exhibits his imaginative ability. When the angels created man they suddenly became afraid of him "when he spoke greater things than you would expect from creation, because invisibly was laid into him a sperm from the higher world." To illustrate this Valentinus uses an analogy. A work created by the mortal can become frightening to the very man who made it: "And the angels became terrified and hid their work" (Hipp. *Ref.* VII.20.2). What interests us is not the speculative basis of the comparison which lies in a cosmic relation between "created man" and the "primeval man," but the striking

[12] Hipp. *Ref.* VII.20.2. With G. Quispel ("L'Homme Gnostique," [Eranos: 1948], pp. 89-139) and against H. Stähelin (*Die gnostischen Quellen Hippolyts* [Leipzig: 1890]) and W. Bousset (*Hauptprobleme der Gnosis* [Göttingen, 1901], p. 330) we regard the report of Hippolytus about Basilides as at least basically authentic. As Quispel has convincingly argued, in the relationship between gnosis, mysticism, and negative theology lie the originality and unity of this system. The same position already in J. A. Hort, art. "Basilides," in *Dictionary of Christian Biography* (London: J. Murray, 1877), I, 268 ff. and again in Robert M. Grant, "Gnostic Origins and the Basilidians of Irenaeus," *Vig. Christ.*, 13 [1959], p. 121.

way of meeting an issue in Christian theology. Why does the plasma rebel against its creators? In this nuclear age the actuality of the Valentinian picture is probably better understood than ever before: man may shudder at his own product. Here is a theological argument in an impressive form, plastic and yet profound, appealing and yet refined in language.

The culmination of this creativity in later Gnosticism explains its downfall. In its syncretistic extreme it becomes eccentric. The Chenoboskion MSS add inexhaustible material for mythological syncretism. Babel and Aphrodite are parallels in the Baruch-Fragment; Eloeim, the Hebrew God, one of the two highest principles beside Edem, stands beside Leda and the Swan.[13] The Naassenes use Christ together with Penelope and Hermes and the Fire-God Esaldaios (Hipp. *Ref.* V.30-33). We find Naas and Bel (Hipp. *Ref.* V.26 ff.), Achamoth and Abraxas (Ir. *Adv. Haer.* I.5 ff.), and of course Osiris (Hipp. *Ref.* V.9.8). The *Paraphrase of Shem* cannot make up its mind whether it means Seth, Melchizedek, or Shem.[14] All this is utterly unchristian. But for all its eccentricity this syncretistic foolishness is a poetic utterance of a new faith. It reveals life and courage. More than that, it reveals imagination and adventure. How boring theological literature can become! Here it gushes in bizarre eccentricity. Soon, however, it begins to play. The secret, the absurd, the mythological take over and the Chenoboskion texts prove the rapid degeneration of the syncretistic mythology.

However, the very eccentric Ophite sect, mentioned in the preceding paragraph for its syncretistic craze, has preserved for us another pertinent quality of Gnostic language. Hippolytus reproduces a famous Gnostic hymn, the "Psalm of the Soul." After the

[13] Hipp. *Ref.* V.26.20; and 26.28; 26.35. Jaldabaoth as Saturnus in Origen *Contra Celsum* VI.31 (cf. Bousset, *op. cit.*, pp. 351 ff.). Πάνδημος 'Αφροδίτη and κοινωνία μυστική are on the same level in Clem. Alex. *Strom.* III.4.27! Gnostic gods, affirms *Apocr. Joh.*, "have also other names" (40.19), "double names" (41.12). Noriah and Noah in Epiph. *Pan.* XXVI.1. Already *Arist.* 16 postulated that Zeus and Dis are other names for the Jewish creator God. All these utterances belong to the mythological type of Gnosticism which F. C. Burkitt (*The Church and Gnosis* [Cambridge: The University Press, 1932], p. 40) has distinguished from the philosophical type. Coptic texts like *Apocr. Joh.*, with their combination of mythical syncretism and a theistic philsophy of negation, show how close the two really are.

[14] Doresse, *op. cit.*, p. 155.

description of the triad—firstborn spirit, chaos, soul—the psalm sings of the fall of soul in tragic verses:

> At times, she views light as one who rules;
> at times, she weeps, thrown into misery;
> at times, she is bewailed and joyous;
> at times, she bewails and is judged;
> at times, she is judged and dies.

This is the story of man, sung in heavy cycles, with the agony of despair expressed in rhythmic enhancement. One can feel with the poet both judgment and death. Yet this is only the first part of the Gnostic preaching. The Savior enters into the drama and petitions God to let him begin the redemptive act:

> Send me, Father!
> Holding the seals I will descend,
> through all the aeons will I wander,
> showing the shape of the Gods,
> the hidden way to the holy—
> —they call it Gnosis—I will hand down.
> —*Hipp. Ref.* V. 10.2

What happened in the psalms of the Old Testament and the hymns of Luke and of Revelation touches here the Gnostic sect. Faith becomes hymnody; theology turns into music; the drama of redemption is clothed in poetic beauty. The actual text of Hippolytus is in an abominable condition, yet through all distortions and translations the original imagination still shines through.

There exists a similar hymn by Valentinus, again transmitted by Hippolytus.

> The whole of the ether I see adorned with Spirit,
> As carried by Spirit I perceive the All,
> Flesh clings to the Soul
> Soul is borne by Air,
> Air hangs to ether,
> From the depth fruits are lifted up,
> From the womb a child is raised.
> —Hipp. *Ref.* V.36.7

This is again artistic manifestation of theology. The message of faith melts into poetry, not losing its content thereby but, rather, converting it into a veiled artistic unit. Imagination has converted the language of theology into theological poetry.

The poetic creativity in Gnostic theology could have a double impact upon the life of the community. Although the first has never been realized, one text at least points in this direction. In the Old Testament the theologian is a prophet and the prophet is a poet: Hosea, Jeremiah, the Second Isaiah. In the last book of the New Testament, the prophetic-poetic unity in theology springs forth once more with fabulous imaginative abundance. Creative language may become, therefore, the transmitter of a prophetic claim. "As indelible spirit I greet the indelible ones. I bring you knowledge of unspeakable and unpronounceable and supercelestial mysteries." (Epiph. *Pan.* XXXI.5.1) In this rare instance, the poetic language of Gnosticism makes a prophetic claim. It is the most important in that it may represent an archaic Gnostic fragment.[15] The Gnostic world was not born to achieve this. But here is one indication that Montanism is not the only place to look for prophetic language in the second century.

In a less technical way, the Gnostic language does have a prophetic dimension. The Gnostic theologian proclaims a special revelation, bringing an alien world to a lost humanity. The claim he makes is that of a unique truth revealed to the elect *hic et nunc,* in an historical uniqueness. The prophetic force in Paul's language of revelation reappears in the great Gnostic theologians of the second century. But the eschatological, the ethical, and the communal aspect of the prophetic address have become completely neglected for the sake of the first and last, the proclamation of gnosis. The Gnostic knows that the language of revelation is what will later be called *verbum alienum.* Because of the inherent dualism, the kerygma of this alien word can never reach prophetic concreteness.

A second aspect of the creativity in Christian theological language lies in the realm of the liturgy. Certain Gnostic groups make im-

---

[15] Karl Holl (Epiphanius, *Panarion I* [GCS, Vol. 25], [Leipzig: 1915], p. 390) puts this fragment beside the poem in Hipp. *Ref.* VI.36.7 and sees in the monistic denominator of both an indication for old Valentinian theology.

portant attempts in this direction. The *Acts of Thomas* preserves a number of liturgical hymns, one of which is the following:

> Come, thou holy name of the Christ that is above every name.
> Come, thou power of the Most High, and the compassion that is perfect.
> Come, charisma of the Most High.
> Come, compassionate mother.
> Come, communion of the male.
> Come, she that revealeth the hidden mysteries.
> Come, mother of the seven houses, that thy rest may be in the eighth house.
> Come, elder of the five members, mind, thought, reflection, consideration, reason; communicate with these young men.
> Come, holy Spirit, and cleanse their veins and their heart, and give them the added seal,
> in the name of the Father and Son and Holy Ghost.[16]

The *Gospel of Truth* has a hymnic passage of which Van Unnik remarks justly that it is the work of a skilled orator.[17] It is again theology of the Word in rhythmic form, and the Coptic translation witnesses to the original poetic quality of the passage:

> His wisdom ponders the Word,
> His message becomes expression,
> His Gnosis become manifestation.
>
> His restraint means his garland,
> His joy is mingled with him,
> His majesty he exalted.

[16] The most famous of these hymns, although too long to be quoted here, is the "Hymn of the Pearl" in *Act. Thom.* 108-113 (Jonas, *Gnosis und spätantiker Geist*, I, 320 ff.). But the most beautiful poetic passage of the *Acts of Thomas* is right at the beginning, in the "Song of the Bride" (6-7):
"The girl is the daughter of light."
To be sure, we may have pre-Christian literature in both (Alfred Adam, *Die Psalmen des Thomas und das Perlenlied als Zeugnisse vorchristlicher Gnosis* [Berlin: 1959], pp. 48 ff.). We are looking forward to the publication of Nr. 30 of the Chenoboskion documents, Doresse, *op. cit.*, p. 188. An impressive hymn is in *Unknown Copt. Work* 22.270 ff.: "I praise thee, Father of all Fathers of Light"; a hymn of repentance in *Pist. Soph.* 32.47 ff.; the moving description of the human situation in an erring cosmos in *Unknown Copt. Work* 19.260 and 1.226.
[17] Van Unnik, *op. cit.*, p. 63. The Coptic text in rhythmic structure in Kendrick Grobel, *The Gospel of Truth* (Nashville: Abingdon Press, 1960), p. 87.

His image he revealed,
His rest he enclosed within him,
His love he embodied in him,
His faith had grasped him.
—*Evang. Ver.* 23.18-33

The *Revelation by Dositheus* of Chenoboskion ought to bring us new hymnic material. Jean Doresse quotes one stanza of respectable quality:

Let us rejoice,
Let us rejoice,
Let us rejoice!

We have seen,
We have seen,
We have seen

What truly was in the beginning,
What truly was,
What was the first eternal, the unbegotten.

From thee came forth the eternals and the
perfect aeons.
—Doresse, *op. cit.*, p. 188

We are witnessing here one of the important transformations in the life of Christian faith. The content of theology is expressed in rhythmic form. It becomes address, praise, petition. This does not occur, however, for beauty's own sake, but for the praise and adoration of God. The language of faith is pronounced and recited in an act of corporate worship. Something is wrong with theological language when it is incapable of turning into prayer and hymn. If the speech of theology is to have any meaning for the life of the church, it must enter liturgy because this transformation takes it out of the intellectual realm into the worship of the congregation. In the liturgical hymn, like the psalm, chorale, or canticle, the creative potential in Christian language finds one of its important realizations.

When Christ broke into the human situation he created a new being. From death and despair he redeemed the distorted creature.

30

Should not the speech of this Christian reflect the newness of his existence? There are rare instances in Gnostic literature where this newness shines through in theological, poetic, or liturgical form.

The material presented here has been treated only in a paradigmatic way. It is the purpose of this essay to illuminate some of the crucial issues behind the conflict with Gnosticism. Here are the Gnostic contributions to the problem of semantics and communication as the second century faces it. These contributions are made sporadically. What one thinker confirms, another denies. What appears as the contribution of one passage may not be the general intent of the author at all. Yet at times the Gnostics see, while the rest of the church is blind. Not that there is such a thing as a Gnostic program, a Gnostic principle concerning the language of faith. The great issues in history evolve in a fashion much more subtle than this. What we have noticed in the Gnostic speech is a potential which lies in its literary fragments. This potential lies in overcoming the factitious mediocrity of theological language by spontaneous semantic newness. The creative possibility in Gnosticism lies buried beneath less fortunate strata. Eccentricity suffocates what has begun to breathe, and its dualism prevents the dramatic from reaching down to the concrete earthly scene, such as the agony of the cross or the triumph of Easter Day. Creativity dwells either in the excesses of mythology or in the realm of abstraction. It is our next duty to examine by what non-Christian forces this Christian potential has been rendered powerless.

THE BIBLICAL WORD IN GNOSTIC LANGUAGE

Gnosticism exposes the conflict between biblical and nonbiblical speech within Christian faith. In understanding either itself or its salient documents, Christianity must use simultaneously two languages in amalgamation, the word of the New Testament and the word of its own generation. What has to be determined is the nature of their mutual relation. Can the mixture assume a character which annuls Christian faith? This is the question of the second century.

We will try to illustrate the dilemma by selecting certain test cases—an artificial procedure; yet a study like this cannot deal with generalities, nor can it discuss an endless list of examples. The paradigmatic approach must suffice as a means of introduction. It will be seen immediately that the specific use of Christian terminology lies at the heart of the Gnostic problem. Here Gnosticism presents one of the most vital, and at the same time most intricate, problems of Christian thought.

God the Father

The New Testament uses the term πατήρ over four hundred times.[18] Many of these references belong to cardinal statements of biblical faith. "You . . . must be perfect, as your heavenly Father is perfect." (Matt. 5:48.) "Father, I have sinned against heaven and before you; I am no longer worthy to be called your son." (Luke 15:21.) "I am the way, and the truth, and the life; no one comes to the Father, but by me." (John 14:6.) "And because you are sons, God has sent the Spirit of his Son into our hearts, crying, 'Abba! Father!'" (Gal. 4:6.) "Father" is understood basically in Semitic terms: the personal sovereign, and, at the same time, caring, merciful father.[19] The Father-God of the Old Testament has become the Father as revealed in the Gospel of John, which contains more references to the Father than any other New Testament book. In Christ, who is one with his Father (17:21), who comes from the Father (16:28), and who will be glorified by the Father (17:1), God the Father has revealed himself (8:19), not God as cosmic power or the psychological force of mystic experience, but God as electing and loving person (3:16). From the Lord's Prayer to the doxologies in the book of Revelation the New Testament presents us with the unique Christian fatherhood of God as brought to man in the redemptive act of his Son, Jesus Christ. One may call this the theme of New Testament faith.

Here begins the conflict. The Father concept meets the Gnostic

[18] Robert Morgenthaler, *Statistik des Neutestamentlichen Wortschatzes* (Zürich and Frankfurt: 1958), p. 130, and the article πατήρ by Schrenk and Quell in *ThWNT*, V, 964-1024.

[19] God is the Father in heaven (Matt. 5:16) who judges (Matt. 6:15) but who also has mercy upon his children (Luke 6:36). Therefore, Paul can address his Roman community in the peace of God the Father (Rom. 1:7) by maintaining both the mercy (Rom. 8:15) and the creatorship (I Cor. 8:6) of the Father.

sphere of thought. From the one passage in the *Evangelium Veritatis* 24:7 to the latest documents of syncretistic Gnosticism, we notice a constant infiltration of the mother principle into the meaning of God's fatherhood. This infiltration differs in degree. The parallelism between Father and Mother seems at first harmless, almost poetic (*Evang. Ver.* 24.7).[20] As time passes, it reaches the full-fledged realm of fertility religion. Beside God steps a mother deity (Hipp. *Ref.* V.26.5). Christ becomes the son of a "Mother of life" (Iren. *Adv. Haer.* I.30.1). The Barbelo Gnostics do not hesitate to adore this mother principle.[21] "Mother" has become a primal deity (*Act. Thom.* 50), "the mother of all creatures" (*Act. Thom.* 39), to which one prays and in whose name the blessing is said (*Act. Thom.* 139).[22]

[20] Kendrick Grobel, *op. cit.*, p. 91, n. 206 tries to get rid of this *hapax legomenon* by suggesting another understanding of the Coptic ΜΕΕΥ, although the definite article speaks clearly against it. This is unnecessary. The text belongs exactly as it is in the period of early Gnosticism where we can witness the breakdown of the Father concept. Many further observations in the *Gospel of Truth* will prove this to coincide with the whole language of this Valentinian meditation.

[21] On the Barbelo Gnostics, see Burkitt, *op. cit.*, pp. 58-61, especially on Iren. *Adv. Haer.* I.29. Arriving in heaven, a Chenoboskion manuscript tells us, the prophet is welcomed by a "supreme mother" (*Treatise of the Great Seth*, in Doresse, *op. cit.*, pp. 149-50). In the thought of Ptolemaean Gnosticism the father has two wives, Ἔννοια and Θέλημα (Iren. *Adv. Haer.* I.12). Christ is the son of a first man, a second man, and the mother of life (I.30.1). The same triad appears in the baptismal formula of the Marcosites: "Into the name of the unknown Father of the Universe, into Truth the mother of all things, into Him who descended on Jesus" (I.21.3). A "Father of Truth" beside a "Mother of Wisdom" in *Act. Thom.* 7. "Come hidden mother" is the petition in *Act. Thom.* 50. Father-mirror of cosmos-mother is the triad at the depth of reality (*Unknown Copt. Work.* 2.229).

[22] A "Primal Mother" (πρωτογενέτειρα) also in *Sophia J. Chr.* 99.10, a document which consequently proposes a male-female revelation (103.1). For *Apocr. Joh.* the Holy Spirit is "life" and "mother" (38.10) and Christ is "father, mother, and son" (21.20). The hymn of *Act. Thom.* 27 names side by side: Holy name of Christ, merciful mother, communion with the male, revealer (*fem.*) of the hidden mysteries, mother of seven realms. The biological-sexual is implicit or explicit (Iren. *Adv. Haer.* I.30.1) in this metaphor. Robert Pierce Casey (*The Excerpta ex Theodoto of Clement of Alexandria* [London: 1934], p. 16) claimed that we have here a projection of nothing else than biological conditions into metaphysics; we have to agree with F. Sagnard (*La Gnose Valentinienne et la témoignage de St. Irénée* [Paris: 1947], pp. 182, 387 ff.), who affirms the redemptive quality in Valentinianism as the cardinal trend of thought. This does not deny, however, the importance of what Quispel (*Gnosis als Weltreligion*, p. 34)

We are witnessing a far-reaching transformation. The Father concept is no longer understood uniquely in the father-child relation, vertically, theologically, but also in the father-mother relation, biologically. The natural analogy against which the Old Testament fought so violently has been drawn. God as Father of Israel has lost his uniqueness and his sovereignty and has been dragged down to the biological, generative realm. He is no longer one, the one Lord of his people, but one of two, of three, or of many.[23] The consequence of this terminological transmutation is inevitable: with such a deflated concept, later Gnosticism must lift God above fatherhood. "Father" can no longer remain the ultimate designation for the Christian God; he is in reality προπάτωρ, a deity above fatherhood.[24] Because the realm of nature has gotten hold of the concept "Father," Christian theology must create another revelatory uniqueness—at least as long as it desires to escape mere pagan polytheism—and this is the "God beyond."

There is a second transformation, related to the first. Gnostic literature moves the concept "Father" into the realm of cosmology. The world exists in cosmic spheres; this ontological framework is most pertinent to the Gnostic understanding of the self, of fall and redemption. Being has stages. Nature and spirit, cosmos and God, are layers of a structured universe.[25] Several ways are open to relate God's fatherhood with the cosmic stages. We can speculate about a cosmogonic process: what is the genetic relation between the

---

called *"Mysterium der Geschlechtlichkeit,"* a fact which is easily demonstrated in the sexual outlets of later Gnostic cults, Leonhard Fendt, *Gnostische Mysterien* (München: 1922), pp. 8 ff., 41 ff. and Hans Leisegang, *Die Gnosis* (Stuttgart: 1955), pp. 186 ff.

[23] Hipp. *Ref.* V.26.1. Opposite to a mother principle (26.5) he is only one of three highest ἀρχαί and creator of twelve good gods (26.3-4), a father who can fight (26.21 ff.).

[24] *Unknown Copt. Work* 16.258; *Sophia J. Chr.* 90.17; *Pist. Soph.* 93.214. Beside the Father in *Apocr. Joh.* (20.11) steps more and more the Mother (53.1; 71.6) until finally, Father is no longer the ultimate (*Soph. J. Chr.* 90.16; Iren. *Adv. Haer.* I.5.2; and *Epistle of Eugnostos* (Doresse, *op. cit.*, p. 193).

[25] Typical is the term αὐτοπάτωρ in the "Valentinian Letter of Instruction," Epiph. *Pan.* XXXI.5.2, and in *Unknown Copt. Work* 16.258 (together with προπάτωρ). God represents a realm in himself, he is "Father and Mother to himself alone" (2.228). Typical also is the designation of the sun as "Father of Light," Clem. Alex. *Strom.* III.6.1. As Bertil Gärtner (*The Theology of the Gospel of Thomas* [London: 1961], p. 127) points out, *Apocr. Joh.* is above all interested in the *nature* of God.

cosmic Father and the visible world? [26] At this point cosmogony must resort to the biological phenomena of the natural world. We can intellectualize the Father concept, spiritualizing it by emptying it of all historical connotations, a process already at work in the *Evangelium Veritatis* with its abstractions like "Father-Gnosis" (18.25). Or, in the most sublime philosophical approach, we can pass over the concept and create a new vocabulary for God.[27] In every one of these possibilities, the personal, concrete Father is adjusted to a certain ontological frame. In Gnosticism this ontological frame is the key to existence. Therefore, we have either cosmogonic mythology or cosmological abstraction! Because the Father-God must fit a structure of being, the Gnostic will seek a metaphysic definition and call him "unbegotten" (*Exc. ex Theod.* 45.1), "solid and unyielding in nature" (*Exc. ex Theod.* 30.1), or "beyond unpronounceability" (οὐκ ἄρρητον) (Hipp. *Ref.* VII.20.3). God is the "first principle of the All" (*Ptolemy to Flora* 7.8). "I am the eternally being," says God in *Apocryphon Johannis* 22.1.[28]

This "eternal being"—how long can it remain a Father? The *Evangelium Veritatis* permits us to observe the subtle deviatory process in its beginning. Certain passages presuppose a personal Father, kind, merciful, choosing his people and withholding his will in his freedom.[29] The whole meditation of this Valentinian theologian emphasizes revelation, the Son bringing to the fallen

[26] In answer to this question rise the various cosmogonic explanations of the Valentinian schools which in *Unknown Copt. Work* lead to an absolute breakdown of the Father concept in favor of polytheistic mythology.

[27] Consistent with his whole thought, Basilides does not use πατήρ but mentions υἱός at times (Hipp. *Ref.* VII.24.2). What he really means in the latter, however, is υἱότης, the "sonship" as abstraction instead of personal designation (23.4, 25.1, 26.1). Basilides replaces the realm of the fatherhood by a whole new vocabulary, πανσπερμία, υἱότης, οὐκ ὢν θεός. *Unknown Copt. Work.* breaks down the Father concept by a plurality of fathers on one hand (6.233) and by the abstraction "fatherhood" on the other (17.259; *Myst. Log.* 33.83).

[28] "The Logos having a message *from the one who is* (τοῦ ὄντος)" (*Exc. ex Theod.* 25.1), is understood in metaphysical meaning as the context indicates. "Father" is described in the first *Psalm of Thomas* (1.1-3) as "joyous light," "glorious light," "glorified light"; the "Sons" are likewise cosmic forces, "sons of light," "aeons of peace," "aeons of rest."

[29] The Father is merciful (*Evang. Ver.* 18.4; 36.18), good (36.35), and sweet (41.2). Nothing happens except by the will of the Father (37.22). Gnosis is given to man by the Father (19.5).

world the hidden knowledge about the true Father.[30] But in what does the knowledge consist? The knowledge is the Father; it is identified with him. But what is its content, its specificity, its meaning? God is perfect, to be sure (35.14). What more? As soon as we seek for more, we are driven step by step into the realm of cosmology, abstraction, and negation. To begin with, the *Gospel of Truth*, as is quite normal and to be expected, stresses the infinity (31.19) and imperishability (35.14) of God. God is of absolute foreknowledge (37.34), a unit within himself (20.20), identical with gnosis (19.16). In the last two we have the beginning of the shift. We would expect unknowing to end with the knowledge of the Father who *is* this knowledge. This knowledge would therefore be identical with both Father and revelation. At times gnosis is indeed the termination of forgetting. But in other contexts, it is not. Let us look at the *"name* Meditation."[31] Originally, in the Jewish background of the work, the "name" has to be the Tetragrammaton, Yahweh. In the second *name* passage (38.8 ff.), there are two seemingly contradictory lines in constant tension. The first is Johannine in character. The "name" of the Father is "Son" (39.25), which is an attempt to stress the centering of Christology in revelation. Christ is himself "Lordly Name" (40.8), who alone, spoke the name of the Father (40.22), revealing and pronouncing him in absolute uniqueness (38.23-25). But then, at the same time, the name of the Father is invisible (38.17). "Name does not belong to the class of words (39.3) and the unengendered (ἀγέννητος) God has no name (39.11). We expect the first to be the revelation of the second—but all we get is an abstraction, "Son," a name which leaves the Father concept without any character. If "Son" is the "name" of the Father, the designation "name" does not mean anything any more. We can say "reflection," "imprint," "image," or any other Platonic symbol to describe vertical relation, but to say that the Son is the "name" of the Father is a meaningless abstraction as far as the word "Father" is concerned. This is exactly

---

[30] "The Gospel of Truth is a joy for them who have received the boon, through the Father of Truth, of knowing it" (*Evang. Ver.* 16.31). 39.7 and 39.23 point also toward a unique revelation in Valentinian Gnosticism. *Epist. of Eugn.* (Doresse, *op. cit.,* pp. 192 ff.) confirms the absolute newness of Revelation for some Gnostic circles.

[31] For the Gnostic concept of the "name" see Gärtner, *op. cit.,* pp. 121 ff.

the point toward which the Gnostic thinker steers. What we really *can* say about the Father is *beyond* communicability. His essence cannot be pronounced. The invisible God has actually no name, and human words can never suffice to express his essence. These are the two stages in this treatise, side by side: the name is "Son," and the name is beyond word. One is mere abstraction; the other has left the realm of reasonable communication. Both times "Father," as a concrete concept, has ceased to exist.

What we have witnessed is the third transformation. Loss of concreteness leads to abstraction, and abstraction leads to negation. What begins to take place in this document will take over all the theologically creative Gnostic systems: the fatherhood of God must succumb to abstraction and to negative attributes about God. The more theology defines, the less definable does this fatherhood become: "without substance" (ἀνούσιος Hipp. *Ref.* VII.21.1), "superior to all thought" (*Evang. Ver.* 17.9), *innommabilis* (Iren. *Adv. Haer.* I.29.1). The gnosis of the Father is man's means to ascend to God; when it reaches God it ceases to be. In lack of knowledge (ἐν ἀγνωσίᾳ) are all things contained within God, says the Valentinian *Letter of Instruction* (Epiph. *Pan.* XXXI.5.2). Definition is no more.[32] This "Father," emptied of attributes, is no longer a Father in the biblical sense but the highest stage in a universe. He is a magnificent peak in religious ontology but not the personal Father of the gospel who provides love and judgment for his creatures. The Father who acts in freedom has been replaced by the father of the universe.[33]

---

[32] "The unthinkably Incomprehensible One who is superior to all thought" (*Evang. Ver.* 17.9). Valentinus in Hipp. *Ref.* VI.29.2 ff., especially in 30.8: ἄμορφος καὶ ἀκατασκεύατος οὐσία; Simon in VI.12 ff.: ἀγέννητον πῦρ. Basilides in VII.25.4 and the Naassenes in V.8.5. Typical is V.8.6-7: ἀλάλῳ λαλοῦν σιωπῇ and V.7.33: the Logos is "without distinctive mark" (ἀχαρακτήριστος). The Coptic texts confirm throughout that the phraseology of Hippolytus is authentically Gnostic. There are two beautiful passages of negative speech in *Apocr. Joh.*, pp. 23 ff. (*cf.* Till, in the Introduction to the work, pp. 38-39) and in the hymn of adoration at the conclusion of *Unknown Copt. Work* 22.270. Gilles Quispel ("L'Homme Gnostique," *Eranos*, 1948, p. 138) sees in this negative language the oneness of all Gnosticism because it represents the typical expression of the Gnostic religious experience.

[33] The loss of God's freedom opens the way for the Hellenistic ἀνάγκη (David Amand, *Fatalisme et Liberté dans l'antiquité grecque* [Louvain: 1945]) to stream into the Gnostic thought, found symptomatically already in *Evang. Ver.* 21.19

We have confronted the biblical-Hebraic fatherhood of a God-man encounter with the cosmology of Greek theism and the cosmogonic deity of the East, as it comes to the surface in the various systems in the specific "Gnostic" consciousness which, despite all discrepancies, contains certain clear uniform trends. Fertility and cosmology both lead to the *negative goal* in the ascent of man through gnosis. Fertility and cosmology help each other in establishing cosmogonic relations between the Father and the world. In the same field belongs the widespread Gnostic attempt to raise God above the male-female dialectic. While all this cosmogonic-sexual symbolism is alien to biblical thought, ever since Elijah fought the fertility religion of Baal, the cosmological aspect is not! LXX translated Exod. 3:14 with ὁ ὤν, throwing the Hebraic God into the midst of cosmological terminologies, and producing by this translation an interpretation of far-reaching consequences.[34]

(see the article by E. Peterson, "La libération d'Adam de l'Anankè," *Rev. Bibl.* 55 [1948], 199 ff.). As ἀνάγκη and τύχη have been the two forces of life in Greek thought (J. Festugière, *L'idéal religieux des Grecs* [Paris: 1932], pp. 66 ff., 101 ff., and Paul Wendland, *Die Hellenistisch-Römische Kultur* [Tübingen: 1912], pp. 106 ff.), so already *Stob. Herm.* XXVIII.38 formulates ἀνάγκη and ἔρος as the two forces of life. Hans Jonas (*Gnosis and spätantiker Geist*, I, 156 ff., 172 ff.) has pointed toward the separation into the necessity of destiny and predestination in Gnostic thought which is, however, not unilaterally achieved, Cf. Hipp. *Ref.* V.26.14; 8.12; VII.22.1; *Exc. ex Theod.* 67.2; Clem. Alex. *Strom.* III.3.2; Iren. *Adv. Haer* I.21.2. Concerning the whole concept of the Father in Valentinanism, see the excellent survey in Sagnard, *La Gnose Valentinienne*, pp. 325-33.

[34] The Hebrew original of Exod. 3:14 contains Hebrew "presence" over "eternity" in speaking about God (Edmond Jacob, *Theology of the Old Testament* [London: Hodder & Stoughton, 1958], pp. 51-52), not "aseity" and "self-existence" (as Paul Heinisch, *Theology of the Old Testament* [Collegeville: 1950], p. 55, in a peculiar anachronism of scholarship formulates) but in the striking formulation of Von Rad, "much less Being than Event" (*Theologie des Alten Testamentes* [München: 1957], pp. 142 ff.). LXX has created the possibility of a Greek metaphysical interpretation of the biblical God by its translation of ὁ ὤν; "I am who I am" now can become Philo's τὸ ὄν (Erwin R. Goodenough, *By Light, Light; The Mystic Gospel of Hellenistic Judaism* [New Haven: Yale University Press; London: H. Milford, Oxford University Press, 1935], pp. 23 ff.), the *Ipsum esse* of Augustine (*De Civ. Dei* VIII.11) and the *qui est* of Thomas (*Summa Theologica*, I, p. 13: *Utrum hoc nomen "qui est" sit maxime nomen dei proprium*). Exod. 3:14 can be explained by Platonic metaphysics, as in *Novus Thesaurus Philologico-Criticus* of Friedrich Schleusner (Tübingen: 1821), V, 575 (it means ὄντα ἀεί and ὅ ἐστι τὸ ὄν) and in the misunderstanding of Thorleif Boman, *Das Hebräische Denken im Vergleich mit dem Griechischen* [Göttingen: 1954], p. 37: God as the *"seiende, ewig wirksame."*

God is "eternally being," according to *Apocryphon of John.* An early Christian creedal statement confesses God as the Father from whom the All came.[35] The book of Revelation praises God, "Who is and who was and who shall be" (1:8), in categories typically influenced by Hellenistic ontology. To claim biblical fatherhood to be only a statement about an "act," about redemption, is therefore simply not true. The New Testament is touched throughout by categories which we discover in Gnosticism. The difference between the Father of the New Testament and the Gnostic Father lies in its *pole of force.* It is not a question of *either-or* but of the center. Any cosmological implication in the New Testament fatherhood of God is subordinate to the redemptive encounter, which occurs in Christ, in the community of faith, in the coming of the Kingdom. The theistic creed of I Cor. 8:6 has a christological second part. There is no biblical cosmogony! There would *have* to be one if cosmology were an essential part of its theology. The pole of force can permit cosmological particles but it cannot accept the cosmic generation. It can permit statements about creation, the Lord of the universe, the Father of the all, because above these the main interest lies in the act of the Father: in history, in the congregation of the saved, in the ethical decision of the individual, in the coming of the Kingdom.

What has happened to the concept is a shift which looks quite slight at first sight. This shift is the crucial issue between Christian and Gnostic faith. What has existed at the edge has received emphasis. And the peripheral has destroyed the pole. When the gospel speaks to the Greeks it does touch their categories; it uses Hellenistic speech about cosmos and generation.[36] This is part of the gospel and its tension. It is part of its thrill to enter the borderlines. But the gospel speculates nowhere about cyclic forces, generative relation, aseity, or existence. When the speech of the Gospel touches cosmic or naturalistic speech, it is not frightened

---

[35] I Cor. 8:6 (Oscar Cullmann, *Die ersten christlichen Glaubensbekenntnisse* [Zollikon: 1943], p. 27). Jewish Diaspora theology already moved toward cosmological theism (Peter Dalbert, *Die Theologie der hellenistisch-jüdischen Missionsliteratur* [Hamburg: 1954], p. 126).

[36] κόσμος *can* be "universe" (John 1:10; Acts 17:24; *cf.* Sasse, *ThWNT,* III 883 ff.), and there *is* a vocabulary on rebirth (Matt. 19:28; Tit. 3:5: παλιγγενεσία; I Pet. 1:3, 23: ἀναγεννάω; and John 3:7: γεννηθῆναι ἄνωθεν).

because it does not subordinate itself. In its tension and in its movement it preserves the center: "Father, forgive them; for they do not know what they do." A Father to whom the Son prays! A Father whom his child fears and whose love the child knows.[37]

Righteousness

Clement of Alexandria preserves for us a fragment from Carpocrates which furnishes another example for the problem of Gnostic language, extreme in character but excellent for the demonstration of the issues in Christian language. It is the passage about the meaning of "righteousness."

Righteousness in the New Testament has several connotations. It concerns man's righteous act vis à vis the justice of God (Luke 1:75). This righteousness as God's will demands obedience (Jas. 1:20). Yet this righteousness is that of the kingdom of God (Matt. 6:33), and this dimension leads to the famous Pauline usage. Righteousness is justification which cannot come by works of the law (Gal. 2:21) but which is God's own holy act, forensic (Rom. 3:25), realized in the cross of his Son (Gal. 3:13), revealed through faith toward faith, as the Epistle to the Romans formulates it (1:17). In all the differences throughout the New Testament we see one main motif: the judging and merciful act of God the Father toward his children, and the response of his children to his merciful and judging will. While Paul proclaims the redemptive quality of this justice, James stresses the necessity of response; and even though the concern of Paul does not live very deeply in the latter, righteousness stands for both in relation to the will of God, in forensic justification, or in ethical obedience.

[37] Hans Lietzmann, *Geschichte der Alten Kirche* [Berlin: 1953], I, 317: "In der Gnosis erhebt sich mit Macht der Gott der östlichen Mystik gegen den Vater im Himmel, zu dem Jesus seine Jünger beten gelehrt hat." Quispel (*Eranos*, 1948, p. 138) observes that Gnostic theology does not understand the *love* of God in a biblical sense. W. C. Van Unnik ("The Gospel of Truth and the New Testament," in *The Jung Codex* [London: Mowbray and Company, 1955], p. 128) remarks that the "fear of God" is lacking in the *Gospel of Truth*. All three observations, by Lietzmann, Quispel, and Van Unnik, bring out aspects of the one main trend, the absence of the biblical Father. *Cf.* also T. Evan Pollard, "Cosmology and the Prologue of the Fourth Gospel," *Vig. Christ*, 12 (1958), 147, who concludes that even a verse like John 1:3 is not so much concerned with cosmology as with the activity of God; "everything happens through him" (p. 152).

The famous passage by the aggressive young Epiphanes, advocating free enterprise in the realm of love and battling the legalistic evil of "monogamy," is usually quoted by the historians of the church to demonstrate the evils of Gnosticism. At this moment we are less interested in the specific nature of this spectacular system than in its underlying principle, which is more coherent than it appears to be at first sight. The treatise "About Righteousness" attempts to explain δικαιοσύνη; it will be wise to translate the Greek term from here on as "justice." The beginning of the fragment defines such justice sharply as "communion with equality" (κοινωνία μετ᾽ ἰσότητος). "Equality" means cosmic proportion without discrimination, the unrestricted distribution of the sunlight over all seeing creatures.[38] Poor and rich, female and male, free and slave, they all share alike—favor would be injustice—in the reception of light (Clem. Alex. *Strom.* III.6.1-3). The second aspect of justice lies in its universal quality, in Greek κοινότης. Justice is "the common," the "universality," in creation. As the sun nourishes all life in equality, letting food grow for all without prejudice, so everything partakes equally of the "common." Sharing in the universality in life is partaking of justice (III.6.4).

At this moment the Father concept breaks in. The Father of the all has given to all creatures in common (κοινῇ) and in equal proportions (ἐπ᾽ ἴσης) an eye to see. His justice lies in establishing creation equally and commonly. With a daring turn of language, Epiphanes now calls this equality and common basis of natural life "the law," no code but inborn dynamic of life, in polemic and sarcastic distinction to any legal or ethical understanding of this concept. Law is cosmic balance, a cycle of light but at the same time human emotion springing forth from the cosmic law: desire, love, life itself (III.7.1 ff.).

At the beginning of this passage stands a triad of concepts:

Justice—Equality—Universality

Justice is immediately tied to cosmology: "justice" means equality, and equality means that which created life has in common. This emphatically nonethical justice is cyclic, natural, cosmic, but in no degree historical. As a matter of fact both man and animal share

[38] On ἰσότης in Philo see Goodenough, *op. cit.*, pp. 64 ff.

in the definition of the concept. Such is the denial of the event (between God and man, and between man and man) by consequent Carpocratean cosmology: the justice of the cosmos needs no history.

Yet what about God? Epiphanes speaks of the divine realm without hesitation:

Father of Cosmos—Creator—Lawgiver

is his next triad. Christian theology could operate quite well with such terminology! We soon realize, however, what each of the terms signifies. The Father of the cosmos has established creation, and now it stands in its eternal equality. There is no possibility of a justice outside this established realm. The tie between God and his world is purely cosmic. Justice is only natural distribution in cyclic relation. "Law" is an indwelling, natural biological force, never written, never transmitted, only existing as far as God gave it to the cosmos at the beginning of creation. There is no encounter or event beyond this, no ethical code, no demand, and no obedience—only the cosmic force.

It does not take much to understand that we have in this chain of speech

Justice—Equality—Universality—Father—Creator—Law

actually another language than that of biblical faith. The chain is conceived purely in terms of a natural cosmology; and therefore, every single concept placed in this frame stands in conscious denial of both philosophical ethic and Christian history. Unchristian is any "justice" which lacks not only the Pauline justification but even any emphasis on obedience to God's demand. Unchristian is *nomos* in its opposition to the covenant relation between God and his people in the Mosaic law; it is instead a natural imperative, not even toward an ethical goal but toward life itself—absolute contradiction to the historical claim with which God met the natural realm of Canaan.[39] Unchristian is "equality," in the New Testament an equality with Christ, not in a cosmic equilibrity but as free equality within the body of Christ (II Cor. 8:13-14). "Father" turns out to be an impressive divine force at the beginning of the cosmic cycle—as Boethius will praise him in his poetry—but he

[39] The difference becomes obvious by a comparison of Clem. Alex. *Strom.* III.7:1-2 with Rom. 3:21, Judg. 5:11, Deut. 32:4, and Ps. 111:7-9.

has no contact with the Father of Israel who asks justice because he loves and chooses his people.

In our examination of the Father terminology of Gnosticism we noticed the shift in the meaning of a term sometimes drastic, sometimes slight. Here we are confronted with a considerably more obvious process. The whole chain of speech is void of biblical signification. Less obvious than this observation is the conclusion. The biblical nature, the Christian essence, of this theologian's speech is not affected by the fact that he speaks more or less in Christian terms. It is true, he does use terms which are alien to biblical semantics and which bear certain non-Christian Hellenistic connotations (universality).[40] He also uses concepts which are obviously remote in the literature of the New Testament (equality). Yet this is not his problem (he uses *nomos* in absolutely un-Hellenistic ways). The whole speech is alien in its basic nature! And therefore the familiar, biblical concepts (justice, father, the Pauline "sharing" κοινωνία) hold the key to the reversal of meaning of seemingly biblical terms. *There* lies the breach! Justice, law, the Creator, the Father—any biblical theology could use these concepts. Epiphanes has not one biblical connotation in these seemingly biblical words. Only secondarily is the seriousness of the problem increased by the fact that certain concepts (equality and universality) are central to this system which are not so in the proclamation of the gospel. They are not responsible for but only aggravate the fact that in the chain of speech in Epiphanes the biblical word is nowhere understood.

Christ and Gnosis

The *Evangelium Veritatis* has remarkably biblical concepts and phrases concerning Christology. "The Father's Name is not spoken but it is revealed by a Son" (38.22). Nobody except the Son "was able to pronounce" this name of the Father (38.25). The uniqueness of the revelatory event persists throughout the meditation.[41] God's name was "unnamable, unutterable, until the moment when He who is perfect spoke it to him [the Son] alone" (40.16). The

[40] κοινότης in Philosophic literature: Plato, *Theaet.* 208 D and Arist. *Pol.* 1274 b 10; again in the *First Ennead* of Plotinus 3.4.
[41] So rightly Grobel, *op. cit.*, p. 55 n. 72, to *Evang. Ver.* 18.35.

teaching of Christ proceeds from the unique revelation (30.32) because the will of God "is characterized by the revealing of His word" (37.6). This shows a deep insight into Christology. The center of all Christian life lies in the unique coming of the Father in his Son. Such coming has one reason only: "He abolished the separation" (34.28). Revelation means bridging the abyss between God and creature. Here lies the way, and here lies the truth of life (18.19).

These phrases, astonishingly relevant for Christian theology, immediately indicate that in early Valentinian literature we are confronted with a serious Christian interpretation, serious not merely in the sense of theological and intellectual quest, but also of biblical concern. The Gospel of John and the Pauline corpus have few phrases which express this one aspect of a unique revelation more attractively. Whoever wrote the *Gospel of Truth* understood one of the key issues in Christian faith: the gospel is not man's but has come through a revelation (Gal. 1:11-12). And this revelation is "what no eye has seen" (I Cor. 2:9).

How is this deeply biblical speech about the revelation of God in his Son continued? What are the ties in the *Evangelium Veritatis?* Again, we discover biblical language. Christ is the "Savior," sent for the work of redemption (16.37); he is the shepherd and "sought after [the one sheep] which had strayed" (32.2). His death meant life for many (20.13); "he was nailed to a tree" (20.25; 18.24); he endured suffering (20.11). Here are all biblical allusions to the life of Christ. The author knows the canonical Gospels and paraphrases Paul, although he sometimes reverses a metaphor (20.25).

If we compare the second group of citations with the first we notice instantly the uneven distribution of the language about God and Christ. Our gospel commentary contains numerous excellent comments on the character of revelation, yet its remarks concerning the earthly life of Christ are sporadic, almost incidental. 20.10-14 reveals a certain knowledge about the life of Christ, yet it nowhere reaches the pivotal interest exhibited in revelatory concern. It would be absurd to place the scanty remarks about the historical Christ on the same level as the forceful statements about revelation. Even if the writer's mind "was full of New Testament imagery," [42] the concrete earthiness of Christ is not central to his speech. That this is no coincidence but part of the whole structure of his thought becomes clear when we examine the relation of his language about the Christ to that about gnosis. Christ is "Gnosis for those who were a-Gnostic" (31.30). This concept as such could merely be an expression of the Pauline-Johannine affirmation that Christ is the truth of life. We are going to show that it means more.

"He was nailed to a tree; He became a fruit of Father-Gnosis." (18.24.) This is a revealing parallelism. The nailing in the death on the cross is immediately put beside knowledge. The edge of death is cut off promptly by knowledge. The same happens in the second passage about the "nailing to a tree": "He fastened the testamentary disposition from the Father to the Cross" (20.25). One should not be concerned about the twisting of a biblical metaphor. Why should not theology have the freedom to do this? But again death is removed to the realm of abstraction and symbolic speech.[43] The sharpness and the sting of death are immediately weakened by a symbol. Could it be that the biblical concept of death does not fit into the theology of our author?

A second observation points in the same direction. In the language of revelation one of its cardinal concepts is gnosis, the revealed, esoteric, saving knowledge. Gnosis annihilates *Plané* in the cosmic battle (26.24) and conquers the torments of existence (31.27). The great alternative to error is gnosis, the equivalent of truth (32.36). Reunion in knowledge is the goal of faith, the triumph over ignorance and want (24.32 ff.). One cannot be cautioned enough against the modern misunderstanding that such gnosis is rationalism. Gnosis for the Gnostic is intellectual experience, visionary reality of the sphere of mind; gnosis is thought as

---

[42] Grobel, *op. cit.*, p. 63, n. 108.

[43] This may be the case, even in Col. 2:14, which is the basis for *Evang. Ver.* 20.25. But for Paul, death is also a reality in its earthly horror and consequence, having come through sin (Rom. 5:12), through one man (I Cor. 15:21). What is conquered in death is its sting (I Cor. 15:56), not only lack of knowledge. All Pauline proclamation about the death of Christ (I Cor. 11:26) has in mind the "obedience unto death" (Phil. 2:8). The *Gospel of Truth* in its concept of salvation as recovery of knowledge misses both the physical misery of death and the physical triumph of eternal life breaking in with Christ.

metaphysical entity.[44] Nevertheless, such reality—although not in post-Kantian understanding—is that of the mind. The Christ of the *Gospel of Truth* stands in close affinity to this "Gnostic" concern. He breathes into the faithful that which exists in the divine thought (30.34), since "Reunion is due to perfect Thought" (34. 33). His mission is illumination, the illuminating of those who live in darkness through forgetting (18.17). All this speech connected with the Christ remains on the level of the abstract. Since "gnosis" is metaphysical reality, it pulls all christological theologumena into the metaphysical realm.

As a consequence of this, all the earthly concreteness of Christology is neglected. We cannot say it is nonexistent, since there is the teaching, the seeking of sheep, the cross. Yet concretization is an onerous process. It is passed over as in the passage 20.10-14, not with contempt, but with a feeling that it is traditional but not essential. Why should this be so? Because all through the relation of Christ and gnosis there is a crypto-Docetism. The speech concerning Father-Son, begetting (38.10) and becoming (39.22), the emergence of the word (37.9) and its passing through the aeons (23.33) is nowhere historical or earthly in any plastic sense. The christological language remains in the realm of the ideal. Christ draws himself downward to death "while eternal life encloses him" (20.28). Incarnation is *immediately* paralleled by eternal life *during* Christ's lifetime; again the seriousness of death is not acknowledged. Whatever the exact wording of 31.5-8 may have been, the text brings "flesh" and "indestructibility" in opposition to each other.[45] That this is docetic is proved by the context: the flesh stands related to Hyle, matter (31.1). And that Hyle is a concept of Gnostic dualism does not need to be proved. Such Docetic dualism is not alien to this meditation, as 25.16 proves: Gnosis "eats up Matter." [46] The language about Christ and gnosis pertains to the perpendicular. We cannot say that it denies the earthly angle of this God-man reference but it pays no heed to its importance.

[44] Wilhelm Windelband, *Lehrbuch der Geschichte der Philosophie* (Tübingen: 1935), p. 97. This already becomes important for *Evang. Ver.* where truth is not a "value" but a metaphysical reality.

[45] The textual difficulties are discussed in Grobel, *op. cit.*, pp. 123 ff.

[46] Reading with Grobel, *op. cit.*, p. 101, n. 234, "it" instead of "he."

There is no Incarnation! Where there seems to be, it is only a "coming down" (20.29).

A comparison with a New Testament passage will focus the issue even more clearly. Let us take what may be the most nearly "Gnostic" passage in Paul, I Cor. 2.6-9. The language contained in this passage is no different from certain Gnostic usages: "We impart a secret and hidden wisdom of God, which God decreed before the ages for our glorification." One could show further Gnostic parallels to the following statements: "No one comprehends the thoughts of God except the Spirit of God" (2:11). Paul has not received the Spirit of the world but the Spirit of God (2:12). Does this in any way differ from the language of the *Gospel of Truth?* It certainly does! We cannot merely compare particle with particle; the man who wrote I Cor. 2 also wrote I Cor. 1. And there we are told unmistakably that Christ is a real historical figure and that the cross is not a mere symbol (1:17). For Paul Christ is crucified (2:2), a stumbling block to the Jew (1:23), preached as risen from the dead (15:12). In speaking about Christ, Paul does not hesitate to use plastic physical metaphors: the body is meant for the Lord, and the Lord for the body (6:13). All possible Docetism is given its final denial with this emphasis on sanctification. The Christian is God's temple (3:17), and the entire sixth chapter makes it unmistakably clear that the whole of man is understood by this. "Glorify God in your body." (6:20.) There is the suffering of the Christian, not merely gnosis; sentenced to death, as fool for Christ does the apostle live (4:9-10). And there is finally the congregation of believers (5:4), torn in strife (11:18), yet one body in joy and suffering (12:26), eating the bread and drinking the cup (11: 26).[47] What distinguishes Paul from the *Gospel of Truth* is not the use of mystery, gnosis, and pleroma. Language can only live in context, as a chain, as a man's total expression. We may find heterogeneous particles and alien concepts. The "Gnosticism" of Paul (in a broad sense of the term) is radically different from the

[47] The person and work of Christ and redemption as faith and love (not as knowledge) mark the decisive distinction between Paul and the Gnostics. The best discussion concerning "Gnosticism" in Paul can be found in Wilson, *op. cit.,* pp. 71 ff., esp. p. 76.

Gnosticism of the *Evangelium Veritatis,* even though in certain ways this meditation understands excellently Paul's concern.[48]

The same can be shown in relation to the Gospel of John. Here the problem seems even more intricate. Is not the language of this book like the language of the Gnostic gospel? "I am not of this world." (8:23.) Darkness has not accepted the light (1:5). The prince of this world is judged (16:11). Do we not have the same uniqueness of the vertical (1:18), the same language about the fruit (15:4), the same emphasis on knowledge (16:3)? The difference lies again in the context. The language of the vertical is continuously paralleled by language stressing the historical, the concrete, the community. In the midst of all the discourses there are the pericopes about the life of Christ; after the theological prologue, immediately the historical prologue concerning the Baptist. Throughout the work, the drama of redemption builds up, an earthly history, leading to the two most dramatic chapters of the book, the Passion. It is a fatal misunderstanding to break up this gospel into levels;[49] even if there were levels originally, the very essence of its Christology lies in the antithesis between the horizontal and the perpendicular. Whatever gnosis there is in this gospel must endure its antithesis: the drama on earth, and in history.[50] This is why Johannine dualism is never Docetic. The Christ in gnosis is only part of the total Christ.

In the *Evangelium Veritatis* the accents have shifted; the relation

---

[48] See the excellent example in the comparison between *Corp. Herm.* XIII.14 and Rom. 7:24 in Günther Bornkamm, *Mythus und Legende in den apokryphen Thomasakten* (Göttingen: 1933), p. 122.

[49] To use late Gnostic and Mandaean sources to prove the origin of the gospel as Heinz Becker has done (*Die Reden des Johannes-evangeliums und der Stil der gnostischen Offenbarungsrede* [Göttingen: 1956]) is one of the most peculiar anachronisms in modern research of church history. E. Percy (*Untersuchungen über den Ursprung der johanneischen Theologie* [Lund: 1939]) has already emphasized that Mandaean sources ought not to be used. Moreover, scholarship must be more cautious before reading back one or two centuries; the time has gone in which the orthodox Protestant scholar can naïvely read all Renaissance in the light of the ninety-five theses. In this respect, the protest by Wilson (*op. cit.,* pp. viii-ix) against W. Schmidthals (*Die Gnosis in Korinth* [Göttingen: 1956]) was timely.

[50] For this insight into the Johannine gospel I am especially grateful to my colleague Ernest W. Saunders. See also C. Milo Connick, "The Dramatic Character of the Fourth Gospel," *Journ. of Bibl. Lit.* 67 (1948), 159 ff.

between Christ and gnosis, despite all the biblical language, is Gnostic in the second-century sense. The historical Christ is non-descript; the language about him cannot excite us because it does not live. If the author's mind was full of New Testament imagery, this imagery has no life. It is no coincidence that "Jesus Christ" as a formula of faith plays only a slight role in the vocabulary of this theologian. Gnosis is stronger than the Christ.[51]

Mysterion

When Sophia recognized the male angels sent forth with the Christ, "she felt ashamed," and therefore she covered her head with a veil. Because of this mystery, say the *Excerpts from Theodotus*, Paul advises the Corinthians that the women ought to cover their heads "because of the angels" (I Cor. 11:10 in *Exc. ex Theod.* 44.1-2). The term *mysterion* is the last concept whose transmutation of meaning we want to analyze.

The term *mysterion*, appearing already in the Qumran literature, is not frequently used in the New Testament.[52] Whenever it appears, however, it has great bearings, which indicates that the issue is of much greater weight than the term. "To you it has been given to know the mysteries of the kingdom of heaven." (Matt. 13.11.) The whole parabolic proclamation, the veiling of the kerygma, is enclosed in this phrase. The apostle is the "steward of the mysteries of God" (I Cor. 4:1) and teaches the "ignorant" Romans concerning the mystery (Rom. 11:25). This "mystery" is nothing else than the gospel (Eph. 6:19), the saving plan of God (Eph. 3:9), the revealed truth which in faith, in daring paradox, Paul calls "wisdom" (I Cor. 2:7). We notice without difficulty that mysterion is merely the Hellenistic word for the revealed character of the gospel, that it means Christ (Col. 1:27), hidden to the world and opened to faith.[53]

There is not one univocal use of *mysterion* in Gnostic literature.

[51] Doresse (*op. cit.*, p. 193 to *Epist. Eugn.*) speaks about a "principle of knowledge." On gnosis, which alone can save, see Wilson, *op. cit.*, p. 88, n. 44.

[52] R. E. Brown, "The Semitic Background of the N. T. Mysterion," *Biblica* 1959, pp. 70 ff. For the Qumran texts see B. Rigaux, "Révélation des Mystères et Perfection à Qumran et dans le Nouveau Testament," *New Test. Stud.*, 4 (1957), 237 ff.

[53] We leave out all incidental meanings of μυστήριον.

What we can trace, however, is the orientation of the term. *Mysterion* is a general concept for the esoteric tradition, designating the secret truth which is accessible only to the initiate.[54] As such it becomes unpronounceable (Hipp. *Ref.* V.8.7). This esoteric unpronounceability of the mystery in the Naassene text already represents a major shift. Because, nevertheless, the mystery has a content (the myth of primal man), unpronounceability means the objective superrational dimension of Gnostic truth, accessible only to the perfect. *Mysterion* is gnosis, but gnosis in so far as it is withheld, that which the Christ opens by bringing gnosis (Hipp. *Ref.* V.10.2). *Mysterion* is the untouchable in the act of ascending knowledge. It is therefore both content and veiling, object as esoteric transmittance and object as unpronounceable mystery. This double quality lies at the heart of Gnostic salvation.

In what does this shift lie? *Mysterion* in the Synoptic quotation and *mysterion* in the Naassene fragment mean first both one and the same thing: faith teaches faith, and faith understands faith. The language of faith is taught, communicated and understood by faith; this means: by a *mysterion* which, formerly hidden, has become revealed at this time (Col. 1:26-27; Eph. 3:4). The communication through the parable to the disciples is therefore a communication between understanding and veiling. "To you it has been given," says Jesus, and then the gospel proceeds to explain the parable! All New Testament language about the mystery, however, must be interpreted within the context of Christology and theology. It never becomes *opus operatum;* it is nowhere permitted to push aside the sovereignty of God. *Mysterion* is *not* a principle of salvation, but at the most an expression of the basic hidden dimension in the saving act of God through Christ. To use the remarkable phrase coined by Bornkamm: *mysterion* is the "gift of a free acting grace." [55]

What is lost in Gnosticism's use of *mysterion* is nothing more or less than the christological and theological context. Mystery, in its symptomatic Gnostic double dimension of the unpronounce-

[54] Epiph. *Pan.* XXXI.7.8. Material in the art. μυστήριον by Bornkamm, *ThWNT,* IV, 818 ff. The most excessive accumulation of references is in *Pistis Sophia.*

[55] Bornkamm, *art. cit.,* p. 825.

able hidden and of the knowable and the revealed, turns into an *opus operatum*. It designates the *opus* of salvation. *"Mysterion* knows," *mysterion* possesses (*Pist. Soph.* 91.203-211). We understand this if we turn back to the terminological shift of the Father concept. Because the Gnostic God, even with all the references to the Father in the *Gospel of Truth*, has lost its fatherhood in favor of a cosmic-ontic principle, a principle of being or of generation, the mystery itself loses its connection with a free acting, gracious, loving, and judging Father. Once this ligature is torn, the way is wide open for the mystery cult to take over. The mother brings the mystery (*Act. Thom.* 50). Now *mysterion* can become again, as it was in pre-Christian literature, a term for ritual rebirth and the cult of deification.[56] Does the mystery save? It *must,* once the acting Father God is removed!

The shift of *mysterion* marks the renunciation of Christology in favor of a Christosophy in which redemptive history becomes myth. The *mysterion* is Jesus; Jesus is the *mysterion.*[57] In the light of our discussion on Christ and gnosis we understand how such a statement grasps only one direction of faith, the mystery as intellectual and spiritual object, the mystery as an expression of the perpendicular in religion. As justice is understood in terms of the cosmic static law and not *sub specie Dei agentis,* as part of the divine act in love, so does the mystery stand as such, as metaphysical entity, rational and superrational at the same time, yet always the ontological object which man can grasp. We see the four concepts analyzed fall into one line. It will be our next duty to look for the dimensions of Gnostic speech.

THE ESSENCE OF GNOSTIC SPEECH

Gnostic language can be highly theological, penetratingly philosophical, or excessively mythological. From banality to exclusive intellectual refinement we meet a wide scale of religious communication. What we try to find next are certain common denominators which enable us to phrase the peculiarity of Gnostic language.

[56] The paralleling of Christian μυστήριον and Eleusian rites in Hipp. *Ref.* V.8.39 ff.

[57] *Act Thom.* 47 and *Pist. Soph.* 10 are symptomatic examples.

The Sphere of Knowledge

Gnostic language endeavors to transmit truth. There must be communication because God has called his people in his grace (*Evang. Ver.* 16.32) and wants them to know the divine truth (16.33). Salvation and eternal life come through revelation; if revelation is to bear fruit of any kind and be meaningful in any sense, there must be transmittance of revelation. Gnostic language must be, therefore, highly informative. Once man has perceived the cosmogonic and redemptory myth as a unique, saving knowledge, he is compelled to pass on this faith. Hence the didactic quality which we observe throughout this whole literature. As Christ in one of the passages of the *Evangelium Veritatis* appears as the great teacher (19.18 ff.), so does Gnostic language strive to illuminate (18.17). The antithesis between forgetting and gnosis demands enlightenment in the wake of a revelatory vision, and therefore is compelled to impart instruction.

But what is this speech which conveys knowledge? It attempts to communicate answers to the quest:

> Who we were and what we have become,
> where we were and where we were thrown,
> whither we hasten, from what we are redeemed,
> what birth is, what rebirth.
> —*Exc. ex Theod.* 78.2

This language addresses man in his earthly existence as a whole. This is not merely intellectual language in an abstract sense. Such language, communicating intellectual knowledge, creates a focus of existence, throws man into a perspective where he suddenly becomes aware of himself, of his past and his future, of his entanglement with the cosmos and of the prospect of salvation. "To know" is, for the Gnostic, by no means an analytic process but perception of truth in being grasped by it, knowledge as sharing in the object of knowledge. I cannot see how one can deny the presence of some Platonic realism in the Gnostic understanding of knowledge.[58]

[58] Cf. the delightful definition by Simone Pétrement (*Le Dualisme chez Platon, les Gnostiques et les Manichéens* [Paris: 1947], p. 129): Gnosis as "*platonisme romantique.*" There is not only Platonic language (Richard

Gnostic language is the communication of *apophasis,* of the oracle (Hipp. *Ref.* VI.18.2). Since we are dealing with a vehicle of divine communication and not of analytic reflection, and since the communication is itself more than pronunciation of letters and vowels, speaking in terms of this vehicle is only part of what really goes on in the man who grasps it. Oracular speech is the expression of an experiential movement as well, and expects such a movement from one who grasps the oracle. "To know" is to ascend.[59] To grasp truth is to be buoyed by it from the sea of ignorance and oblivion. What seems to be rational language is therefore only part of an abstract-experiential communication between revelation and man. The above quotation from the *Excerpts* expresses, not merely a promise of knowledge, but one of salvation at the same time. If I perceive these answers through knowledge, I will rise to a state where I see myself, in my cosmic perdition and potential redemption, and this perception means elevation into a realm of perfection, of knowledge, of the saved; this perception is existential ascendancy over cosmic disaster. Here we have the double dimension in Gnostic language. On one hand, it communicates truth—objectively, intelligently, abstractly, mythologically; on

---

Reitzenstein, *Historia Monachorum und Historia Lausiaca* [Göttingen: 1916], pp. 97 ff.) beside Stoic language (Sagnard, *op. cit.,* pp. 579 ff.), but there is a Platonic background in both Valentinus and Basilides (Quispel, *art. cit., Eranos,* 1948, pp. 99 ff.). Platonic is the understanding of truth as metaphysic reality and the perception of knowledge as rediscovery. Of course, the Gnostic knowledge as "illumination" and "knowledge of God" (Rudolf Bultmann, art., γνῶσις, *ThWNT,* I, 693 ff.) is no longer Socratean knowledge, Platonism having moved east since Plutarch's work on Isis and Osiris (Lietzmann, *op. cit.,* I, 284 ff.). Quispel therefore demands a clear distinction between Platonic elements and Platonism (*art. cit.,* p. 111), and Sagnard's conclusion is a "double language," philosophic and Eastern (*op. cit.,* p. 616). The Eastern impact is heavier than the Greek.

[59] *Evangelium Phil.* (Epiph. *Pan.* XXVI.13.2), the ascent of the soul into heaven. *Odes of Solomon* 38.1; *Evang. Mar.* 16.3; *Evang. Thom.* 49; *Sophia J. Chr.* 105.12. Such ascent is a rising into the realm of thought (*Apocr. Joh.* 54.7), by the initiated (48.2), to whom Christ has revealed himself (86.7). The goal of this knowledge through ascent is "rest," *Evang. Mar.* 17.5; *Apocr. Joh.* 68.12; *Sophia J. Chr.* 110.7; *Evang. Thom.* 60. Cf. the line in *Evang. Thom.* 2: seeking—finding—to be troubled—to marvel—to reign, and in *Stob. Herm.* VI.18: νοῆσαι θεόν—θεάσασθαι—μακάριος γενέσθαι. Also *Corpus Hermeticum* IV.2, X.15, and XIV.4. *Revelation of Zostrian and Zoroaster* (Doresse, *op. cit.,* p. 157): "Then I ascended into the perceptible world."

the other hand, it only accompanies truth, it hides truth within its oracle. Mystery is revealed fact, and mystery is unpronounceable.

This double dimension parallels the obvious—yet at first sight so puzzling—fact that Gnostic language is both visionary and instructive. The spectral touch of unreality in the midst of didactic speech is an expression for an experience beyond language. Such speech is not mystic in a proper, but only in a derivative, sense because ascending occurs in the grasping of knowledge and nowhere else. Nor is it experiential in the sense that emotion comes first, for Gnostic religious experience stands in no antinomy whatsoever to the intellect but is absolutely tied to it, to "intellect," of course, related and defined by the revelation itself. Formulations like "mystic," "abstract," "experiential," are no more than approaches to the inner essence of Gnostic language. They all attempt to explain this peculiarly theological as well as mythological, abstract as well as imaginative, speech. Such must be the language that communicates the Gnostic concern.

This double dimension explains why such didactic speech consistently lapses into negation. Because to explain "who we were and what we have become" is only to verbalize a visionary-intellectual operation of the human spirit, language takes refuge at regular intervals in intimating what cannot be expressed: the absolute transcendence of the deity which is responsible for the mystery of language. Negative language in Gnosticism is the breath that prevents this speech from becoming rationalistic. It would be a grave mistake to apply the numerous statements concerning the uncommunicable divine essence solely to a realm *ante gratiam* as if in revelation what there is to say about God has been said. The *Gospel of Truth* makes this already quite clear, let alone works such as the *Apocryphon of John* or *Pistis Sophia*.[60] Negative language accompanies abstract; it is its shadow, its reflection, its mystery. Only when they both meet will the Gnostic be in possession of a means of communication.

Why should there be any problem with such language? Is this not exactly how the kerygma should be communicated? This specific nature of a speech that conveys truth in words, yet the truth in

---

[60] A good example lies in the juxtaposition of negative and pantheistic formulations in *Unknown Copt. Work*—for instance in its final hymn 22.270 ff.

not merely words—this echoes the Pauline tension that faith comes from hearing (Rom. 10:16), yet all knowledge may be useless (I Cor. 13:2). Could not Paul have affirmed exactly this: that all knowledge which must be preached is never knowledge for its own sake but is only "in Christ" (I Cor. 2:2), in a realm beyond the merely abstract and intellectual—knowledge as part of carrying the stigmata (Gal. 6:16)? Moreover, does Paul not use language ("to depart" in Phil. 1:23; "to be in Christ" in II Cor. 5:17) that expresses the same perpendicular movement of Gnostic knowledge? And finally, has not Paul also negative language at certain crucial places in his letters, in the final verses of Rom. 11 and in his account of a vision in II Cor. 12:4? The "Gnostic" understanding of language contains a profound element of truth for the communication of Christian faith.

The problem breaks open as soon as its various aspects are examined, namely its dualistic, cosmological, and—tied in with this—its non-Hebraic connotations. We enter the issue of "ontological" language by showing what takes place when the Gnostic makes use of numerical symbolism.

Language and Ontology

THE GNOSTIC USE OF NUMBERS

It would be a mistake to deny the symbolic use of numbers in the Bible. The very opening of Genesis has a numerical structure and the last book of the Bible is again full of symbolic numbers. When Gnosticism makes such a vast use of numerical symbolism, it can obviously appeal to biblical precedents. When Barnabas uses 318 in symbolic fashion (9:8), as Revelation veils its secret truth behind 666 (13:17-18), why should the Gnostics then not refer to 365 (Hipp. *Ref.* VII.26.6; Iren. *Adv. Haer.* I.24.3)?

Biblical numbers have primarily two dimensions. They are related to the meaning of the Old Testament and to the newness of faith in the New Testament. In the first instance, there is the number "twelve." This is obviously connected with the twelve tribes (Matt. 19:28). The number twelve originates in Israel, even though the symbolism does not always make this explicit. However, this symbolism turns into a New Testament symbol in its own right. Contemporary study indicates a twelvefold structure in the Gospel of Mark.[61] The "twelve" in the second sense points not only toward the Old Testament—toward Israel which it represents —but also toward the "Twelve" whom Christ elected and who are the twelve apostles of the Lamb in the Eschaton (Rev. 21:12, 14). The same is true with the number "four." Its relation to the Tetragrammaton, the perfect number of God's name, is the first case in point. The Matthean Apocalypse even quotes the Old Testament reference to the four winds (Matt. 24:31; Zech. 2.6; Rev. 4.1), and the symbolic animals of Revelation go back to Ezekiel (Rev. 4.1; Ezek. 1.10). But at the same time four is the number of the Gospels, an implicit fact which became extremely popular in the early church and in the history of art to our very day. The four parts of the seamless robe of Jesus (John 19.23) and the four days of death in the story of Lazarus (John 11:17) are now connected with the life and work of Christ. The number seven has a close relation to creation. The number of the seven churches, spirits, and angels in Revelation is the number of the days of creation.[62] But it is also the number of miracles in the Gospel of John and the amount of bread in the feeding of the four thousand (Matt. 15.34). "Seven" is connected with the work and sacrament of the Christ. It is a New Testament symbol in addition to its Old Testament background. New Testament symbolism becomes most obvious in the number three. The Old Testament symbol for God is four, conditioned by the consonants of JHWH, and the number three plays only a minor role. The New Testament uses the number three from very early times, explicitly in the three days of Paul's blindness (Acts 9:9) and the three loaves of bread (Luke 11:5), implicitly in the Pauline blessings, the first Epistle of John, and the Matthean formula at the end of his Gospel.[63]

---

[61] Austin M. Farrer, *A Study in St. Mark* (New York: Oxford University Press, 1952), pp. 69 ff., 80-81 (the twelve healing miracles).

[62] Rengstorf (*ThWNT*, II, 629) shows that the symbolism of the "seven" exists in places where seven planets were not known and therefore must be seen as symbolism for the four times seven days to the phase of the moon.

[63] Jesus uses "three" in the parable (Matt. 13:33). We have three days (Luke 2:46; Mark 8:2; Acts 5:7), three months (Luke 1:56), three years (Gal. 1:18), in addition to three angels (Rev. 6:6), three evil spirits (16:13), and three plagues (9:18). The triadic formulas II Cor. 13:13 (and I Cor. 13:13), I Pet. 1:2, I John 5:7-8, and Matt. 28:19 are not trinitarian formulas (*cf.* Schrenk, *ThWNT*, V, 1013), but because of their liturgical foundation play a

It can hardly be affirmed that the use of numbers in the New Testament is void of any cosmological associations. Implications about the four points of the compass and the four basic elements of life may or may not have been present. The number seven in Revelation reveals cosmic concepts. If there is a relation of this symbol to the one in creation, a cosmological tie is established. This dimension, however, is a secondary one throughout the New Testament symbolism of numbers. There is not one planetary speculation, not one indication of cosmogonic references on the part of these numbers. The elements are sharply rejected (Col. 2:8; 2:20). The symbolism with regard to creation is never used in any sense of a natural theology or pantheistic law, as in the Hellenistic *Tyche* or the astrological syncretistic theology.[64] New Testament symbolism is rooted in, and primarily directed toward, a sovereign God and the free act of redemption.

In the Gnostic numbers another symbolic world scintillates. Already in Simon, whoever he is, numbers have a cosmological dimension. The number of creation is used for Simonian cosmogonic speculations and therewith belongs in priority to the cosmic spheres. The double triad divides the six days of creation and stands for the dichotomy heaven and earth, *nous* and *epinoia* (Hipp. *Ref.* VI.14.1 ff.). The numbers express a cosmic relation, as "four" and "one" in the empyreal world represent basic principles of existence (Hipp. *Ref.* V.9.5). The secret names of Abrasax and Meithras in the construct of Basilides which result in the figure 365 are clearly symbols of the cosmic structure. Abrasax is the cosmic power who comprehends the 365 heavens.[65] Whatever

---

considerable role in the establishment of fourth-century trinitarian thought (Harnack, *op. cit.*, I, 175). Beside the basic number four, the OT, of course, knows and uses the three all along, from Gen. 18:2 to Jonah 1:17.

[64] Cf. F. Sagnard, "Extraits de Théodote," *Sources Chrétiennes* (Paris: 1948), XXIII, 226.

[65] *Acta Archelaus* 3; Iren. *Adv. Haer.* I.24.7; Hipp. *Ref.* VII.26.6; *Cf.* Walter Völker, *Quellen zur Geschichte der christlichen Gnosis*, pp. 45 ff. Typical for Gnostic speculation is the combination of seven plus twelve, *Psalms of Thomas* 1.22; 1.31; 1.42; *Sophia J. Chr.* 77.13 (seven women and twelve disciples follow Christ); *Apocr. Joh.* 39.10 (there are seven angels for each of the twelve aeons). The old man in the *Gospel of Thomas* asks a question of a child of seven years (*Evang. Thom.* 3), and in the act of wrath there are seven participants (*Evang. Mar.* 16.4). On cosmological meaning of speculations with numbers cf. W. Bousset, *op. cit.*, pp. 358 ff. and K. Stahle, *Die Zahlenmystik bei Philon von Alexandria* (Tübingen: 1933).

subordinate cosmic relation may have existed in the biblical numerical symbolism has here become an essential feature in a natural cosmology. Numbers here contain ontological qualities in themselves: the elements have asserted themselves as principles of life. "Seven" and "fourteen" reflect the "primal nature" in the "primal sperm" (Hipp. *Ref.* V.7.21). The twenty-four letters of the alphabet are emanations which symbolize the original triadic force.[66] "Twelve" points toward an aeonic choir (*Act. Thom.* 6-7). The clearest exposition of this new status of numerical symbolism can be found in the Valentinian cosmogony with its thirty aeons. The number thirty is reached by two different processes: the original eight emanate a tenfold (Logos and life) and a twelvefold (*anthropos* and *ekklesia*) aeon circle (Iren. *Adv. Haer.* I.1.2), a number also reached through the mystical and symbolic addition of 1 plus 3 plus 6 plus 9 plus 11 (Iren. *Adv. Haer.* I.1.3). The cosmic law in its manifold ramifications is deducible from two presuppositions. Both prove the celestial order. Yet the second, a deduction from the famous parable of the workers in the vineyard, is used primarily to express the heavenly constellation. Now, even if the New Testament parable contains the number thirty, and even if in this thirty some heavenly constellation or stellar mythology be implied, the parable is told to show the grace of the Lord and not to teach metaphysics. In Gnosticism the biblical orientation toward the redemptive event in using the symbolism of numbers is replaced by an ontological symbolism in its own right.[67]

[66] Iren. *Adv. Haer.* I.14.5. *Apocr. Joh.* 39.6: Jaldabaoth creates twelve angels, every one in his aeon, according to the twelve incorruptible aeons. Number is reflection of the structure of truth, but as cosmic reflection since truth is cosmic. *Exc. ex Theod.* 25:2: Christ with Apostles=sun with zodiac. Orig. *C.C.* VI.35: seven circles of seven cosmic rulers in the Ophite cult. Seven planetary zones already in *Herm. Trism.* I.25. Speculations play with numeric additions in *Apocr. Joh.* 39 (leading either to 360 in the MS of Till, *Pap. Ber. 8502,* p. 43, or 365, in Chenoboskion, Doresse, *op. cit.,* p. 203) and in Iren. *Adv. Haer.* I.16.1: 1 plus 2 plus 3 plus 4 equals the number 10. There is extensive numeric symbolism in *Pist. Soph., Myst. Log.,* and *Unknown Copt. Work;* see the diagrams of numeric emanations in Walter Till, *Koptisch-Gnostische Schriften,* pp. 268 ff.

[67] Numeric symbolism is cosmic symbolism (Christ sends three disciples each into the four directions of the world, *Pist. Soph.* 148.385) but is at the same time expression of the forces of life and death (Doresse, *op. cit.,* p. 147, n. 2). *Stob. Herm.* XXVII.16 knows sixty grades of quality of souls. The crucial point of divergence between Christian and Gnostic numeric symbolism has been

Early Christianity loves to play with numeric symbolism. Let it play! The issue is not whether it should enjoy doing this but whether numbers become entities in themselves (explaining the world by numeric metaphysic proportionality) or whether they remain subservient to an inner-Christian faith. In Gnosticism, the Christocentric symbol (Abraham's circumcising 318 people) has become a cosmocentric one (forty-six years of building the temple as a mystic symbol).[68] Once the symbol is rooted in, not merely touched by, cosmic relation, once it explains existence from stages of being, then it has deprived Christian faith of its primacy of redemption. When man's fourfold existence is *conditioned* by the four heavens (*Exc. ex Theod.* 51.1) and Adam has "derived qualities" from the fourth of these stages, called "paradise" (Iren. *Adv Haer.* I.5.2), then the redeeming word of Christian faith has become subordinate to the structure of the universe.

THE GNOSTIC COSMOS

We have observed in numeric symbolism a proneness to an autonomous metaphysical essence of the symbolic number. A similar bent captures the concept of the cosmos. The Old Testament did not possess a term for the "world" when the authors of the LXX introduced *kosmos* into biblical speech.[69] For the New Testament, however, it is a familiar word, in most places. The disciples are the light of the world which God has loved but which will pass away.[70] Paul is crucified to the world and its wisdom, yet the gospel bears fruit in the whole cosmos whose Savior is the Christ.[71] Kosmos occurs

---

formulated by Farrer, *op. cit.,* p. 79: for Mark, the numbers "were his instrument and not his masters." In *Unknown Copt. Work* 2.228, the twelve depths (βάθη) represent the ground of being. Cosmic number is meant to be a reflection of ultimate reality.

[68] *Barnabas* 9.8 versus Heracl. *Fragm.* 16. How the number can become cosmic principle can be further studied in the role of "four," cf. *Till, Pap. Ber. 8502,* p. 28; Sagnard, "Extraits de Théodote," p. 165; Heinrich Schlier, *Religions-geschicthliche Untersuchungen zu den Ignatiusbriefen* (Giessen: 1929), p. 107; and Sagnard, *La Gnose Valentinienne,* pp. 337 ff.

[69] Rudolf Bultmann, *Theologie des Neuen Testamentes* (Tübingen: 1953), p. 250 and G. Florovsky, "Eschatology in the Patristic Age," *Patr. Stud.* II, [1955], 240 ff.

[70] Matt. 5:14; Phil. 2:15; John 3:16; Rom. 3:6; I Tim. 1:15; I John 4:9; I Cor. 7:31; I John 5:4.

[71] Gal. 6:14; I Cor. 1:20; 2:12 (Heb. 11:38 and I John 3:13); Col. 1:6; Rom. 1:8; John 4:42; II Cor. 5:19; I John 4:14.

throughout the New Testament. The observation that the Old Testament has no word for the world does not seem to help much. Or does it?

The Gnostic seizes upon the fact that *kosmos* is a favorite term, especially in the Johannine literature. We know of a special prologue to this gospel in the Valentinian school.[72] The extraordinary interest of the Gnostic in this concept points immediately toward our concern: *kosmos,* since the New Testament, has undergone a transmutation of context and of importance. The world becomes a metaphysical entity. Part of the kerygma is communication about the cosmic structure, because *kosmos* is part of the whole structure of being to which man belongs. There is a deep inner relation between cosmos and man's own inner cosmos (κόσμος ἰδικός).[73] Cosmos is the basis for existence; the cosmic sperm brings forth the threefold sonship.[74] Christ reveals its nature and its mysteries; man must know the cosmogony because when he fathoms the coming into being of existence he understands himself. The New Testament never teaches cosmology as part of its saving message; as a matter of fact, it does not possess one specific cosmology. Nowhere does it teach a cosmogony, a fact which expresses lucidly the lack of interest in the cosmos as a metaphysical principle. Knowledge concerning the cosmos contains no redemptive value of any kind; the redemption is Christ, and never Christ's *mysterion* concerning the shape of the cosmos. The Gnostic cosmos makes a statement about salvation. Because it is a part of a plan involving God and the world, and because there is an inner connection between its nature and man's, man must perceive its essence in order to ascend. Ascent takes place within the cosmos. The cosmos is part of God's own structure of being, as the Hermetic Corpus phrases it in his famous sequence:

GOD—AEON—COSMOS—TIME—GENESIS.[75]

[72] Iren. *Adv. Haer.* I.8.5-6; *cf. Herm. Trism.* I.4 ff.

[73] Hipp. *Ref.* V.8.5; *cf. Herm. Trism.* X.14 and VIII.2: the cosmos, having been made immortal, by the eternal God, is the "second god" (VII.1), the material god (X.10), to which man is subject (X.22).

[74] Hipp. *Ref.* VII.22.7. The play with words κόσμος—κοσμεῖν (*Exc. ex Theod.* 41.4) stands in strong contradiction to the dualism of *Evang. Thom.* 56 ("The one who has perceived the world has found a body") ; *cf.* Casey, *op. cit.,* p. 135.

[75] *Herm. Trism.* XI.2. *Mysterion* of Jesus as detailed revelation concerning

This is the consequent subservience of redemption to being in the Gnostic use of language.

No Christian theology can formulate its witness without an ontological terminology. In a church which addresses Hellenistic civilization and its countless future parallels, the language about heaven and earth, creation and world, nature and being, is inevitable for the communication of biblical thought. As a matter of fact, this has been so, not only since the language of the Old Covenant moved into the sphere of the Greeks, but ever since there has been theological language at all. The situation is only aggravated after the one linguistic step that reinterpreted the Old Testament by a new code of semantics; ὁ ὤν (Exod. 3:14). The new Testament uses flesh-spirit, pleroma-aeon-heaven-cosmos; and its God appears as "the one who is and who was and who shall be" (Rev. 1:8). This is *ontological* language in a broad sense, *i.e.,* language that lends itself to a study of being, language in which the "abstract," or "the essential," or the "metaphysical" can be grasped, formulated, and brought into coherent systematic shape.[76]

The New Testament uses such language constantly. So does the Gnostic. The issue between them lies in the place, emphasis, and relation which the ontological word or phrase can—or cannot—maintain. Can there be a doctrine of being which comprises God-cosmos-man in a metaphysic vision? Does the statement about heaven and earth, generation and fall, and the language concerning stages and differences of being *dominate, determine,* and *explain* existence? Must you have a metaphysical understanding of the language of being of cosmic stages and generic natures, in order to understand yourself as a creature in need of redemption? Here lies the split. In the New Testament there is no cosmogony, there

---

cosmic facts, pleroma and aeons through the late *Pist. Soph.* (16 ff.). A profound insight can be found in Hans Jonas' *The Gnostic Religion* ([Boston: Beacon Press, 1958], p. 254) where he opposes "Christianity's own acosmic tendencies" to the Gnostic language of principle.

[76] "Ontological" in the antithesis coined by August Dell, "Imago Dei" (*Festschrift für Gustav Krüger* [Giessen: 1932]): *"ontologische Daseinsanalyse"* versus *"theologisches Daseinsverständnis."* Wilhelm Kamlah (*Christentum und Geschichtlichkeit* [Stuttgart Köln: 1951], p. 92) has made an important distinction between antique and modern (scientific) ontology.

is no "specifically biblical" cosmology; there is nowhere any instruction concerning the nature of heaven and there is no metaphysic of flesh and spirit.[77] Ontological language does not yet mean ontology! Of course, the New Testament often uses the Greek categories of flesh and spirit, and at times they come close to becoming a metaphysical pivot; yet always the ontological will be crossed out by the christological concern, by theocentric relation.[78] There is in the Book of Revelation an apocalyptic imagery which presupposes heavenly structures; but the drama of the work does not depend upon, does not even need for its fulfillment, the specific nature of the heavenly structure. The ontological language of Gnosticism, however, establishes a frame of being from which existence is derived and understood (*Evang. Ver.* 21.11).[79]

Here we have reached the heart of Gnostic language. The basic experience of the Gnostic is his being thrown into a lost world.[80] In a new vision of man at the twilight of the ancient world—not Greece, not Persia, but between the two—gnosis sees the hopeless situation of man, severed from an alien, unpronounceable deity, a "God" who is in reality this man's own fallen self, self being neither body nor soul but pneuma. All Gnostic religions have one goal in common: to present to man redemption from his tragically bereft existence. For this earthly existence of his, the Gnostic is given a cosmic explanation.[81] The dualistic Gnostic language furnishes the frame by which I understand myself as thrown into the lost world. In understanding why the aeons fell, I understand my own hopeless situation; hearing why and how and by whom

[77] Already in *Evang. Thom.*, as Gärtner has shown (*op. cit.*, p. 141), the question about the *nature of Jesus* comes to the fore.

[78] Eduard Schweizer, *ThWNT*, VI, 413 ff., and his article, "Die hellenistische Komponente im neutestamentlichen σάρξ—Begriff," *Zeitschr. f. neut. Wiss.* 56 (1957), 237 ff. and Samuel Laeuchli, "Monism and Dualism in the Pauline Anthropology," *Bibl. Research* 3 (1958), 15 ff. *Cf.* also Gärtner, *op. cit.*, p. 169, on the somewhat dualistic life-death antithesis of the New Testament which has been turned into a "decisive antithesis" between two worlds, hyle and aeons.

[79] Symptomatic is the Gnostic use of "root"; the place toward which the Gnostic directs his thought is his root (*Evang. Ver.* 41.23) because the roots of God's emanations are in him (41.16). The same concept again in *Paraphrase of Shem* (Doresse, *op. cit.*, p. 147).

[80] Hans Jonas, *Gnosis und spätantiker Geist*, I, 140 ff.

[81] Cf. Gilles Quispel, "La Conception de l'Homme Valentinienne," *Eranos*, 1947, p. 249.

Adam was created, I no longer wonder about my drunken stumbling in a world of darkness. Into this dualistic gap redemption penetrates. Pneuma, the inner self, erring, wandering, crying for hope, can be redeemed and reascend to the unpronounceable realm of the divine. Cosmology and cosmogony are the necessary background for this scheme because they make understandable the coming down of primal man and the going up of the pneumatic substance.

Such dualistic language is both the product and interpretation of existence. On one hand, what is Gnostic dualistic language if not the projection of the situation of natural man upon a screen of cosmic mythology? The dualism which I perceive is the dualism within my own self. Yet we are dealing with more than merely a projection. In a brilliant modern interpretation of Gnosticism, based partly upon Martin Heidegger, Hans Jonas introduces the concept of transcendence. I do not only project my dualistic experience within me into mythology, I also find in this projection an "objectification," the objectivity of my existence.[82] Dualistic language as construct (interpretation) and dualistic language as projection (expression) are the two aspects in the dualistic semantics of Gnosticism which must be seen together in order to perceive Gnostic redemption. Pneuma fell: dualism is explained; the Soter came down: dualism is challenged; pneuma ascends through gnosis: dualism is conquered. You can still describe this process as "mythological projection of the experience within the self" (*Mysthische Projektion der Selbsterfahrung*)[83] but it must be understood in two senses: an experience which the self makes (as subject) and an experience which takes place within the self (as object).

Throughout this literature we find monistic and dualistic language side by side. In our discussion of the Father concept in the *Gospel of Truth* we already concluded that the two cannot be severed temporally. The *Gospel of Thomas* presents us with two excellent examples for the proximity of two conflicting ontological trends: "Woe to the flesh which depends upon the soul; woe to the soul which depends upon the flesh" (112) versus the famous

[82] *Op. cit.*, II, 4 ff.
[83] Quispel, *Gnosis als Weltreligion*, p. 17.

Logion 77 "Cleave a (piece of) wood, I am there; lift up the stone and you will find me there." Gnostic ontology combines existential dualism with ultimate monism.[84] These two languages struggle violently with each other. One could write a history of Gnosticism by establishing the borders between these two types of speech, from extreme Iranian dualism to the pantheism exhibited in the Logion 77 just quoted. The meeting of dualism with monism, or the mutual penetration of the two, is *conditio sine qua non* for Gnostic redemption. Were it not so, it would not be my pneuma which is saved!

Here lies the ontological problem of Gnostic language. The nature of pneuma is "one in kind and single [μονοειδής and ἑνική]," says Heracleon in Fragment 37. How can pneuma be one in a dualistic ontology? This is what made Plotinus so furious with the Gnostics.[85] They break the universe asunder, yet postulate ontological layers in this universe through which Soter descends.

> Why should this down-shining take place unless such a process belonged to a univeral law? Either the process is in the order of Nature or against that order. If it is in the nature of things it must have taken place from eternity; if it is against the nature of things, then the breach of natural right exists in the Supreme also.—*Plotinus Ennead* II.9.13.

There goes forever the dream of ontological coherence in Christian theology! This strikes home at the inner contradiction of ontological theology. The Christian Gnostic is caught in the friction of two conflicting ontologies. If pneuma which saves me is pneuma within me, then God is both pneumatic substance in me and pneumatic substance coming down; such a God is no longer the biblical God. Gnostic dualistic language negates in practically every concept its Hebraic root. Gnostic pneuma is "one in kind and single,"—this attempt at a religious coherence fails both philosophically and theologically. Plotinus rejects it. It is not coherent; but biblical faith has to reject it: its pneuma is not conceived in ontological coherence. Pneuma of God versus pneuma of man is a statement of faith, of an encounter, of an address, of a relation, and of a dependence—and, we must add, of worship between for-

[84] Harnack (*op. cit.*, I, 261) coined the well-known phrase that the Gnostics are dualists on the lower and monists on the higher level.

[85] C. Schmidt, *Plotin's Stellung zum Gnosticimus* (Leipzig: 1901), pp. 37 ff.

giveness and praise. As soon as it becomes more, i.e., is molded into
a framework of ontology, pneuma will strangle the biblical God
in his sovereignty and in his mercy. In Gnosticism the identity and
coherence of pneuma belong to the essence of redemption. This is
why the biblical God has been constricted.

Dualism is mythological "objectification of existence." It is not
the purpose of this study to survey and sift the different Gnostic
schools. Dualism, the common denominator of Gnosticism,[86] can
take on different shades, starting from the light-darkness motive,[87]
through dualistic anthropologies to a hermaphrodite principle of
revelation,[88] or to extreme dualistic ethics.[89] Almost always,

[86] Oscar Cullman, *Le problème littéraire et historique du roman pseudo-Clémentin* (Paris: 1930), p. 191 and Hans Jonas, *op. cit.*, II, 94 ff.) Helmer Ringgren (in Ringgren-Ström, *Die Religionen der Völker* [Stuttgart: 1959], p. 381) divides the whole of the Gnostic literature in a Manichaean-Mandaean and a Syriac-Egyptian dualism.

[87] A few references must suffice. The important early document is of course the *War of the Sons of Light with the Sons of Darkness*, 1.1, XII (XIII.1-6). (We have left the Qumran references out completely since they are temporally far removed from the collision between church and gnosis in the second century; for the same reason Hermetic references, *Psalms of Thomas* and *Pist. Soph.* are only used secondarily.) Light-Darkness in *Evang. Mar.* 16.6; *Evang. Ver.* 30.6; *Evang. Thom.* 25; *Apocr. Joh.* 59.21, and, in Chenoboskion, *Par. of Shem.* (Doresse, *op. cit.*, p. 147); *Second Treatise of the Great Seth* (p. 150); cf. also *Corp. Herm.* I.28 and *Pist. Soph.* 126. The paraphrase of the creation story (*Unknown Copt. Work* 18.261) is in dualistic phrases.

[88] *Evang. Thom.* 114; ἀρσηνόθηλυς Hipp. *Ref.* V.7.14, Iren. *Adv. Haer.* I.18.2. The male-female aeon does not grow old (*Apocr. Joh.* 28.2) and the divine spirit is male and virgin at the same time (37.5; 75.11; and *Sophia J. Chr.* 94.11, already in "Simon," Hipp. *Ref.* VI.18.6). The communion of the female principle with the male of *Act. Thom.* 27 and 50 comes back in *Arkhangelike:* the male-female death (Doresse, *op. cit.*, p. 167) and the male-female eros (p. 168). The dualistic view of man exists everywhere, in Valentinianism (Iren. *Adv. Haer.* I.5.5; *Exc. ex Theod.* 51.1); in Ophite circles (Hipp. *Ref.* V.26.32); in Menander (Tert. *De Resurrectione Carnis* 5). χοϊκός is earthly corruption, *Myst. Log.* 4:43. Pneumatic versus somatic is the great antithesis (Iren. *Adv. Haer.* I.6.1-4) whereby the pneumatic is saved and the psychic will be destroyed (*Exc. ex Theod.* 56.3). Revealing anthropological terms are πτῶμα (*Evang. Thom.* 60, 80, 87) and ὕλη (*Evang. Ver.* 25.17; 35.9; ὑλικός *Exc. ex Theod.* 47.3; 56.2; *Apocr. Joh.* 52.17; 55.7). The difference between Gnostic ὕλη and biblical σάρξ is the difference between dualistic ontology and dualistic language that does *not* represent a dualistic anthropology (against Grobel, *op. cit.*, p. 123, n. 329). Typical are Hipp. *Ref.* V.7.40 (ἡ κάτω κτίσις-θνητή, ἡ ἄνω κτίσις-ἀθάνατος) and *Ps. Thom.* 14.8-11 (where ὕλη is the evil mother of this earth). In *Unknown Copt. Work* 13.251 ὕλη is manifestation of evil.

[89] We have on one hand Gnostic libertinism (Clem. Alex. *Strom.* III.18.2 and

dualism coerces Christology into Docetism.[90] Dualistic ontology in conflict with a monistic metaphysic calls for countless variations. The transmutation of one into the other can be clothed in magic syncretism or delicately phrased in philosophical finesse, in a search for ultimate reality; apocalypticism and philosophy, superstition and theology of revelation will fight to determine the hinge of ontological unification. The labyrinth will increase with forthcoming Gnostic manuscripts. From the perspective of a biblical language they have all one common denominator: dualistic ontological language holds a metaphysical primacy over the Christian understanding of language, because the starting point for all its speech is the human situation, namely the dualistic experience. We have inquired into the division between Christian and Gnostic language; what has the refined mind of Basilides in common with the flimsy intelligence behind *Pistis Sophia?* That for both, seen from a biblical perspective, the dualistic experience of man in its transcendental objectification created a (metaphysical or philosophical) dualistic language which precedes and channels biblical semantics.[91]

The language of the gospel is the speech of redeemed existence. For the faith of the New Testament, Christian existence is rooted in the event of Jesus Christ, in his kerygma about the kingdom, in his coming down from the Father, and in his merciful righteousness. Language communicates the fact, promise, and truth of this encounter with the Christ. Language is witness to this encounter, by the man who shares in it. As an expression of the earthly and personal confrontation, it is dominated by one goal: to communicate this confrontation. This confrontation means redemption, and redemption is life in Christ. Speech is expression of, and wit-

---

II.26.3); on the other, denial of the sexual realm (Marcionite marriage called *spurcitiae,* Tert. *Adv. Marc.* I.19; the devil tempts Eve but not Adam in *Slav. Hen.* 31.6; the male principle as truth and the female principle as error, *Clem. Homilies* III.27). Both are consequences of dualistic anthropology.

[90] The Valentinian fragment Clem. Alex. *Strom.* III.59.3: Food which Jesus ate was not corrupted because Jesus had no corruptibility in him. Consistent with dualistic ontology the Logos departs from Jesus before the passion, Iren. *Adv. Haer.* I.26.1; *Evang. Pet.* 19.

[91] A symptomatic case is the Marcionite change of Luke 12:51 in which his dualistic experience makes Marcion change the text; Christ does not give, he *throws* peace on earth.

ness to, a living relation: "It is no longer I who live, but Christ who lives in me" (Gal. 2:20). Between such use of language and the Gnostic use lies the grace of Christ, lies the dimension of a historic faith, lies a personal and acting God. What prevents such biblical language about being (which, of course, it also is) from becoming metaphysical is nothing else than the core of biblical faith itself: a free-acting God, mercy as freedom, grace as gift. Redemption must be expressed by some kind of semantics but it must never be dominated by semantics as a metaphysical entity. In Gnosticism, redemption is part of a cosmic frame, and part of understanding redemption is to understand the frame.[92] Biblical speech has never drawn out the lines to the Gnostic frames which its language obviously contains. Creation is what redeemed existence faces but not that by which it is conditioned.

Language and History

The last paragraph leads us to the next point. We determined what Gnostic language has become; we proceed by asking what is forfeited in this metamorphosis when assumed by Christian theology. The use of allegory will serve as introductory example.

THE GNOSTIC ALLEGORY

In the *Gospel of Truth*, a biblical parable receives a peculiar interpretation. Christ "is the shepherd who left behind him the ninety-nine sheep which had not strayed" (*Evang. Ver.* 31.35). He found the lost one and "rejoiced when he found it" (32.4). Obviously we have here the Synoptic parable of Matt. 18:12-14 and Luke 15:4-7. The change from the number ninety-nine to the number one hundred is, in ancient popular arithmetic and the superstition of folklore, the transition from odd to even, from imperfect to perfect. Ninety-nine by ancient arithmetic sign language is indicated by finger positions of the left hand; according to popular notions, however, the left hand is sinister and the right hand favorable. Only one is therefore missing in ninety-nine (a position

---

[92] If you discover the beginning you discover the end: because where the beginning is there the end will be (*Evang. Thom.* 18). Hans Jonas, *Gnosis und spätantiker Geist*, II,I, pp. 131 ff. has summarized the issue in his distinction between the Gnostic "*Heilswelt*" and the Christian "*Heilstatsache.*"

of the left hand) to reach the right hand positions of the hundreds. This is what Jesus achieves in finding the one-hundredth sheep (32.6)! [93]

This allegory is symptomatic for the interpretive principle in Gnosticism. At the outset, there is the desire to understand a biblical passage or word. The explanation, however, cannot abide by the historical text, but moves immediately into the realm of the absolute. The parable indicates constellation, relation, perfection. As Gnostic salvation promises the deliverance of man from forgetting and want into a perfect relation with the ground of being through a perfection of knowledge, so does the parable point to this recovery of a totality, of a perfect relation. The language of the parable is understood in metaphysical concepts: as the communication of an abstract truth. The recovery of the even is the reinstallation of divine, perfect relation.[94] Faith offers the recovery of the self through participation in this perfection by means of an ascending knowledge.

The failure of such allegory exposes itself when we ask what it does *not* express. "He rejoiced when he found it." (32.4.) Why does He rejoice? Because "the entire sum is won" (32.8). This is most symptomatic. The interest is centered not on the one as one but on the one as having attributed to the recovery of the whole! The concern lies with the totality, or at least with the constellation. Such emphasis loses all sight of the shocking preference of Jesus for the one over all those who never went astray: "He rejoices over [the one] *more* than over the ninety-nine." (Matt. 18:13. Italics mine.) The interpretation is not interested in the uniqueness of this finding, and in its importance for this one-recovered individual as such. Neither does it elaborate on the finder, the Christ, nor on his act of finding, nor on the specific meaning of this recovery either in the place of Israel or in the locus of the Christian community. It does not, of course, touch on any ethical consequence

---

[93] A discussion of the parable by Grobel, *op cit.*, pp. 129-35, and Van Unnik, *Newly Discovered Gnostic Writings*, pp. 60-61. For the finger counting see the article by H. I. Marrou, "L'Évangile de Vérité et la diffusion du comput digital dans l'antiquité," *Vig. Christ.* 11 (1958), 98 ff.

[94] Grobel's suggestion that the circle means perfection makes sense (*op. cit.*, p. 133, n. 357). In every case some metaphysical meaning must be implied in 32.15-17.

which may or may not be implied in the parable. In any case, the parable has no interpretation in the earthly realm concerning the meaning of concrete forgiveness within a Christian church, or the relation between the righteous and the sinner, or the proclamation of the Kingdom by the person of Christ and the preaching of the church. Any one of these could reveal an understanding of the meaning of Christ's recovering the lost one. But none of these interpretations would fit the Gnostic concern. The shock of grace is replaced by the metaphysic quest.

This example of *Evangelium Veritatis* is symptomatic for Gnostic allegorization. "I am the door," is brought by Theodotus into an ontological frame, the separation of male and female seeds, a separation at the beginning of the fall *(Exc. ex Theod.* 21.1-2). At the end of the cycle, this separation dissolves and the female parts are changed into male (21:3); there is a boundary line (ὅρος) which marks the opening to the pleroma, the divine world (22:4).[95] "I am the door" means, therefore, *I am at this limit where this change of female into male seeds occurs and where the spiritual seeds enter the pleroma* (26:2-3). The problem of this interpretation does not lie in the fantastic imagery as it appears to the modern mind; to one who thought in these categories this was a natural trend of thought. The problem lies in the consequent metaphysical transformation of a biblical metaphor which now no longer considers the earthly Christ, the earthly body of Christ, and the earthly existence of the one who comes to the door. All interpretation refers to man's mind, to his experience and gnosis, and to the world grasped by this gnosis. Such interpretation has long ceased to be historical. It lacks the concern for the historical and for the concrete verbal meaning of a biblical word. Not that Gnosticism does not know Christian redemption or the existence of the Gospel.[96] But all this is spiritualized; it is "cosmic" in the

[95] For the identification of ὅρος with σταυρός, cf. Sagnard, *Extraits de Théodote,* p. 103, n. 2.

[96] Εὐαγγέλιον was the title of Marcion's gospel (Ch.-H. Puech in Hennecke, *op. cit.,* p. 258) and the word appears frequently in Gnostic writings, *Evang. Ver.* 17.2; *Evang. Mar.* 8.22; *Sophia J. Chr.* 98.10; *Hipp. Ref.* VII.26.5 (for Basilides); Iren. *Adv. Haer.* I.8.4 (for Valentinus). Valentinianism especially is akin to this concept and has therefore been called "mysticism of grace and election" (Quispel, *Eranos,* 1947, p. 262). But already in *Evang. Ver.* we discover

Gnostic sense. "The Holy Spirit will come upon thee" is seen as the descent of power and light from the sonship through Ogdoas and Hebdomas to Mary, a process which in the future is reversed by the upward movement of the lowest sonship toward purification (Hipp. *Ref.* VII.26.8-10). Such allegory has no understanding of the concrete and historical. All history—if you could ever call it such—is abstract and cosmic. This, however, is no longer history; the earth, the physical congregation, the sequence of events are only included as far as the abstract and cosmic event touches them.[97]

Gnostic interpretation means the adaptation of a biblical text to a metaphysical frame by either denying, or at least laying aside, the aspect of history. We can show this in the realm of anthropology. Adam is the offspring of the marriage between pleroma and eloim, a product of two conflicting forces, on the borderline between pleroma and creation (*Exc. ex Theod.* 41.4; Hipp. *Ref.* V.26.8; 26.23). The body of Adam is formed from evil matter.[98] The creation of the woman is the emanation of *ennoia* from the first man (*Apocr. Joh.* 59-60). All three examples use biblical metaphors to demonstrate anthropological facts: exegesis as the presentation of an anthropology. Interpretation is in reality the elaboration of a metaphysical concept of "man" with the tools of biblical language. "Primal man" in all the frequent and manifold elaborations of Gnosticism means the "Principle of manhood" in mythological shape.[99] It is the *principle* which the Gnostic is prone to show, and not the history. Because "primal man" is a metaphysical principle, so is the "second man"; there is a direct line from the metaphysical concern in exegesis to Docetism in Christology.

This anthropological primacy over history shows up in the anthropological dualism which is forced at all levels into the biblical

how "grace" and "election" are transplanted from a sphere of a God acting in this world to a sphere of "acting being."

[97] H. E. W. Turner, *The Pattern of Christian Truth* (London: Mowbray & Co. Ltd., 1954), p. 237: "In general, Gnostic exegesis bears all the traces of the flight from history which characterizes their systems as a whole." This is the nonhistorical denominator analogous to the dualistic one.

[98] Hipp. *Ref.* VI.34.4 and 14.5 ff.; *Exc. ex Theod.* 50.

[99] Only secondarily, primal man receives a soteriological dimension (Kraeling, *op. cit.*, p. 127).

text: *Corpus dicunt esse carcerem* (Iren. *Adv. Haer.* I.25.4). The Gnostic divisions into body and mind (*Gospel of Thomas* 80), female and male (*Gospel of Thomas* 114), or flesh and soul (*Gospel of Thomas* 112), with its countless additional metaphysical dualistic possibilities dominate the historical and christological passages. Hosea's words against the harlotry of the land; Christ's saying about the eunuchs; the Pauline words about the conflict between law and spirit—all must be molded to fit some dualistic concept of man, even though the specific metaphysics of one dualism varies from another.[100] Gnostic interpretation does not see any need for seeking to understand a text in its historical setting[101] because it cannot understand man as a whole, within a community of believers, in the tradition of Israel. The language of a biblical text is therefore meaningless to the Gnostic unless it fits his structure of thought, namely the dualism of his existence within his Gnostic self-consciousness. Language must assimilate itself to Gnostic metaphysics, otherwise it is not worth being pronounced.

The natural result of this forcing of a biblical word into a metaphysical pattern is the change of its meaning at will. Because Hyle is diabolical, exegesis must spiritualize any hylozoistic text. "Apart from the law" (Rom. 7:9) designates the pre-bodily existence of man (Origen *Ad. Rom.* V.1). The seventh commandment means libertinism once dualism is understood in its consequent metaphysical dimension (Clem. Alex. *Strom.* III.9.1-3). When Christ announces his death, he actually speaks of another person (Mark 8:31 in *Exc. ex Theod.* 61.4). "Blessed is the one who was before he became" is a clever reformulation of a familiar biblical theme in the *Gospel of Thomas* (19). Apocryphal gospels do not hesitate to introduce this principle of transformation into biblical documents themselves: "My power, my power, why hast thou forsaken me" is the famous cry of Jesus according to the *Gospel of Peter* 19. This is the replacement of biblical language

---

[100] Hipp. *Ref.* V.27.4 (on Hos. 1:2); Clem. Alex. *Strom.* III.1.1 ff.; *Exc. ex Theod.* 52 and the *Evang. Egypt.* (Clem. *Alex Strom.* III.4.5, 63 and 91 ff.; cf. Hennecke, *op cit.*, pp. 109 ff.) all pronounce a sharp dualism of male versus female which is modified in *Exc. ex Theod.* 67.

[101] The Jewish allegorical background is presented by L. Heinemann, *Altjüdische Allegoristik* (Tübingen: 1935). For the Greek counterpart see Wendland, *op. cit.*, pp. 115 ff. For the whole see Kamlah, *op. cit.*, pp. 91 ff.

by an acceptable Gnostic language in which dualistic metaphysics triumphs over Incarnation as concrete event.

Such Gnostic allegory is void of any typological interpretation. Typology differs from allegory in application.[102] The biblical word is not primarily understood in anthropological, psychological, or cultural patterns but from within God's own historic events on earth. Typology focuses exegesis on the core of biblical faith: God's redeeming history, *Heilsgeschichte*. Thus Adam points, not to anthropological truth, but to the second Adam, following the first (Rom. 5:14). Adam as Typos, leaving aside any modern critical concern about saga or myth in the creation story, means allegory channeled into the horizontal level of the divine act. The language of creation is understood by the language of historical Israel, the redeemed community. When it speaks of promise and fulfillment, first and second event, type and antitype, typology takes biblical language seriously in its meaning for the history of Israel and the Incarnation. This does not mean that every New Testament quotation can be neatly separated from allegory and classified as typological. As we examine the texts, it is simply not so. "You shall not muzzle an ox when it is treading out the grain." (Deut. 25:4, in I Cor. 9:9 ff.) Paul mastered rabbinic allegory to his heart's content! Yet that the whole of New Testament interpretation belongs in a broad sense to some typological kind of exegesis is proved by Gnostic allegory, where there is no attempt at typology. Exegesis neither focuses on the historical Christ, nor concerns itself with the fulfillment of history. Neither is the object the present community of Christ as the locus of the Holy Spirit, which would look to the incarnate act of the earthly Christ. Typology is plainly impossible for the Gnostic because the frame within which exegesis operates has no history, because his dualism cannot accept the Old Testament, and because his anthropology rejects Hyle. The only possibility for exegesis under this axiom is a thoroughgoing reinterpre-

---

[102] L. Goppelt, *TYPOS: die typologische Deutung des AT. im Neuen* (Gütersloh: 1939), and the two essays in *Stud. in Bibl. Theol.* 1957 by G. W. H. Lampe ("The Reasonableness of Typology") and K. J. Woolcombe ("The Biblical Origins and Patristic Development of Typology"). The question was reformulated by Walther Eichrodt: "Ist typologische Exegese sachgemässe Exegese?", *Theol. Lit. Ztg.* 81 (1956), 641 ff. Also Hugo Rahner on Barnabas, "Das mystische Tau," *Zeitschr. f. kath. Theol.* 75 (1953), 385 ff.

tation in metaphysical terms. "God has made heaven and earth" (or Gen. 1:1) becomes: "The Demiurge has created psychic and hylic beings" (*Exc. ex Theod.* 47.2). Exegesis is explanation of one language by another. Because Gnostic speech is exclusively dualistic, negative and experiential, the concreteness of the biblical language is suppressed. The difference between the two exegetical principles of pure allegory and typological allegory does not merely lie in a greater or lesser degree of "arbitrariness" (typology can be very arbitrary at times) but in the approach to the historic concreteness of the word of God.[103]

What are the steps from Christian speech to Gnostic speech?[104]
1. *The loss of the language about Jesus Christ.* In the Coptic *Gospel according to Mary,* the prologue to the "Apocryphon of John," Christ appears as the Savior (7.2) who speaks in an apparently historical situation; Peter asks him questions, Christ answers them (7.10 ff.). More than this, he greets the disciples, he pronounces his peace over them, and he sends them out to preach the gospel (8.12 ff.). The Coptic manuscript opens with what seems to be a real scene in the life of Christ. Traces like these appear throughout Gnostic writings. Suddenly we hear of the passion, of a parable, even of Pontius Pilate.[105] Some texts prefer to speak of Jesus, some speak exclusively of Christ [106] but many pretend that

---

[103] Gnosticism neither needs nor knows actual history; what seems to be history is rather *"symbole pour désigner un processus intérieur,"* Quispel, Eranos, 1948, p. 125.

[104] For the specifically linguistic aspects of this problem consult the contributions by Christine Mohrmann. "Linguistic Problems in the Early Church," *Vig. Christ.* 11 (1957), 11 ff. lists several of her publications which are often inaccessible. We hope that soon there will come a comprehensive monograph from her pen on this subject.

[105] *Exc. ex Theod.* 23.3; the mustard grain in Basilides (Hipp. *Ref.* VII.21.3); and the Naassene fragment (V.9.6).

[106] *"Christ"* for instance in Iren. *Adv. Haer.* I.2.5 (Valentinus); I.21.3 (Marcus); Hipp. *Ref.* VII.26.2 (Basilides); V.7.33 (Naassenes); in *Sophia J. Chr.* 114.14; *Apocr. Joh.* 30.17. In Ptolemy's letter "Christ" appears only once in a quotation (5.14), while the word is fully absent in the syncretistic fragment of the Gnostic Justin. "Jesus" is rarer; appears, however, throughout Gnostic texts, *Evang. Ver.* 20.23; *Apocr. Joh.* 77.8; *Sophia J. Chr.* 127.12; *Exc. ex Theod.* 36.2; Iren. *Adv. Haer.* I.2.6 (Valentinus); I.21.3 (Marcus); Hipp. *Ref.* VII.27.12 (Basilides); and V.10.2 (the Naassene Psalm). This evidence shows that the problem of speaking about Jesus Christ is not merely one of mentioning him or not mentioning him, but of *how* this name is used.

73

they know the history of Jesus and refer to it naturally. Perhaps they do! *Evang. Ver.* 20.10-14 certainly gives the appearance of doing so. But even *if* they do, what they say about the historical Jesus is never more than background scenery which *nolens, volens,* the Gnostic feels should be used in his elaboration of gnosis. The historical scene of the *Gospel of Mary* is only the prelude to the vision which Mary tells she has had after the Savior has gone, and which she communicates as a Gnostic mystery to the disciples (10.10 ff.). The relation of the historical allusion to her revelation is as clear as it can be: Mary who has been loved more than all other women (10.2) communicates to the disciples that which is hidden to them (10.8). History is merely—shall we say—excuse or pretense, or shall we say apologetic device? In any case, the Mariological revelation of truth needs the preceding historical hinge only in order to justify itself. That this is its ulterior motive is neatly demonstrated by the following "Apocryphon of John." There, as in the preceding Coptic revelation, a historical situation is drawn out at the outset: John meets a Pharisee in the temple who asks him about his Master (19.13). The Master is not there! The Pharisee slanders the Nazaraios by calling him a deceiver and the disciple John turns away to a desolate place. *Here*— neither in Jerusalem nor in the north, neither with the other disciples nor in the temple—but here, in timeless solitude, he receives the glorious vision, "the heaven is opened" (20.20) and the child as the "Father, the Son, and the Holy Spirit" (21.20) comes to him to bring him the extensive revelation recorded in this book.

This Christ has no terrestrial reality of flesh and blood. He is Savior and Redeemer but he does not live as real person. He cannot live because Gnostic language cannot grasp him as living being. Abstraction—yes; hypostasis—indeed. History—never. A historical tale, in which the earth is touched by the hand and feet of a breathing human life, cannot permeate the imagination of the Gnostic.[107] He does not possess the vocabulary in which to re-create the tale. If he knows the vocabulary, he does not live in it. His religious language must place Christ elsewhere.

---

[107] Gärtner, *op. cit.*, p. 75; as a consequence of the interest in the mediation of knowledge, already in *Evang. Thom.* the earthly life of Jesus becomes less interesting for the collector of biblical material.

No one can deny that the Gospel of John uses concepts which occur frequently in Gnostic literature. What then is the difference, say, between the Fourth Gospel and the *Gospel of Truth?* It is that no matter what sources scholars try to sift in order to understand the formative process of the Fourth Gospel, the whole book contains ← a living picture of a living and historical Christ. The passion story of this Gospel is a drama, told in the vividness of a progressive enactment. Jesus acts (2:1 ff.) ; he throws out the merchants (2: 13 ff.), and combats the Jews in pungent dialogues (7:25 ff.) . The liveliness and visualization in the resurrection narratives have inspired the visual arts throughout history. The numerous speeches of this Gospel which transmit revelation by Christ are supported by particles of earthly reality, by selected stories, and by presupposing the Synoptic accounts; thus they draw the picture of a tangible earthly figure. In the *Gospel of Truth* the historical Christ stands somewhere in the background of the meditation, but He is not a reality of flesh and blood.[108] The author is simply not concerned about the earthliness and terrestrial realism of this background. When Bach wrote his *Passion According to St. John,* he found enough dramatic and realistic material in this Gospel to create his baroque masterpiece. He could not have done this even in a most sketchy fashion with the historical evidence of the *Gospel of Truth.* One may object that a great deal of the Johannine language could not have been used either. A great deal is not the whole. This is just the point. The extensive revelatory speech of the Fourth Gospel is erected on select blocks of an underlying tale, and this tale means life and flesh. "And the word became *flesh,* and *dwelt* among us." (Italics mine.)

2. *The loss of the language about man.* Gnostic language is incapable of communicating the historical reality of Jesus Christ because of its anthropology. The reason for this failure lies in the absolute loss of the Hebraic-biblical view of man. The unity of man in the Old Testament sense has broken asunder. Man

---

[108] Wilson (*op. cit.,* p. 169, n. 74) is correct there is no *outspoken* Docetism in *Evang. Ver.;* but the Christ of this gospel has no life at all and comes close to Docetic notions. The interest in the Christ is exclusively the interest in the knowledge which this Christ brings. He comes to open the book, "this is why he appeared" (*Evang. Ver.* 20.24) ; Till's Coptic Berlin manuscript shows the same indifference toward the earthly person and ministry of Christ.

stands in a desperate battle between spirit and flesh. This dualistic thinking is not altogether alien to the New Testament, for there are traces of dualism in the Fourth Gospel and in Paul. But these dualistic motives never create a dualistic anthropology; next to what appears as an ascetic chapter, Paul denies any principal dualism with his famous "Glorify God in your body" (I Cor. 6:20). The New Testament has no definitive anthropology but only different anthropological levels. It maintains what I would call the Hebraic barricade against dualistic anthropological speech which is strong enough to prevent any dualism—the product of a personal experience in life—from becoming ontological. (By "Hebraic" we do not mean "Hebrew" or Judaistic in opposition to Hellenism but, rather, the heart of Old Testament prophetic thinking between Moses and the exile.) Hebraic roots always bar Pauline theology from setting up a metaphysical structure: pneuma versus Hyle, mind, soul, body in clearly defined ontological distinctions.[109]

In Gnostic language this Hebraic barricade against dualistic anthropology has fallen. Σωματικός receives (as it never did in the New Testament) a meaning equivalent to χοϊκός and ὑλικός [110] (Exc. ex Theod. 51.1, as in Stob. Herm. XV.7). The chain which belongs to the familiar terminology of the New Testament—pneuma, nous, logos—is given a dualistic twist; now the weight lies on a realm opposite to the physical world, the created cosmos of this aeon (Evang. Ver. 31.1).[111] Man is divided; soma is cloak of

[109] "Barricade" is a more emphatic term for what Wilson (op. cit., p. 256) called "control."

[110] ὑλικός-ἀριστερός Iren. Adv. Haer. I.5.6; Exc. ex Theod. 56.3. This dualistic anthropology is the antithesis of the Christian understanding of man (Phil. 1:20) in which the Christian is "always carrying in the body the death of Jesus so that the life of Jesus may also be manifested in our bodies" (II Cor. 4:10; italics mine). C. H. Dood, Man in God's Design according to the New Testament (Newcastle: Valence Drome, 1953). This is the alternative to Gnostic anthropology: "Das Christentum beansprucht die ganze Menschheit und den ganzen Menschen" (Quispel, Gnosis als Weltreligion, p. 25).

[111] The difference between Christian and Gnostic understanding of this terminology can be studied by a juxtaposition of I Cor. 2:4 and Exc. ex Theod. 57. For the Gnostic πνευματικός belongs to a realm which is saved by nature (this is not yet sufficiently analyzed, however, concerning Evang. Ver.) and needs μόρφωσις, while ψυχικός has to be saved and needs μετάθεσις. For Paul, πνευματικός is the Christian who has received the spirit while ψυχικός is opposed to faith, knowledge, and truth in Christ; ὑλικός does not appear at all in Paul.

76

darkness; the generic act is rejected.[112] Created matter is, as Hyle, diabolic, antipode to spirit and reason, to Logos and God (*Exc. ex Theod.* 47.3). The christological consequences are fatal; what is addressed in man by the revelation in Christ, and what is re-created by the new faith, is mind, consciousness, experience, but it is not the person in his psychosomatic comprehension. The nous between soul and spirit can see God in the divine vision (*Evang. Mar.* 10.20). When Christ lives for a Gnostic, he lives indeed, but he lives as a mysterious entity, as a fascinating reality of abstraction, or as a revealed theologoumenon. Christ as a man of flesh and blood cannot be meaningful because Gnostic language cannot grasp man as a creature of flesh and spirit in unity.

Once the barricade has fallen, anthropology as a metaphysical faith crushes the I-Thou relations between God and man. The Gnostic thinks of man in terms of anthropological essence.[113] The first concept which has to go is sin, in the biblical sense. As in the New Testament, sin is deprivation and separation. But deprivation and separation are both ignorance. Deprivation of glory and separation from the Father have been narrowed into the Gnostic channel of "knowledge" as the conquest of "forgetting." [114] "There

[112] *Herm. Trism.* VII.2.6; Epiph. *Pan.* XXVI.13.2-3 (*Evang. Phil.*). "Sperm" and "death" are together in *Apocr. Joh.* 57.5 but can also become the substance of the father which fills the light (*Evang. Ver.* 43.13). It is evident that such dualism in itself prevents any notion of a resurrection of the body, since "the nature of matter" dissolves itself (*Evang. Mar.* 7.1-8) and any idea of creation; hence metaphors like "tree of life" (*Apocr. Joh.* 59.19) and "creation from the rib" (59.9) become poetic expressions for dualistic cosmogonies.

[113] An example is *Fragm.* 24 of Heracleon. The nature of God is ἄχραντος, καθαρός, and ἀόρατος; the pneumatics who worship God (John 4:24) are of the same nature! Werner Foerster (*Von Valentin zu Herakleon* [Giessen: 1928] [with an enumeration of fragments different from the more complete one by Voelker]) comments on this passage: "Das ganze Wesen des Pneumatikers ist ein naturhaft gegebenes."

[114] Through knowledge, forgetting is destroyed (*Evang. Ver.* 18.4); knowledge through mysteries leads to election (*Op. Copt.* I, a); ignorance died (*Evang. Mar.* 16.20). (R. Reitzenstein, *Die hellenistischen Mysterienreligionen* [Leipzig: 1910], p. 166). This "error" in the Gnostic sense in *Ode Sal.* 38 (Robert M. Grant, "Notes on Gnosis," *Vig. Christ.* II (1957), p. 150) and in *Evang. Ver.* 26.19; 22.21; 17.29) as antipodes to knowledge demonstrates Pauline gnosis (Phil. 3:8; Eph. 3:19; I Cor. 8:1; II Cor. 8:7) to be another concept (J. Dupont, *Gnosis, La Connaissance religieuse dans les epîtres de St. Paul* [Louvain: 1949]). The Gnostic birth as weakening and forgetting stands far removed from any Pauline anthropology (*Pist. Soph.* 11.282).

is no sin," says the Savior to Peter in a lucid statement (*Evang. Mar.* 7.13). The loss of the concept of sin breaks in with the Gospel of Truth.[115] The first Gnostic texts already show the intellectualizing and spiritualizing of sin and miss its ethical and existential completeness.

With this barricade fallen, and with the encounter between the Father and man effaced, the anthropological language of Gnosticism easily falls into monistic formulations. It is not a total pantheism but one of God and pneuma. Pneumatic cosmos and the soul are one. The person possessing gnosis takes this gnosis which is his own and brings it back to himself (*Evang. Ver.* 21.11). "If one is a Gnostic he is from on high" (*Evang. Ver.* 22.3); such a phrase sees an inner connection between the spiritual and mental on the one hand and the divine world on the other. Ascent into the realm of the spirit is ascent to God, which is ascent to the world of the soul itself. Light comes back to light (*Ps. Thom.* 9.13). The Infinite is at the same time the one "who fills the All" (*Unknown Copt. Work* 18.259). "I am you and you are I; and wherever you are I am, sown into everything; and wherever you will, you harvest me, and if you harvest me, you harvest yourself." (*Epiph. Pan.* XXVI.3.1.) This is the ultimate expression of a monistic-pantheistic trend in Gnosticism,[116] understandable from the cardinal definition of gnosis itself. Is the latter not throughout this literature both subject and

---

[115] Despite Grobel's protest (*op. cit.*, p. 163, n. 479), Van Unnik's remark stands that the main distinction between the *Gospel of Truth* and the NT lies in the former's lack of the concept of sin (*The Gospel of Truth*, p .126). It is true the word does appear and Van Unnik can no longer say that sin is not even mentioned (*Newly Discovered Gnostic Writings*, p. 68); yet he is right, the Gospel in its antithesis of forgetting vs. knowledge does not reckon with "sin" in the biblical meaning of the word. Sin is "error" (32.37) and has no concrete meaning beyond this (35.26).

[116] A typical formulation is given by Hipp. *Ref.* V.8.4: κατεμέμιχε καὶ κεκέρακε πάντα πᾶσιν. Cf. the σύμπας of Ptolemy to Flora, 4.1 (already *Stob. Herm.* XXIII.62); "in whom the All is" (*Evang. Ver.* 18.34); *Evang. Thom.* 77. *Herm. Trism.* XI.2: aeon is God, cosmos is aeon, time is cosmos, genesis is time. An early example of the dualistic-monistic relation of speech is the second *Psalm of Thomas*. Monistic and dualistic speech next to each other has been studied by Th. Zielinski ("Hermes und die Hermetik," *Arch. f. Rel. Wiss.*, 1905, pp. 321 ff., and 1906, pp. 25 ff.) who tried to lead them back to Peripatetic, Platonic, and pantheistic trends (pp. 25-26 of 1906). "How could it happen that the Lord of the All wandered through us without our knowing it?" *Pist. Soph.* 13.22.

object, knowledge which I grasp and knowledge that grasps me? When knowledge is *really* saving knowledge[117] it represents the ultimate opposition to any nominalistic limitation of objectivity; then the realm of knowledge in me is really the realm of God himself.[118]

This loss of the biblical view of man illuminates the failure to grasp Jesus Christ as a human figure. Since man is a creature deeply split between evil Hyle and the authentic pneuma coming from the aeonic world, Christ must fit this scheme; hence the hidden or overt Docetism throughout. But why does the Christ speak to me, how does he redeem me? His pneuma—as does mine—comes from aeonic worlds, there I feel homogeneity. In a common ground of being dwells our mutual identity.[119] If anything has meaning for the Gnostic it is truth, kerygma, pneuma, but it can never be the life of the One who stood by the lakeside and called the fishermen to follow him.

3. *The loss of biblical realism.* The want of the Hebraic barricade leads to the elimination of New Testament realism in language. Gnosticism systematically replaces realism by symbolism. Hebraic speech never loses sight of the concrete even in its nonconcrete statements because there is a basic unity of existence on earth. This unity stands against the symbolic way of thinking which from Hellenistic circles infiltrates both the New Testament and its

---

[117] Iren. *Adv. Haer.* I.21.4. Cf. Jonas, *Gnosis und spätantiker Geist,* vol. II, 1, pp. 150 ff. Here lies the point of contact between Gnosticism and Hermetic literature (*Corp. Herm.* X.15), even though the way of gnosis is not the same.

[118] Gnosis becomes "knowledge of oneself" which the soul reaches after its ascent (ἐπέγνων ἐμαυτήν, *Evang. Phil.;* Epiph. *Pan.* XXVI.13.2). In the beautiful gown, the man in the "Hymn of the Pearl" sees and perceives himself (*Act. Thom.* 112). In it (μονάς), the All exists, in it the All found itself and perceived itself (*Unknown Copt. Work* 12.251). As the Logos is unpronounceable (Hipp. *Ref.* V.733) the human brain is unpronounceable (V.8.13). Kraeling (*op. cit.,* p. 49) points toward the double meaning of such identity: mind contains the cosmos, and mind is contained within the cosmos "as active agent and indwelling principle." "What is fundamentally, Gnosis?" ask C. H. Puech in "The Jung Codex and Other Gnostic Documents" (*The Jung Codex* [London: 1955], p. 29) ; "An experience or a theory which has reference to some definite interior mental happening . . . [The Gnostic] knows or reknows himself in God, knows God and becomes conscious of himself as effluence from God."

[119] Adam, *op. cit.,* p. 82: "Das Lebensgefühl des Gnostikers hat seine Mitte in dem Bewusstsein, dass sein eigenes Selbst identisch ist mit dem Wesen der Erlösergestalt, des salvator et salvatus."

predecessor, the LXX. One of the most far-reaching terms which Gnosticism introduces into the vocabulary of Christianity is *symbolon*. Despite many Greek terms which the New Testament takes over, either by transformation or by simple assimilation, from the Stoic vices to the terminology of the mystery, "symbol" interestingly has no place among its words, although the term had been widely known and used for centuries.[120] To be sure, the *res* may be there even though the term is lacking. Yet the acquisition of the new expression is symptomatic. The Hebraic concreteness of language which shines through the Greek New Testament terminology, as in *sphragis* and *arrhabon*, is swept away by the symbolic concept of language. Gen. 1:26 becomes *eikon* and *symbolon* (Hipp. *Ref.* V.26.9). Even in the exegesis which is closest to biblical faith, in Ptolemy, *symbolon* tends to replaces *typos;* one part of the law Christ has eliminated while another part is "image and symbol" *(Epistle to Flora* 5.8 ff.). The movement from typology to symlism in Christian exegesis is nothing spectacular at first sight; the two appear frequently to be one and the same thing. One could further argue for symbolic allegory in the New Testament and for traces of typology among the Symbolists of the early Church (Origen). Nevertheless, the appearance of *symbolon* marks the Gnostic attack against biblical typology. Symbol needs no history.[121] Symbolic understanding of language can dissolve the realism of Hebraic thought: the symbol points, it sees images, it draws shadows of the parable of the cave. The New Testament makes use of this technique without hesitation at times: "Now we see in a mirror dimly" (I Cor. 13:12). But the same Paul puts beside such language his pivotal Hebraic sentence: "When the time had fully come, God sent forth his Son" (Gal. 4:4). The Hebraic roots prevent Paul's language from ever becoming immersed in cyclic symbolism.

[120] Walther Eichrodt, "Vom Symbol zum Typus," *Theol. Lit. Ztg.* 81 (1957), 509 ff. For the meaning of the symbol cf. J. Gonda, *Deiknymi* (Amsterdam: 1929).

[121] Gnosis and *mysterion* are used as symbols: *Ptolemy to Flora* 6.5; Orig. *C. C.* VI.31 (although the formula might well be Origen's own); *Sophia J. Chr.* 124.5; Papyrus of *Deir el-Bala'izah* (Hennecke, *op. cit.,* p. 245). In Jewish Diaspora theology, spiritualization has set in without breaking altogether historical continuity. When later Gnosticism denies the symbol, it is not for the sake of *typos* but for the opposite reason; in its ultimate nature, the soul is without symbol since it is without answer and without apology (*Pist. Soph.* 98.242; 109.278).

There is a significant consequence to this loss of realism. The disintegration of realism through a symbolic understanding of faith calls for a misuse of biblical concrete language in the interest of magic. Rationalistic symbolism brings along its shadow, superstitious realism. Gnostic terminology, aided by esoteric constructions, impelled by popular religiosity, falls in its later stage into the application of Christian and non-Christian language for magic purpose. Secret proper names receive magical power (Epiph. *Pan.* XXXI.6.10; already *Corp. Herm.* XVI.2); the words become magical formulas for the initiated (Epiph. *Pan.* XXXI.7-8);[122] in vicarious baptism the liturgical words are efficacious even in death (Chrysostom *Cat.* 310; Epiph. *Pan.* XXVIII.6.4; Tert. *Adversus Marcionem* V.10). Only at first sight does the connection between magic and symbol appear peculiar. Rationalistic symbolism cannot live in itself (except as the sublime philosophy of a very few, such as Basilides); it cries for physical reality. After the extinction of the Old Testament realism of language, magic realism steps as a natural force beside the theological intellectualism of Christian faith.[123] Is this not the key to the Eucharistic controversy all through history?

Because of this shift into superrationalistic symbolism, Gnostic language has forever lost the possibility of communicating biblical eschatology. One of the most obvious symptoms of Gnostic language is the consequent spiritualizing of eschatological terminology. The

[122] Cf. Hans Lietzmann, *Gnosis und Magie* (in *KleineSchriften*, [Berlin: 1958], pp. 84 ff.), on Gnostic magical amulets. With his ἐπίκλησις Marcus changes the white wine into blood (Iren. *Adv. Haer.* I.13.2 ff.). The belief in the power of the word, practiced in exorcism (Orig. *C. C.* I.6; I.24; VIII.58) could lead to performances of Eucharistic miracles. On the replacement of faith by magic formulas, cf. Burkitt, *op. cit.*, pp. 37 ff., and R. Gauschinietz, "Zur Eucharistie der Marcosianer," *Zeitschr. f. wiss. Theol.*, 1914, pp. 45 ff. From a biblical perspective, early nonritualistic Gnosticism (Till, *op. cit.*, p. 38, and Jonas, *op. cit.*, vol. II,1, pp. 19. ff.) and the ritualistic Gnostic systems have in common the lack of a realistic biblical view of life, history, and man. The trend already exists in ancient philosophy; after philosophic criticism had undermined religious belief, magic and superstitious cults followed Hellenistic rationalism, cf. Wilson, *op. cit.*, p. 259.

[123] F. Sagnard (*La Gnose Valentinienne*, p. 614) is correct that especially Valentinian Gnosticism is free from magic. The opening wedge, however, is alchemy and astrology, which Sagnard goes on to name; they will lead to the magic rituals which Leonhard Fendt has described in his book. Once the realism is broken, we have to go either into sacramental magic or to Areopagite transcendentalism.

whole *Gospel of Truth* is directed toward "rest" (ἀνάπαυσις), but this rest is only in a heavenly paradise; paradise is the spiritual realm; the kingdom of God is pleroma.[124] The metaphysical twist killed any realistic understanding of a "new heaven" and a "new heart." Because of its dualistic presuppositions, Gnostic language cannot endure eschatology. Apocalyptic interest—whatever there may be—is forever servered from history, society, and man. Dualism coerces it into heaven, knowledge, mind. This is one of the aspects of the departure from the Old Testament in early Jewish Gnosticism.[125] The Gnostic attempt to escape from physical reality can only speak about an earthly future in pessimistic images.[126]

4. *The loss of the Old Testament.* The first thing which the student of Christian history learns is the denunciation of the Old Testament by virtually all Gnostic schools, with the exception of Ptolemy's letter. It is the revelation of a demiurge. We understand at this point the profound inner connection between the denial of the Hebraic revelation and the language of Gnosticism. What

---

[124] *Evang. Ver.* 40.30; 41.4; 41.13; 41.25; 42.22-37; 43.1. Heracleon *Fragm.* 33. "Rest" is spiritual repose according to knowledge, *Par. of Shem* (Doresse, *op. cit.*, p. 149). Typical is the juxtaposition of "resurrection" and "rest," *Unknown Copt. Work* 6.234. The judgment and condemnation of the chaotic Gods (fortieth document of Chenoboskion (Doresse, *op. cit.*, pp. 169-70) betrays an apocalyptic background which, however (*Ps. Thom.* 2.37-51), is soon conceived dualistically and becomes finally exclusively spiritualized, as joy and rest (*Act. Thom.* 50). Robert Frick (*Die Geschichte des Reich-Gottesgedankens in der Alten Kirche bis zu Origenes und Augustin* [Giessen: 1928], p. 46) is correct: Gnostic ascent of the soul means replacement of early Christian eschatology. (Cf. also Gärtner, *op. cit.*, p. 265 on "rest" in NT and Gnosticism.) I disagree with Jonas, *Gnosis und spätantiker Geist*, Vol. II, 1, p. 11 when he claims *"Dieses Weltbild ist nicht so sehr das Bild eines Seins als eines Geschehens,"* and therefore calls the Gnostic world view "eschatological." Here modern existentialist concepts are projected into antiquity. This is not *"Geschehen"* and it is not "eschatological," both of which presuppose history on one hand, the totality of life on the other. As Jonas himself expresses so well, we are confronting a *"Heilswelt"* with a *"Heilstatsache";* there is *"Geschehen"* in the latter but the being is much more important because the Gnostic *constructs* the stages of being in order to explain and grasp whatever spiritual event there is (fall of the soul, the coming down of the Savior, the levels of man). Here lies the difference between gnosis and existentialism; and it is therefore not farfetched to compare the Gnostics rather with the frame of thought of C. G. Jung, as Quispel has been doing in his *Eranos* publications.

[125] Robert M. Grant, *Gnosticism and Early Christianity*, pp. 27 ff.

[126] Pessimism in eschatology is also partly the product of the connection with rebirth (Doresse, *op. cit.*, pp. 112-13).

the Gnostic rejects in the Old Testament is the earth, God's act in both flesh and spirit. Salvation and judgment for the prophets occur among people and cities. The word of God addresses Israel, a nation, a political unit, a land. Egypt, Canaan, the fall of Jerusalem—this graphic sequence is rejected because its history does not coincide with the split between body and spirit within man. "The earth is the Lord's and the fulness thereof" (Ps. 24:1) cannot be perceived by the language of a man who thinks of salvation as a mental and mystical redemption. The earth is not the Lord's —this is where the Gnostic stands; this he understands because he has experienced it. The Old Testament psalm contradicts his awareness. The rejection of Israel is the outgrowth of an existential, dualistic experience.[127]

The loss of the Old Testament is therefore, among other things, the loss of its language, not merely the replacement of the Hebrew by Greek, philologically, but rather the renunciation of the Old Testament mode of speaking about God, man, and world. Hebraic roots—even in the Greek translation and throughout the New Testament—have kept Christian language in the dimensions of time and person instead of space and nature.[128] For this reason they bar the development of a thoroughgoing ontological language in which being is grasped in terms of space and nature. This does not say that the New Testament does not know spatial terminology (cosmos) or that it is not concerned with the realm of nature (restoration of cosmos). The New Testament stands within the tension of the language of Judaism since it entered the Helenistic

---

[127] "Loss of the Old Testament" does not necessarily mean rejection; *Evang. Ver.* in its unpolemic nature would not reject the OT but it assumes a unique revelation which does not reckon with it (see Søren Giversen, "Evangelium Veritatis and the Epistle to the Hebrews," *Stud. Theol.*, 13 [1959], p. 91). The rejection is pronounced *expressis verbis* in *Apocr. Joh.*, where Christ with a smile rejects Moses (45:7), the story of creation (58:16; 59:17), and Noah (73:3). This is an honest declaration of Gnostic allegory. In his rejection of the OT, the Gnostic rejects any notion of a linear time element within salvation. *Moses* is reported to reveal the holy *revelation* to a *disciple* in the *temple* of Jerusalem (*Arkh.* Doresse, *op. cit.*, p. 171)!

[128] C. H. Puech, "La Gnose et le Temps," *Eranos*, 1952, pp. 57 ff. has shown that the Gnostic concept of "time" is not merely the Hellenistic cyclic alternative to the Christian time but a cyclic understanding which sees the vitality of "time" but contains a solution to escape from it. See also Jindrich Manek, "The Biblical Concept of Time and our Gospels," *New Test. Stud.* 4 (1959), pp. 45 ff.

world. But the Hebraic roots in early Christian communication prevent the ontological aspects from taking control over the realm of faith. Theology and Christology are thus safeguarded from becoming metaphysics or Christosophy. In Gnosticism there is no longer any safeguard. As the Old Testament falls, the barriers fall. Cosmological vocabulary takes over, *Victus victori legem dat*. The alien speech, conquered by the faith of Yahweh, forces upon Yahweh its metaphysics. Even though Gnostic texts still use Old Testament vocabulary, this vocabulary is no longer understood.[129]

The loss of the Old Testament language leads inevitably to the loss of the Creator. This is so obvious that we need not dwell on it. One aspect, however, becomes significant at this point. On the top level of the Gnostic language lies the unpronounceable realm of the deity. Basilides, philosophically the most perspicacious of all the Gnostic thinkers, develops this in language of rare subtlety.[130] Negative attributes such as Basilides uses are found in many places of the canon: "invisible," "inexpressible," and "unapproachable," beside the two famous attributes, "unsearchable" and "unscrutable" at the end of Rom. 11.[131] In the difference between Paul and Basilides concerning the transcendence of God we recognize what "loss of the Hebraic speech" means. There is negative terminology in the New Testament, parallel to many modes of Hellenistic theology or cosmogony. In the last phases, man has to become silent before God; his language begins to fail. This failing is expressed by negative terminology. Such language is for Paul final expression in

[129] All through Gnostic literature we find Hebrew terminology and terminology resembling Hebrew proper names. Gnostic formulas use "Hebrew names," Irenaeus reports, *Adv. Haer.* I.21.3; there are Ἰάω (I.4.1; Pist. *Soph.* 7.12), Ἐλοεῖμ (Hipp. *Ref.* V.26.7), and especially Ialdabaoth (Robert M. Grant, "Notes on Gnosis," *Vig. Christ.* II (1957), pp. 148-49, and Doresse, *op. cit.*, p. 166). All this betrays a Jewish terminology which is no longer understood theologically. The Adam-Christ scheme can even bypass the OT (Hipp. *Ref.* VI.35.3).

[130] Liechtenhahn (*op. cit.*, pp. 105 ff.) "defended" the original Basilides against the report by Hippolytus—unnecessarily so. This philosophic aspect makes this fragment so valuable. The same unity of mystic and negative language, in a much less philosophic genius, appears in the Naassene document: ἄρρητος αὐτοῖς λόγος καὶ μυστικός Hipp. *Ref.* V.7.21.

[131] Rom. 11:33-36; II Cor. 12:1-4. What stands as final hymnic praise at the end of Rom. 11 appears at the outset in *Evang. Ver.* 17.7 and 17.22; the incomprehensibility and inconceivableness of God begin to maintain metaphysic priority in theological thinking.

hymnody; for Basilides it determines the principle of thought. Only once does Paul reluctantly tell of his ecstatic experience; had his enemies not forced him into it, we might never have heard of the "unpronounceable words" of II Cor. 12:4. For the Gnostic this Pauline phrase belongs to his salient theological vocabulary. It would be absurd to unravel Paul's language of redemption from the negative terminology; for Basilides, this negative language is the determinative element in the description of the spirit's ascent into its own undefinable origin.[132] This monistic speech concerning the ultimate region of being denies no less than the dualistic speech about man the Old Testament Creator and his presence in Israel, in the territory of Canaan, as the Father of his children.[133]

The loss of the Old Testament surrenders Gnostic speech to extravagant syncretism. The more Chenoboskion manuscripts that become known, the more grotesque is the mythological speech of Gnostic syncretism. In the *Evangelium Vertitatis* the mythological elements are moderate although one could not say that they are absent.[134] In *Arkhangelike* the mythological excesses have no limits. The uniqueness of the God of Abraham must heed to the syncretist heaven of the Near East. Ever since the Old Testament was rendered into the Greek tongue, elements of Hellenistic syncretism have been part of it. Now, however, syncretism of another type appears as compared with which the first cannot really be called "syncretism." The difference between the two lies in the presence or absence of the frame which keeps Judaism or Christianity within the theocentric boundary lines of the Old Testament.[135] This loss of the Old Testament has become an even more striking fact since

[132] The exception is Ptolemy's letter where a typological interpretation shows up (Gilles Quispel, "Ptolémée, Lettre à Flora," *Sourc. Chrét.,* Vol. 24 [Paris: 1949], p. 35). Here lies a step of great importance from which Origen will carry on.

[133] Robert M. Grant, *Gnosticism and Early Christianity,* p. 118, is right in affirming that Christianity was saved from dualism "because it insisted upon retaining the Old Testament more or less as it stood."

[134] There is mythology all through this meditation (against Grobel, *op. cit.,* p. 33, n. 4 and p. 83, n. 173): Truth as an abstract entity (17.25); totality going upward to the unknown Father (21.20); the enraged Plane (18.22); and the destroyed forgetting (18.6). All this is phrased, of course, in indefinitely more moderate form than in most other Gnostic documents especially the new evidence of Chenoboskion.

modern scholarship has demonstrated a broad Jewish background to Gnostic language.[136] This semantics has betrayed one of its own springs from which it was nourished.

(5.) *The loss of the community of faith.* In a passage of the *Evangelium Veritatis,* the author employs the Pauline metaphor of the "body" in order to indicate a relation between God and the faithful *(Evang. Ver.* 18.40). A closer look reveals that this seemingly biblical metaphor is void of biblical meaning.

It appears strange, to start with, that the metaphor is used in reference to God and not to Christ. This *could* merely mean, to be sure, the expression of a Sabellian Docetic Christology which can be detected elsewhere in the gospel.[137] The context points in another direction. A comparison between I Cor. and the *Gospel of Truth* shows two conflicting concepts of the body of the faithful. Nowhere in the latter does the body of Christ have earthly meaning. In I Cor. 12:26, "If one member suffers, all suffer together; if one member is honored, all rejoice together." In the *Evangelium Veritatis* the metaphor is meant cosmologically, as 19.1 ff. proves. The metaphor is applied to the Gnostic's relation to God (19.5) and concerning the All (19.7 ff.) which is precisely what Paul did not have in mind when he spoke of Jews, Greeks, slaves, free (I Cor. 12:13). They belong not to a cosmological body. In the metaphor, the striking Pauline application of diverse gifts and talents between weaker and stronger members (I Cor. 12:22-25) is nonexistent; it has to be, of course, from the Gnostic standpoint. The Pauline passage leads into an enumeration of the members within the body: "Are all apostles? Are all prophets? Are all teachers?" (12:29). The *Gospel of Truth* leads . . . only into the return to the

[135] Such a boundary line accounts for Wilson's pertinent conclusion that whatever syncretism there is in Diaspora Judaism and Christianity is "extremely mild" in comparison with Gnostic syncretism *(op. cit.,* p. 256). Gnosticism shall indeed not be judged merely on the basis of its mythological language *(Harnack, Dogmengeschichte,* I, 252), but mythological syncretism is a symptom for the semantic breakdown in Christian Gnosticism (Bultmann, *Theologie des Neuen Testamentes,* pp. 181-82).

[136] Cf. also Jean Daniélou, *Théologie du Judéo-Christianisme,* (Tournai: 1958), p. 425.

[137] This is the suggestion by Grobel *(op. cit.,* p. 55, n. 74). His whole commentary has an apologetic tendency to soften as much as possible the Gnostic substance of the meditation.

Father (19.5). The whole context proves that the metaphor of the body is understood in no other than a vertical way and that the Pauline "body" is absent.

Gnostic thought has lost, perhaps not the language of the community of Christ which appears at random, but the close kinship between a language of faith and the language of the Christian community. The Gnostics have the *ekklesia*, but for them it is an aeon, pre-existent, heavenly.[138] They do not see the biblical relation between the language of faith and the language of the body of Christ. The *Gospel of Truth* speaks nowhere about the earthly nature of the congregation as a vital matter of Christian faith. The whole meditation is an extensive elaboration of the perpendicular relation between God and man. The faithful are called "children" (27.13; 43.22), but this metaphor does not lead into a "household" of God. Gospel, revelation, salvation—this is Gnostic faith; but the earthly assembly in which this manifestation takes place is of minor importance. The goal is "rest" (24.20), "reunion" (24.26), "completeness" (24.28).

From this we can also understand why the *Gospel of Truth* does not quite know what to do with ethical language. Because the body as the earthly locus of salvation remains absent, language that deals with the interchange between the faithful, and between the Christians and the world, is used only occasionally. You should do the will of the Father, the gospel preaches (33.30). But when we look for the actual meaning of this will, it is never rooted in the community of faith. There is a striking phrase on repentance as a return (35.22); but in what follows, "forgiveness" completely lacks any practical application within the body of Christ. Forgiveness means "to remain behind in the Light within the Lack" (35.28). What this language has lost is the inner relation between wisdom, righteousness, sanctification, and redemption (I Cor. 1:30). Ethical language and revelatory language are drifting beside each other because the uniqueness of the vertical experience has no place left for the earth.

---

[138] Iren. *Adv. Haer.* I.5.6 (ἡ ἄνω 'Εκκλησία), and I.8.6 (in the Valentinian prologue to the Gospel of John); ἡ ἀληθινὴ 'Εκκλησία belongs to the aeonic world, I.30.1.

These aspects of loss are all facts of one and the same decrement. They mutually condition and augment each other. Underneath lies a failure to think in the biblical frame (between the sovereignty of God and the grace of Christ, between the history of salvation and the congregation of redemption), an unguarded openness to peripheral language which may turn biblical faith into theosophy or theism, metaphysics or mysticism. Perhaps we could explain it all from one single issue: its speech about God the Father. The disintegration of the Father concept is the pathway to Gnostic theosophy. Because the concept of God the Father disappears, sin disappears too.[139] What disintegrates is not Hebrew language but the Hebraic understanding of language; and therefore, what fails in Gnosticism is nothing less than the axis of biblical communication about God. The newly discovered Gnostic manuscripts have not modified but proved the point.[140]

CONCLUSION

The texts examined have by no means revealed one language whether philologically or stylistically. There is all the difference in the world between the language of the *Evangelium Veritatis,* the Phebionite rituals, and the philosophy of Basilides. Of the problems presented each one often bears more upon certain Gnostic writings and less upon another. It is impossible to speak about Gnosticism at all without doing constantly *some* violation to *some* system. However, the problem of the Gnostic "atmosphere" of speech can be stated by definite conclusions:

1. The Gnostic vocabulary as such demonstrates a preliminary problem in Christian communication. It would be unwieldy to

---

[139] What breaks asunder is the encounter between Father and man. Van Unnik (*Newly Discovered Gnostic Writings,* p. 68) has put his finger on the crucial point: the *Gospel of Truth* gives only a caricature of Christian revelation "because it starts from a non-Christian God." See also Gärtner (*op. cit.,* p. 73) on the conflict between Christian and Gnostic faith.

[140] Harnack (*op. cit.,* I, 259) spoke about the "trübselige Berichte der Kirchenväter." Our examination has again proved this accusation to be wrong. Harnack should have had access to Chenoboskion! The same conclusion which we find also in Quispel (*Gnosis als Weltreligion,* p. 47) : 'Die Gnostiker waren noch viel schlimmere Ketzer als es sogar die Kirchenväter vermuteten"), and Van Unnik (*op. cit.,* p. 23) was made by Sagnard (*La Gnose Valentinienne,* p. 618) before the discovery of the new Coptic material.

create a Christain exegesis with Yaldabaoth or Bel Achamoth as proper names indicating a heavenly sphere. To have any proclamation of faith without speaking of Jesus Christ, the *ekklesia,* or faith is impossible. The farther the Gnostic text is removed from specifically Christian circles in the second century, the more the semantic breakdown materializes. Without a certain pivotal biblical vocabulary, Christian faith cannot be transmitted.

Such an accusation, however, does not apply to a great many of the Gnostic writings with which we have dealt. They do contain God and Christ, redemption and freedom, grace and the Holy Spirit. The *Gospel of Truth* is the best example of a Gnostic book with Christian terminology. What seems like farfetched Gnostic metaphors may be biblical if seen in another context. The central stained-glass window in the Church of the Holy Trinity in Worms contains a snake as a symbol for the resurrection. This artistic form of 1959 is not the snake of the Ophites but Old Testament *typos* for the risen Christ. Num. 21:9 and not Hipp. *Ref.* VI.16. The context determines the meaning of biblical language.

2. Gnostic language lacks the salient directions of biblical language. The language of God and man is bereft of its one purpose, to express man in confrontation with God, God coming to man in Christ. The communication of an encounter turns into a communication of "nature"—either the nature of heaven (cosmogony), or the nature of Christ (his coming down through the angelic spheres), or the nature of man (dualism). Language about Israel, *ekklesia,* and time is replaced by language embracing heaven, pneuma, and time. The communication of events on earth in their relation to God turns into the communication of theosophy forced into dualistic and monistic frames. The faith-love-hope complex is overpowered by gnosis. Ethical language is not absent but erratic; hope is spiritualized like all other eschatological language in the Bible; faith, the key word in Paul, has been completely conquered by knowledge, the saving *mysterion.* The language of faith has become the language of knowledge.

3. The actuality of the Gnostic problem lies in its subtlety. Peripheral speech permeates the center and becomes the center. Practically every one of the issues observed has traces in the New Testament but is subordinated to the one concern: the encounter

between God and man in the Christ of Israel who is the Christ of his church. Syncretistic, mythological, dualistic, or mystic speech takes over the Hebraic Christocentric terminology of realism, encounter, earth; what has been touched by the semantics of the gospel throughout the New Testament moves into the heart of communication. Hence the fatal consequences: man is cleft asunder, the Father must depart, earth becomes evil. What makes Gnostic language Gnostic is the shift of center.

To speak of Gnostic language in the New Testament is therefore misleading. We can recognize Gnostic elements in a broad sense, yet we have such Gnostic elements in countless documents far removed from any historical Gnosticism. What distinguishes biblical speech from Gnostic speech is nothing less than its very center. The same may be said of "syncretistic" language. In one sense, any speech, ever since the third man uttered exclamations used by the first and the second man, is syncretistic. In a precise sense, however, "syncretistic" means that which unites different streams together. To designate both biblical and Gnostic language as "syncretistic" obscures the extent of two opposed atmospheres and misses the emphasis within the two: the dominant "Hebraic" language, used to describe incarnation and redemption, is replaced in Gnosticism by a language or languages of equal vlaue.

At this point we need to ask what the Christian *canon* means in the controversy with Gnosticism.

1. We have assumed a New Testament type of communication differing from a second-century type. With the outbreak of the great controversy, however, the canon had not yet been defined. How can we speak about a corpus of New Testament writings before they were assembled into a collection? This observation misleads Harnack into his famous mistake in claiming the Gnostics had the first canon. This is only true in a superficial sense; in reality, the substance of the canon exists before either church or Gnostics become aware of a "canon" in a technical sense. *Kanon* is the measuring tape of faith, an apostolic document is the reflection of apostolic witness, living word grasped by written word. The basic material for this "weaver's rod" of Christian faith is present at the end of the first century: "apostolic language" as the authentic Christian communication embracing the triad—Jesus,

Paul, and John—transmitted by the early Christian communities. "Apostolic" should not be understood in an exclusive, literal sense. The Gospels were not written by apostles: the triad, Jesus, Paul, and John, is a genuine reflection of the apostolic event. Such a triad penetrates the second century; when it becomes conscious it becomes canon.

2. Gnostic documents have clarified one issue with perspicuity: "canonical language" cannot be this or that biblical word or formula illuminated by the Spirit. A fundamentalist proof text linguistic is likewise doomed to fail, exactly as Gnostic arbitrariness fails. On a literal interpretation Gnostic speech may be deduced from Pauline and Johannine phrases just as a wild apocalyptic sermon or a dry legalistic exhortation can be preached from both Revelation and the Gospel according to Matthew. "Canonical language" demands the search for the center and the comprehension of the whole. "Canonical language" is only possible in a chain of biblical terminology, never in a catchword or in a set phrase, but in relation of biblical concepts to each other. It is a frame rather than list, a barrier as much as a command. This is just what the Greek word *kanon* means: "the mason's ruddled line" by which the preacher and the theologian of the Christian church must measure their speech. To call such discipline of speech impoverishment would be to reveal painful ignorance concerning the fascinating tension within this frame. "Canonical language" is a restatement of authentic Christian communication between comprehension and precision.

3. When we say "canonical language" we have expressed by this very term the conflict of this language. It does not lie in this or that apostolic word, in one specific type of New Testament speech but in the center which comprehends the whole. For instance: it is christological language within the Hebraic concept of the relation between God and man, and not within the Gnostic theosophical language. By making a statement like this, language of today describes the canonical center. *What* canonical language is can therefore only be determined by exegetical research a posteriori. Yet such language is found to be contained in the canon, a never-ceasing protest against the arbitrariness which is always present in exegetical study. The history of faith is, among other things, a

constant restatement of canonical language. This must be so from the very nature of biblical speech. We have compared the core and the periphery. What is the relation between the two? When does the periphery crush the heart, or when is the periphery lost? There is no package answer that solves the issue once and forever. The language of the gospel—and by this we mean the gospel in the broad New Testament sense of the word—is a language in movement which is sent from the outset on a thrilling quest; it is nevertheless canonical because its quest is not a game but oscillates within given limits, between joy and doom.

We asked at the beginning what was Gnostic in some of the sayings in the *Gospel of Thomas*. We believe we have given answers by which this Gnosticism can be determined. Yet these very answers indicate that Christian speech may fall into Gnostic speech if it is not continuously safeguarded. Just as in the second century the canon is not yet closed, the precise borders of Gnostic versus Christian communication cannot always be drawn. There are Gnostic elements—sometimes even more than this!—in *Barnabas*, in *II Clement*, and in *Ignatius*. For a great many of the second-century Christians, the issue of a canonical faith is not at all clear, and only the ignorant believe this period to be neatly divided into sheep and goats. The *Gospel of Thomas* can set Christian and Gnostic sayings side by side because the two streams run into each other for centuries. The mutual infiltration of these two types of languages in the second century, despite all the polemic on both sides, witnesses to the urgency of the study of the canon in any period. As always in the history of the church, only a few are aware of its bearings in a contemporary issue.

The problem presented is not just a Gnostic one. It is the issue of Christian language in any period. In the exegetical meeting between the faith of the Bible and the Christian of the church, two languages clash. Every generation brings along its natural speech, its ontology, its metaphysics. Unless the word of the Bible infiltrates the vocabulary of the contemporary, there can be no Christian communication. But as the infiltration occurs, the canonical authenticity of this vocabulary is threatened. The study of theology takes place in the struggle of two languages. On every occasion, almost with every meaningful sentence, preaching must fight its way through this dilemma of speech. Christian instruction must convey—unless it is doomed from the outset—the meaning of canonical language to a generation thinking in its own terms. A Christian may believe he is speaking in Christian terms when actually he is betraying the canonical language at every turn. For the entire future of the Christian language, the Gnostic question must be faced: hidden, naïve, sophisticated, or open. The church owes its gratitude to the Gnostics for having brought this dilemma into the open. Once and forever, the lesson has been taught that Christian language depends upon the axis of Christian faith.

Chapter 2

The Language of Post-Apostolic Christianity

   Inquiring into the "language of the church" apart from Gnosticism, we perceive soon that there is no such thing as "Christian language" between A.D. 100 and 180. The church is groping its way in order to establish Christian communication. The story of this search is sometimes erratic; in its naïveté and impetuousness, even embarrassing at times; yet fascinating because of its freshness. We shall not try to present a single alternative to Gnosticism in a uniform frame, but we shall seek to establish certain lines of speech which are symptomatic for the age between John and Irenaeus.

LAW AND GRACE

   The first sphere of communication we want to examine is the one encircling language of law. For the Apostolic Fathers, *nomos* represents a favorite concept, the law which Christ gave to his people and which he received from his Father (Hermas *Similitudes* V.6.3). In Gnosticism we noted, not absence, but the relative unimportance of ethical language; here the picture is reversed. There is ethical speech all the way through! Christ is almost identified with the law (Herm. *Sim.* VIII.3.2). There are numerous parallel concepts to *nomos·* "order" (*Sim.* VIII.4.2) ; "*ordinance*" (*Barnabas* 1.6; *Epistle of Diognetus* 5.3; Ignatius *Magnesians* 13.1) ; "command" (*I Clement* 42.3) ; "mutual exhortation" (56.2); "legal observance" (1.3) ; [1] and, of course, "obedience" (10.1-7). The sig-

---

[1] τὰ νόμιμα also 3.4; 40.4; Hermas *Visions* I.3.4; in classical Greek often synonymous with νόμοι (Pl. *Phaedr.* 265 A), cf. Liddle & Scott, *A Greek-English Lexicon* (Oxford: University Press, 1940), p. 1179B. For the whole realm, cf. S. H. Blank, "The Septuagint Renderings of OT Terms for Law," *Hebr. Union College Ann.* 7 (1930) , 259 ff.

nificance of this language for Christian faith shines through in Hermas' choice of *Mandates* ('Εντολαί) as a title for one of his cycles, a term which is likewise used by *II Clement* (one must "watch the mandates of the Lord" 8.4) and *I Clement* (13.3).[2] To determine the place of *nomos* in the teaching of this period in relation to the New Testament is the aim of the following study. The New Testament uses *nomos* and its synonyms. Are the "end of the law" of Rom. 10:4 and the "new law" of Barn. 2.6 the same?

The Language of Command

The reader of the postcanonical literature is at first sight amazed at the extreme moralistic and legalistic language in much of this literature. The greater part of *Clement*'s letter to the Corinthian community is an exhortation to Christian conduct relieved only by the lengthy quotations from the Old Testament. "Let us obey" (9.1); "Let us look intently" (7.4);[3] "Let us be humble minded" (13.1); "Let us be kind" (14.3); "Let us be imitators" (17.1) —the whole letter is one constant "Let us." *II Clement* continues in the same mood: "Let us turn to God" (16.1); "Let us do the will of the one who called us" (5.1); "Let us do righteousness" (19.3). The exhortation may also encourage spiritual life, as in the mandate for prayer and intercession (*I Clem.* 56.1); yet even then exhortation is aimed at moral achievement: "It is better to confess one's sins than to harden the heart" (51.3). The *Didache's* whole teaching on the Two Ways, taken over from an earlier source, is a perpetual series of direct commands: "Thou shalt" and "Thou shalt not." The emphasis on prohibition gives the teaching on the Two Ways an even gloomier character.[4] Is this all the Christian

---

[2] The Christian faith as "ἐντολή" in I Tim. 6:14 and II Pet. 2:21. Cf. also *II Clem.* 3.4 and *Barn.* 6.1 and 7.3. The decalogue plays a vital role in this period, Robert M. Grant, "The Decalogue in Early Christianity," *Harv. Theol. Rev.* 40 (1947), 1 ff.

[3] ἀτενίσωμεν ("Let us fix our gaze," Kirsopp Lake, in "The Apostolic Fathers," *Loeb Class. Libr.*, [Cambridge: Harvard University Press, and London: William Heinemann, 1945]), a favorite Lukan word, also in the same hortatory subjunctive *I Clem.* 9.2 and 19.2. The style goes back to the homily of the synagogue, Hartwig Thyen, *Der Stil der Jüdisch-Hellenistischen Homilie* (Göttingen: 1955), pp. 90 ff.

[4] *Did.* replaces the hortatory plural of the Hellenistic-Jewish diatribe (μετανοήσωμεν) by the straight command in the second person: τέκνον μου, φεῦγε 3.1.

instruction the people received who were baptized in *Didache* 7? *II Clement* affirms: "to confess" means, first to do what God says; second, not to disregard his commandments; third, to honor him not only with one's lips but with heart and mind (3.4).[5]

On the footsteps of a language of ethical command follows a language of merit. *II Clement* is typically representative of this type of speech. "If we think little [of Christ] we also hope to obtain but little." [6] Eternal rest or eternal punishment depend upon whether we have done the will of Christ or not (*II Clem.* 6.7). "Who shall be our advocate if we be not found to have pious and righteous works" (6.9)? The parable of the slave in *Hermas,* a slave who achieves more than his Lord expects on his departure, is the allegorical expression of this idea of merit. Because of the works which the slave has done, the Lord makes him equal with his Son.[7] It makes no difference to our analysis if *Hermas* has taken over this text from a Judaistic source.[8] It shows enough about his concept of Christian salvation that he *can* take over this parable and build a whole string of explanations around it. The relationship between man and God is one of obligation and wages (Herm. *Mand.* II.6-7). The concept of merit has affected Christology as well as the proclamation of the kingdom of God (*Sim.* V.6.7; *II*

τένον μου μὴ γίνου οἰωνοσκόπος 3.4. For some modern interpretations of the two-way instruction which Harnack tried to reconstruct (*Die Apostellehre und die jüdischen beiden Wege* [Leipzig: 1896], pp. 57 ff.) see Werner Jentsch, *Urchristliches Erziehungsdenken* (Gütersloh: 1951), p. 269, and Thyen, *op. cit.,* p. 110.

[5] Another explanation for ὁμολογεῖν in 4.3-4: 1.) ἐν τοῖς ἔργοις; 2.) ἐν τῷ ἀγαπᾶν; 3.) ἐν τῷ μή . . . . (follows a whole catalogue of virtues and vices).

[6] *II Clem.* 1.2. Also 8.4: "If we do the will of the Father, and if we keep the flesh holy, and if we observe the mandates of the Lord, we shall obtain life eternal." The thought is emphasized by a repetition in 8.7. "We shall receive our reward in this flesh" (9.5). "The reward is not small in turning an erring and lost soul toward salvation" (15.1). The same emphasis in Clem. *Recogn.* I.61.

[7] Herm. *Sim.* V.2.7. V. Schweitzer, "Der Pastor Hermae und die opera supererogatoria," *Theol. Quartalschr.* 86 (1904), 539 ff. The meritorious tendency, already in *I Clem.* (L. Goppelt, *Christentum und Judentum im ersten und zweiten Jahrhundert* [Gütersloh: 1954], p. 239) is reserved in Gnosticism for the lower classes of humanity, Iren. *Adv. Haer.* I.6.4.

[8] Martin Dibelius (*Der Hirt des Hermas* [Tübingen: 1923], p. 565) laments the obscuration of the message of Jesus in this parable; cf. also G. Schlaeger, "Der Hirt des Hermas eine ursprünglich jüdische Schrift," in *Nieuw Theol. Tijdschr.* 16 (1927), 327 ff.

Clem. 9.6). The same trend of speech appears in Ignatius' understanding of his own martyrdom. The desire to suffer as God's
wheat and his urgent request to the Roman community not to
interfere for his sake [9] have one goal: the "attaining of Christ"
(ἐπιτυγχάνω), the achievement of the prize (Ign. *Romans* 6.1-2).
"To attain" is the typical term for this striving toward martyrdom.[10] Suffering is the stipulation for Ignatius' becoming the
freedman of Christ (*Rom.* 4:3).[11] Grace is a reward (*Smyrnaeans*
12.1) ! While in other respects Ignatius represents a unique language
of Christian faith at the beginning of the second century, in this
he shares with *II Clement* the meritorious concept of salvation.
To be sure, *II Clement* has experienced the harsh truth that reward does not come too quickly, a trouble to many a Christian
soul thinking in terms of insurance payments (20.3). But this does
not alter his basic striving to attain merit.[12] Resurrection and
reward are parallel terms for *Barnabas* (21.1). The early Christian
metaphor of the right and left sides has been turned into a metaphor for works of supererogation (Herm. *Vis.* III.2.1).

We observe next a frequent vocabulary of repentance. Already in
the *Didache's* church life, "to confess one's sins" is demanded in
the mutual reproof of Christians as a prerequisite to participation
in the Lord's Supper (15.3; 10.6).[13] The exhortation to repentance
within the Christian life fills practically every page of *Hermas*.
For him "repentance" (*metanoia*) is the focal point of the Christian's daily life. The vision of the tower and the stones which are
either used for building or cast away is directed toward the paragraph on penitence: the rejected stones "have not been thrown
far away from the tower, because they will be valuable for the build-

---

[9] Ign. *Trallians* 4.2; Ign. *Rom.* 4.2; 2.1-2; 4.1.

[10] Ign. *Rom.* 2.1; 5.3. The term can actually mean "to profit," "to gain"
(Xenophon *Memorabilia* IV.2.28); also *II Clem.* 5.6 and Ign. *Magn.* 14 and
Tral. 13.3.

[11]*Rom.* 4.3 is quite explicit: Ignatius' becoming free and his resurrection are
dependent upon his being allowed to suffer: ἐὰν πάθω. On the rising conviction
of eternal life as reward see Harnack, *Dogmengeschichte*, I, 190. This is what
the righteous waits for according to *II Clem.* 20.3.

[12] The emphasis on recompense of a good life by God is built, of course, upon
early Christian preaching about salvation, that God had mercy upon us in
Christ (*II Clem.* 1.7-8) : but it is remarkable how fast *II Clem.* switches from
the language of salvation to the language of reward: 9.5-6.

[13]*Did.* 4.14 and Herm. *Vis.* I.1.3; III.1.5; *II Clem.* 8:3; *I Clem.* 52.1.

ing if they repent" (*Vis.* III.5.5). *Hermas'* whole emphasis in his teaching on marriage (*Mand.* IV); on salvation (*Vis.* II.2.5; *Sim.* VIII.11.1); on the ascetic life (*Sim.* IX.14.1-2) is dominated by a concern for repentance. His book is written with the intent to proclaim one more chance of repentance (*Mand.* IV.1.8; 3.6) which ought to be acted upon immediately (*Sim.* IX.23.2; VIII.9.4). The dire consequences of refusing to repent and the judgment of the "angel of repentance" are preached with the monotonous effect of hortatory language.[14] The repentance of the sins committed in the Corinthian revolt is also the goal of the ethical teaching in *I Clement* (7:5-7, 56:2),[15] and his pseudonymous successor again puts a great deal of emphasis on repentance (*II Clem.* 8.1; 16.1). This penitential language develops related formulations: "to be educated toward repentance" (*I Clem.* 57.1); "to have a 'time' for repentance" (*II Clem.* 8.2); "to have a 'chance' for repentance" (Herm. *Vis.* II.2.5); and "to receive repentance (*I Clem.* 8.5).[16]

This type of post-Apostolic literature has an excessive vocabulary of virtues and vices. Late Judaism has been ransacked for its teaching on good and evil in human life. The vision of the seven women provides a good occasion to present seven virtues: "Faith," "continence," "simplicity," "innocence," "reverence," "knowledge," "love" (Herm. *Vis.* III.8.2 ff.). Countless others exist: "humility" (*I Clem.* 21.8); "indulgence" (13.1); "concord" (30.3); making the catalogues of vices a favorite topic in post-Pauline literature (Herm. *Mand.* VIII.3-5). The lists of vices in the New Testament are augmented, and *Barnabas'* knowledge of evil things transcends, at least theoretically, that of Paul (10.7-8). The *Didache* has an extensive list of vices in its opening instruction (5). The *Mandates* of *Hermas* are the naïve systematic presentation of a number of Jewish-Christian virtues and their opposites—truth, chastity, fear, and doubt.

[14] Herm. *Vis.* V.7; *Mand.* XII.6.1; *Sim.* VIII.9.1.

[15] The goal of *I Clem.* is *metanoia* (Olof Andren, *Righteousness and Peace* [Upsala: 1960], p. 213), a concept which in the second century begins to lose the dynamic nature which it held in primitive Christianity (André Benoit, *Le baptême chrétien au second siècle* [Paris: 1953], pp. 223 ff.) by being formed into a concept of a penitential discipline.

[16] Herm. *Sim.* IX.26.6; for the whole see B. Poschmann, *Paenitentia Secunda* (Bonn: 1939), pp. 134 ff.

Such are, in short paradigms, some of the post-Apostolic trends in expressing the ethical and legal concern of faith. In order to create a sharp focus of discussion, we choose three concepts and analyze them in their mutations between post-Apostolic writers themselves and in their distinction from the main exponents of New Testament faith.

RIGHTEOUSNESS—SIN—GRACE

A case could easily be presented—and many instances can be given—in support of the view that the post-Apostolic church does not relive the New Testament language. A look at the word "righteousness" is revealing. When *II Clement* uses this famous Pauline noun he means "righteous acts" (6.9) which man must fulfill in order to receive the rewards of heaven (11.7); hence we must "practise righteousness in order to be saved at the end" (19.3). According to *Hermas,* the "virtue of righteousness" (*Mand.* I.2) does not lie in external fasting but—in the good tradition of Judaism in the Diaspora—in serving the Lord, walking in his ordinance, and doing no evil (*Sim.* V.1.4-5), "virtue of righteousness" being the consequence of a command (VI.1.4). The *Didache* judges the traveling teachers by their "increasing righteousness and knowledge" (11.2). It is not difficult to note in all three authors the tragic absence of the greatest biblical emphasis on righteousness, that of Rom. 3.21.

The case, however, is more subtle and therefore more interesting. The crucial starting point lies in *Clement*'s epistle. Not only does the author use Pauline literary forms in his letter,[17] he is also familiar with Pauline terminology and, more than that, with Pauline patterns of thought. This holds true even when it comes to the cardinal Pauline concept of righteousness. "We are not made righteous by ourselves," he states, commenting on the blessings given to the Patriarchs, but "by faith through which the Almighty God has justified all men from the beginning of the world" (32.4). Such was the Pauline argument. *Clement* follows even farther in the steps of the great theologian by mentioning the

---

[17] Hans Lietzmann, *Geschichte der Alten Kirche,* I, 202; Albert E. Barnett, *Paul Becomes a Literary Influence* (Chicago: University of Chicago Press, 1941), pp. 89 ff.

example of Abraham (31.2). It has been a grave failure, however, to call the Clementine righteousness Pauline for these reasons.[18] The difference between Rom. 3:21-26 and *I Clement* 30-32 lies on one hand in the latter's failure to grasp the christological meaning of the Pauline righteousness, as the "righteousness of God through faith in Jesus Christ" (Rom. 3:22); the grace freely given "through the redemption which is in Christ Jesus" (3:24); which came through "expiation by his blood" (3:25). That some of these Pauline issues are hinted at elsewhere in the letter of *Clement* does not solve the case; *here,* in outlining righteousness in a Pauline context, the author has missed its profound meaning. The difference lies on the other hand in the fact that *Clement* is nowhere in his letter aware of the conflict between righteousness and law, a conflict which is so obvious not only in Romans (3:21 ff.) but in Galatians (2:21) and Philippians (3:9). The consequence of this omission shows up when Clement quotes, as Paul did in Rom. 4:1-5, the passage from Gen. 15:6 ("And Abraham believed God, and it was counted unto him for righteousness."). Paul quotes this text to demonstrate that faith does not come from works; *Clement* goes on to declare that Abraham received a son "because of faith and hospitality" (10.7)! The conclusion must stand: righteousness for *Clement* is still partly a work, as it had been in Hellenistic-Jewish circles.[19]

Now Paul does not employ righteousness in a libertinist Gnostic sense, as though the work of love were the product of a diabolic force. There is no partnership between righteousness and unrighteousness (II Cor. 6:14). Where then lies the gap between Paul and Clement of Rome? It is that Paul arrives at his positive statement concerning righteousness as obedience through a *conflict with the law* (Rom. 6:14). Between the righteous act of Paul and the righteous act of *Clement* stands righteousness as freedom in

---

[18] L. Sanders, *L'Hellénisme de Saint Clément de Rome et le Paulinisme,* [Louvain: 1943], *"véritablement Paulinien,"* p. 158). It is not a matter of a verse, not even of two or three chapters. One swallow does not make a summer.

[19] Cf. Schrenk, in *ThWNT,* II, 198. Eva Aleith (*Paulusverständnis in der Alten Kirche* [Berlin: 1937], p. 4) is right, the context and especially the OT examples prove that *Clement* has not understood Paul's faith in its depth; and yet I would call ch. 32 more than only *"Verbeugung gegen Paulus."* It is Paul with a wrong center and a wrong accent.

Christ (Rom. 8:10). *Clement* has not gone through the conflict even though many of his statements sound Pauline. This failure to follow Paul in the path of theological conversion and growth to maturity has important bearings; it is exactly for this reason that the letter of *Clement* is written with such legalistic overtones. Rom. 12-15 appears as the organic consequence to Rom. 1-8 ("organic" does not deny that the fruit had to grow through pain); *I Clement* 30-32 seems somewhat lost in an ocean of repetitious exhortation. What is lacking in *Clement's* legalism is nothing less than freedom from the law in Christ (Rom. 8:2). When this freedom is absent, there is no Pauline righteousness.[20]

Of course there are other approaches to righteousness in the New Testament than the Pauline. *Clement* would certainly not feel uncomfortable with Matt. 5:20 or James 1:20.[21] What right have we to compare *I Clement* with Paul? Because the Pauline vision of the Hellenistic *dikaiosyne* is the creative and important biblical contribution and because this is the central contribution of the biblical message. James 1:20 may not be in harmony with Rom. 3:21, but we can understand it as a modification, warning, counteremphasis. Yet not even a rigid proof-text method would dare to declare the meaning in James to be at the center of the New Testament. The newness of the concept in the New Testament is the result of a conflict and its christological answer in the life and thought of Paul. This conflict in Paul is not merely one of his thought, a logical dilemma, but a total one, the turbulent clash in his life. What is lacking in the righteousness of *Clement* is what Schrenk called the "crisis" between law and the act of justifica-

[20] H. E. W. Turner, *The Patristic Doctrine of Redemption* (London: A. R. Mowbray, 1952), pp. 33 ff. In *Sibylline Oracles* III.234-35, δικαιοσύνη is paralleled by ἀρετή. Such is the understanding of Hellenistic Judaism (cf. Strack-Billerbeck, III, 163), exhibited by Herm. *Mand.* XII.3.1. Christian Eggenberger (*Die Quellen der politischen Ethik des 1. Klemensbriefes* [Zürich: 1951], p. 165) was rightly astonished by the lack of ἐλευθερία in an author who pretends to be familiar with Paul's work. This lack is understandable without Eggenberger's theory of a conscious falsification for political reasons; Clement has nowhere understood that between grace and moral command stands for Paul the freedom in Christ (II Cor. 3:17-18).

[21] Franklin W. Young ("The Relation of I Clement to the Epistle of James," *Journ. of Bibl. Lit.* 67 [1948], 339 ff.) has established a direct relationship between the two through an analysis of the Rahab story in *I Clem.* 12.1-4 and James 2:25.

tion.[22] Here lies the basis for Roman legalism. There is no clash in Clement himself.

The distance from the Pauline meaning varies. At times *Clement* is close, at times he is farther removed. Already Barnabas elucidates the Pauline meaning less; "righteousness is the beginning and end of judgment," and joy and gladness are "witness to the work of righteousness" (1.6). In *II Clement* and *Didache,* Pauline righteousness is no longer understood at all.[23] Such is the end of the process which starts with *I Clement.* The course it takes throws light on the place of righteousness in Clement himself. According to *I Clement* 30-32, *Clement* has a glimpse of Paul's "alien" righteousness. But the main body of his letter does not reflect this. We must not, therefore, merely compare one chapter with another; the over-all nomistic atmosphere of *I Clement* suffocates the Pauline touches. The suffocation of Paul by nomism in the Apostolic Fathers is not begun by the elimination of Paul but by an emphasis on the mandates.

Related to our observations on righteousness are the ways in which the Apostolic Fathers use *hamartia.* One particular characteristic of the New Testament faith lies in its specific use of the term "sin." Sin is seen as a breech in the relationship between God and man (Rom. 6:16 ff.), which has been annulled by the victory of Christ (Rev. 1:5), conquered in the sacrifice of his death (John 1:29). This does not make sin merely a physical, nonmoral force in the Gnostic sense; however, it does not leave sin in a purely moral category either. Moral sin is the result of a basic alienation from God. For the Apostolic Fathers, sin is primarily "doing bad," especially for *Hermas.* The family turns away from faith (*Vis.* I.3.1),

[22] Schrenk, *ThWNT,* II, 198 and Goppelt, *op. cit.,* pp. 108 ff. The OT antithesis between law and promise cuts apart the OT synthesis of the two.

[23] Typical are ποιέω δικαιοσύνην (*II Clem.* 11.7 and 4.2; [Matt. 7.21] and πράσσω δικαιοσύνην (*II Clem.* 19.3). "To wait for the kingdom in love and righteousness" (12.1) reveals a touch of biblical righteousness, but 6.9 (cf. 5:7) betrays not the slightest trace of Paul. Neither does *Did.* 11.2. Ps. 106.3 in Herm. *Vis.* II.3.3 is fully directed toward righteousness as an act which man fulfills; if you live in simplicity and temperance you are saved (II.3.2) ! By stating that these Christians are legalists because they did not follow Paul "in his inconsistencies," James W. Parkes (*The Conflict of the Church and the Synagogue* [London: The Sancino Press, 1934], p. 69) fails to understand the Pauline righteousness exactly as did the Apostolic Fathers.

business appears in its unethical wordliness (*Sim.* VI.3.5-6),[24] the wife gossips (*Vis.* II.2.3) and sexual problems arise (*Mand.* XII.2.1). To be sure, it would be just as distressing for an apocalyptic writer to have a gossiping wife. What *Hermas* does not see behind his enumerations of sins is the powerful New Testament understanding of *hamartia* as the human denial of God, as man's separation from the Creator—the aspect of it which the Gnostics understood. This little man's morality misses the biblical dimension of sin as rebellion, sin as breach of a relationship, sin as transgression against the covenant.[25] Paul enumerated sins in his lists of vices; but Paul could never have made such ingenuous statements as: "If you set it before yourself that they [the mandates] can be kept, you will easily keep them, and they will not be difficult" (*Mand.* XII.3.5).[26] This second-century "power of positive thinking," as naïve as its twentieth-century grandchild, misjudges the biblical phenomenon of sin as rebellion and breach. If it is so easy to keep mandates, why did *Hermas* need all the apparatus of apocalypticism to come forth with one, and only one, specially revealed second repentance? Apparently it was not that easy, not even in Rome around 140. And it was not that easy either in Corinth, fifty years earlier, or there would have been no need to conceive a long letter with extensive biblical demonstrations of the results of evil. Now *Clement* is not that naïve; but again, meritorious notions prevent a biblical understanding of sin since nomism has kept righteousness within its claws. "Blessed are we, beloved, if we perform the commandments of God in the concord of love that through love our sins may be forgiven." (50.5.) *Clement* knows of "deliverance" (60.3), but the path of deliverance (teaching, sanctification, bringing man to honor, 59.3) lacks again the Pauline conflict after which deliver-

---

[24] *Hermas* sees rightly the ethical problems for a Christian in wealth (*Vis.* III.9.6), business and worldly activity (X.1.4); he does not see the underlying cause for it. If he uses his family merely as type for the whole church, as Dibelius suggests (*op. cit.*, pp. 445-46), the misconception of sin is still not excused because moral sin has no relation to the body—temple—bride vocabulary.

[25] I Kings 12:19; Lev. 4:13; Ps. 51:6; Gen. 3.

[26] When Paul speaks about "reward," the tone, context, and emphasis are quite different, cf. Preisker, *ThWNT*, IV, 726. The relation between grace and reward in Paul is not as homogeneous as Floyd Filson (*St. Paul's Conception of Recompense* [Leipzig: 1931], pp. 132-35) concludes.

ance remains no longer a mere command not to do evil but becomes the freedom not to sin (Rom. 6:22). *Barnabas* stands closer
than the others to the biblical meaning of sin: "We go down in
the water full of sins and filth"—"We come up, bearing in our
hearts the fruit of fear and having in our spirit the hope in Jesus"
(11.11). Sin as "human foulness" (ῥύπος) reveals a deeper insight
into the biblical word *hamartia* than sin as luxurious living (Herm.
Mand. XII.2.1). And yet it is *Barnabas* who has the questionable
statement about merit (21.1).[27]

A third link in the same chain of biblical concepts underscores
this result when we examine *metanoia,* the biblical word for repentance, and *charis,* the biblical word for grace. *Clement* recognizes
that *charis* denotes a gift of God; man is "made perfect in love by
the grace of God" (50.3), and he comes through Christ "under the
yoke of his grace" (16.17). But why can *I Clement* quote Prov.
3:34 (God gives grace to the humble) in a context which speaks
of grace as a gift (30.2-3)? Because for Clement *charis* has not been
freed from the undertone of merit. God gives grace not to the
proud but to the humble—this throws *charis* back to Judaistic
moralism.[28] Paul was not given grace because he was humble! Here
once more we see precious Pauline insights enfeebled by nomistic
notions. Again, what begins in *Clement* becomes soon prevelant.
For the Two Ways of *Didache, charis* means human reward before
God (1.3);[29] Pauline grace is not even remotely understood. *II*

[27] The eschatological emphasis should not be held responsible for such a
misconception of sin (against Turner, *op. cit.,* pp. 71 ff.), but the nomism which
has become a "principle of life" (Victor Ernst Hasler, *Gesetz und Evangelium
in der Alten Kirche* [Zürich: 1953], p. 42).

[28] Barnett (*op. cit.,* p. 93) has shown in a comparison between I Cor. 2:9 and
I Clem. 34.8 how the unknown quotation is used almost identically by both,
yet by a slight change *Clement* puts an emphasis on future reward into the
text. For the same example (I Cor. 2:9 and *I Clem.* 34.8) see *The New Testament in the Apostolic Fathers* [Oxford: Clarendon Press, 1903], pp. 42 ff.).

[29] Cf. Luke 6:32. Despite 10.6 which contains an eschatological meaning of
χάρις, I simply cannot see Hans Lilje's "Christuszeugnis" in this manual (*Die
Lehre der zwölf Apostel* [Hamburg: 1956], pp. 19 ff.). When the death of
Christ is not mentioned in the Communion prayers, the suffering servant does
not exactly witness for Christ. *Did.* 10.6 is purely eschatological. The few relations between the *Didache* and Paul which Edouard Massaux (*L'Influence de
l'Evangile de saint Matthieu sur la littérature chrétienne avant saint Irénée*
[Louvain: 1950], pp. 647 ff.) has found amount to very little and nowhere represent major thought patterns. Despite the fact that "a great portion of Didache's

Clement knows the concept only in the sense of Luke 6:32 as "credit" (13.4). For *Hermas, charis* is favor before God (*Mand.* X.3.1); indulgence by those who repent (XII.3.3); the acceptance and reward of the servant in the eyes of his master (*Sim.* V.2.10). It is *Barnabas* who comes closer to Paul again, for he knows of a grace which God not only gave to the prophets (5.6) but which appeared at the cross (9.8). The goal of *Clement's* letter is *metanoia* as an act of repentance; the purpose of *Hermas'* literary attempt is likewise *metanoia.*[30] What the two have in common is symptomatic for the post-Apostolic period: the subordination of *charis* to the concern of penitence.

We have observed the development of three biblical concepts toward, and within, some of the post-canonical writers. We notice at once how, here again, we can only speak with caution about unity or even uniformity of language.[31] What we can trace, however, are general trends behind some of the concepts, which reveal distinctions from one group of literature to another. Such differentiation is not merely a matter of comparing a word here with a passage there, but a matter of asking for the relation between a definite

---

language if not of its subject matter" appears to be "founded upon the New Testament Scripture" (F. E. Vokes, *The Riddle of the Didache* [London: S. P. C. K. and New York: The Macmillan Co., 1938], p. 95), there lies an abyss between the language of the *Didache* and the one of Paul and John. Thomas Torrence (*The Doctrine of Grace in the Apostolic Fathers* [Edinburgh: Oliver & Boyd, 1948], p. 42) was right in calling the χάρις of the Two Ways a correlative of merit.

[30] Because of this failure to grasp NT μετάνοια (Torrence, *op. cit.*, pp. 51-52), parallel to the Gnostic failure in which sin has merely become *"résipiscence"* (Quispel, *Eranos,* 1947, p. 261), we cannot place μετάνοια in Hermas and in the NT together under the genus *"Bekehrungsreligion"* (Dibelius, *op. cit.,* pp. 510-13). The radical change of Mark 1 and Luke 13:3-5 is not the μετάνοια of Hermas. (Goppelt, *op. cit.,* p. 242 on what he calls the loss of the inner meaning of μετάνοια in *Hermas;* peculiarly enough, however, Goppelt does not see the same development at work in *Clement* whose repentance he does not believe to be *"Abfall von Paulus,"* p. 239. After all Goppelt says about Paul [pp. 100-120], this must be *"Abfall von Paulus"!*) .

[31] One can only cautiously speak about a *"Théologie du Judéo-Christianisme."* The language of Clement of Rome is quite different from the Ignatian, and the latter's differs fully from the Pseudo-Clementine literature. I feel uncomfortable in having to comprehend all three in Daniéliou's title. The militant anti-Paulinism of *Clem. Hom.* XI.35.3-6 or XVII.13.19 (George Strecker, *Das Judenchristentum in den Pseudoklementinen* [TU 70] [Berlin: 1958], pp. 187 ff.) is quite different from the semi-Pauline nomism of Clement of Rome.

concept in a certain context to the total context of a document. Righteousness in *I Clement* 30-32 and righteousness in Rom. 3:21 are alike; where they cease to be alike is in the context of mandatory speech. Ethical language in Paul collides with a keen new vocabulary of redemption and grace from which it does not reevolve with the same nomistic connotation that it held before. The post-Apostolic period uses the Pauline language of grace, righteousness, and repentance—but without the collision, and therefore without the newness. The "new law" of *Barnabas* 2.6 is not the "end of the law" of Rom. 10:4.[32] Language after Paul is drowned again in nomism because the Christians who use it have not experienced the agony and triumph in Paul's question to the Galatians: "Let me ask you only this: Did you receive the Spirit by works of the law, or by hearing with faith?" (Gal. 3:2).[33]

The Language Which Communicates the Christ

The entire post-Apostolic period stands under the power of a revolutionary communication of faith, and this communication revolves around Jesus, the Christ. "Far be it from me to glory except in the cross of our Lord Jesus Christ." (Gal. 6:14.) This unique

---

[32] Determination of context, immediate and at large, is demanded by the "elliptic use" of Christian speech for which G. Bartelink ("Ellipse und Bedeutungsverdichtung in der christlichen griechischen Literatur," *Vig. Christ.* 10 [1956], 1 ff.) has done a first research paper which we hope will be followed by others; without *"Bedeutungsverdichtung"* in the broad definition of Bartelink there could not be any communication of Christian faith.

[33] The Philonic identification of logos and law (Goodenough, *op. cit.,* p. 58) has undergone in Paul breach and recovery; in Barnabas we do not find either. Moral language, as Hasler saw it so sharply in the early Christian development, has a tendency to become autonomous and independent (*op. cit.,* p. 106). Christianity turned into a *"Tugendlehre"* (Jonas, *Gnosis und spätantiker Geist,* vol. II, pp. 31 ff.) ; *"die Verkündigung wurde zusehends lehrhafter und deshalb immer mehr pädagogisiert"* (Jentsch, *op. cit.,* p. 271) ; and, in the definition of Wilhelm Kamlah (*Christentum und Geschichtlichkeit* [Stuttgart/Köln: 1951], p. 69), *"hellenistisches Moraljudentum"* has become *"katholisches Moralchristentum."* For this reason, the Gospel of Matthew with its didactic purpose (K. Stendahl, *The School of St. Matthew* [Uppsala: 1954], p. 35) plays such a role in this literature (Massaux, *op. cit.,* pp. 647 ff.) . The kerygmatic passages of Matthew, however, the "story" of salvation as it came to this evangelist by way of the primitive congregation, what Edward P. Blair (*Jesus in the Gospel of Matthew* [Nashville: Abingdon Press, 1960], p. 139) called the "portrait" of Jesus, does not live in this literature.

experience of the Christ in the life of the apostle infiltrates and pervades the thinking and preaching of the post-Apostolic Fathers.[34] Christian communication is communication in Christ and about Christ. The dominant figure is Ignatius of Antioch.

In his seven letters, Ignatius presents an extensive documentation of christological language in the wake of biblical communication. Every one of his greetings is full of language about Christ: a greeting to the church in Philadelphia in the blood of Jesus Christ; to a church which belongs to the Lord Jesus Christ; which rejoices in the Passion of our Lord; to a hierarchy which is appointed according to the mind of Jesus Christ (Phil. Inscr.).

The abundance of such language in the addresses is not due to style but reflects a Christ mysticism or a Christ experience in the thought and life of the author. Throughout his letters this Christ-language continues. The terminology about God frequently, though not invariably, draws after it a similar expression about the Christ. Greeting "in the Father" leads to greeting in the Son (Magn. Inscr.); the will of God is the will of Jesus Christ (Tral. 1.1); the church of Smyrna is the community of the Father and of his beloved Son Jesus Christ (Smyrn. Inscr.). There is an extensive vocabulary about Christ, the Lord, the Son, the Word, the Savior,[35] which is elaborated specifically; the doctor (Ign. Eph. 7.2), the bishop (Ign. Rom. 9.1), the new leaven (Magn. 10.2), and the inseparable life (Ign. Eph. 3.2).[36] To communicate Christ is to communicate Christ as man, in violent rejection of Docetic misrepresentations. Spread over all his short letters are allusion to the historical Jesus of the New Testament—his birth, baptism, Davidic descent; suffering, cross, and death in various contexts. These references are

[34] H. Korn, Die Nachwirkungen der Christusmystik des Paulus in den apostolischen Vätern (Leipzig: 1938), and Karl Prümm, Christentum als Neuheitserlebnis (Freiburg i. Br.: 1939), p. 93.

[35] Lord: Ign. Phil. 4.1; Magn. 13.1; Smyrn. 10.1. Υἱός Magn. 8.2 and in the trinitarian passage 13.1. Logos (Smyrn. Inscr.) who proceeded from silence Magn. 8.2; the word without lie, Ing. Rom. 8.2 σωτήρ in the opening of Ign. Eph. 1.1; Magn. Inscr.; Phil. 9.2 and Smyrn. 7.1.

[36] The teacher (Magn. 9.1); the hope (Smyrn. 10.2); the new man (Eph. 20.1); the γνώμη of the father (3.2) and his γνῶσις (17.2). We also should mention several passages naming Christ θεός: in the Inscr. of Phil. and Rom.; in Smyrn. 1.1 and 10.1; Rom. 3.3 and 6.3; Eph. 15.3 and Ign. Pol. 8.3.

crowned by an important group of resurrection passages.[37] The historical allusions are paralleled by others of a theological import —the pre-existence of Christ, his forgiveness and sovereignty.[38] Further we must recognize the frequent language about unity with Christ (ἕνωσις, *Magn.* 13.2), "being in Christ" which Paul had formulated as the expression of Christian newness (II Cor. 5:17). "Remain in Christ" is the final greeting to the young bishop of Smyrna (*Ign. Pol.* 8.3).[39] Christological communication is rooted in the reality which the Christ maintains in the life of Ignatius: "How can we live without him?" (*Magn.* 9.2). This man is not using theological phrases; "to live in Christ" expresses a unity of emotion and thought which underlies his existence as Christian martyr and theologian.[40]

[37] Of *Davidic origin* (not only in the creed of *Tral.* 9.1 and *Smyrn.* 1.1, but also *Rom.* 7.3; *Eph.* 20.2 and 18.2; in the words of Paul, *Rom.* 1.3, which may be in turn a creedal phrase); Christ is *born* (*Magn.* 11; *Eph.* 18.2; *Tral.* 9.1); *baptized* (*Eph.* 18.2; *Smyrn.* 1.1); *unctioned* (*Eph.* 17.1); he *suffered* (*Tral.* 11.2; *Eph.* 7.2; *Smyrn.* 2.1); under *Pontius Pilate* (*Magn.* 11.1; *Smyrn.* 1.2; *Tral.* 9.1). *Cross* (*Phil.* 8.2); *crucifixion* (*Eph.* 16.2); and *death* (*Tral.* 2.1) exist; and parallel to the importance of *Incarnation* (*Eph.* 19.2; *Magn.* 8.2) is the *resurrection* (*Phil.* 8.2; *Smyrn.* 3.2). Birth, suffering, and resurrection are three essentials of Christ (*Magn.* 11.1); his *suffering* is our *resurrection* (*Smyrn.* 5.3). *Life* has christological significance (Cyril Charles Richardson, *The Christianity of Ignatius of Antioch* [New York: Columbia Univ. Press, 1935], p. 28).

[38] *Pre-existence* (*Magn.* 6.1; Ign. *Pol.* 3.2 Christ-ὑπὲρ καιρόν, and *Magn.* 9.2); *forgiveness* (*Phil.* 8.1) and *sovereignty* (*Tral.* 2.1 ἐξουσία,, *Smyrn.* 4.1).

[39] Always the oneness (ἕνωσις) with Christ (*Magn.* 1.1; *Tral.* 11.2; *Phil.* 4.1; cf. Richardson, *op. cit.*, p. 33); the unity ἑνότης) with Christ (*Phil.* 5.2); ἐν Χριστῷ (*Tral.* 1.1); διὰ Χριστοῦ (*Magn.* 5.2); κατὰ κύριον (Ign. *Pol.* 5.2); in the name (*Eph.* 3.1); honor (*Magn.* 15); grace (*Phil.* 8.1); power (*Eph.* 11.2); and faith (*Magn.* 1.1) of Christ: to pray in Christ (Ign. *Pol.* 8.3), and to suffer with Christ (*Smyrn.* 4.2) in whom Ignatius is bound (*Phil.* 7.2).

[40] Heinrich Schlier (*Religionsgeschichtliche Untersuchungen zu den Ignatius-briefen* [Giessen: 1929] has furnished a great deal of Gnostic material in order to demonstrate Gnostic, even Iranian, streams in Ignatius. In development of this material, Hans-Werner Bartsch (*Gnostisches Gut und Gemeindetradition bei Ignatius von Antiochien* [Gütersloh: 1940] pp. 166 ff.) divides Ignatius into three levels: a Gnostic one, a Christian-Gnostic one, and a third, untouched by Gnosticism. What this dissection misses is the kerygmatic unity of the christological proclamation, the thrust of a Christ language which Ed. von der Goltz (*Ignatius von Antiochien als Christ und Theologe,* TU 12 [Leipzig: 1894]) has tried to catch. Despite the latent threat to a Christian proclamation in the substantial (Schlier, *op. cit.*, pp. 180-81) and the Gnostic—sacramental (Bartsch, *op. cit.*, p. 168) language—both a real problem for the second century and for Ignatius—the Christ language of Ignatius is more biblical than Chr. Maurer

Ignatius is the most powerful post-Apostolic witness to Christian language as Christ language. As early as Clement of Rome we find a different kind of communication of the Christ. His address is christological. Important formulations point toward later christological developments and betray insights into biblical thought patterns (46.6 and 42.2-3). His language about atonement conveys faith in Christ who gave his blood for us (49.6 and 21.6) and who is the high priest of the Christian's offering (36.1). The existence of Clement is undeniably related to the Christ and his calling (32.4). Yet it does not take much to feel the difference between Ignatius of Antioch and Clement of Rome. It lies in the urgency and uniqueness of the Christ language. In Ignatius, almost every sentence breathes the fervor of a Christ mysticism, in the language of a man who is held captive to Christ; the language of *Clement* simply does not radiate this fervent concern to communicate the spiritual reality of a Christ. The ecstasy of Ignatius is not absent from Clement; it is not so intense. His didactic purpose hampers his communication of the life and work of Christ; *Clement* writes in order to communicate *metanoia* and not to communicate the Christ. *Clement* prays to God and speaks about him in ways which do not indicate the unique focusing of thought upon Christ. *Clement* has many passages about the Creator's mercy (60.1-4), the will of God (6.1), and the divine commandments (33.1-8), which indicate that not only the urgency but the uniqueness of the Christ experience is one step removed from Ignatius. Two aspects enhance each other: the didactic element weakens the communication of the Christ, and this weakened reality in turn becomes responsible for the didactic overtone. The literature of *Hermas* is the product of such enhancement.

The Christ language of *Hermas* is a sad affair indeed. This is not simply because it is theologically poor. We could forgive an author, untouched by Gnosticism, illiterate in New Testament fi-

---

(*Ignatius von Antiochien und das Johannesevangelium* [Zürich: 1949]) wanted to admit. Of course it is not christological language in purely Pauline sense (W. von Loewenich, *Das Johannesverständnis im zweiten Jahrhundert* [Giessen: 1923], p. 32, against Massaux, *op. cit.*, pp. 117-30 who has assembled extensive comparative material without a sufficiently critical comparison), but it is infinitely more christological than *Clement* or *Hermas*; not to speak of *Didache*.

nesses, for mixing up Christ and the church (*Sim.* IX.1.2), for missing the distinction between servant and Lord in Christology (V.6.1), and for confounding son and pneuma (V.6.5). Terminology about Christ in the New Testament is not always as precise as a Thomist or Barthian theologian would like to have it presented. But the tragedy of *Hermas* is that his opus does not need language about the Christ, not because the writer is so obviously confused about it, but because it does not mean much to him. The confusion is partly the result of a lack of concern. What makes sense to him is pragmatical—the status of the church and his desire to alter it. His language is so thoroughly penitential, admonitory, meritorious, that no type of christological language can live beside it. There are two types of confusions—one at the start, and one at the end of a theological debate. This type represents confusion before the start! The christological language is poor, not because *Hermas* has been confused after serious digging (which is often a good thing), but because the concern was never there. When he makes his one christological effort in the parable of the servant, he explains the Christ allegory with his penitential and meritorious language, which drives him to state the exaltation of Jesus as a reward (*Sim.* V.6).[41] Speech about repentance has replaced the speech about the Christ.

In the *Didache* we encounter a further complication. The second part of this manual uses strikingly authentic primitive Christian phraseology, baptismal formulations (7.1-3), Maranatha (10.6), the "Gospel of the Lord" (15.4). The document coins a witty phrase to brand those who "sell Christ" (12.5). The prayers before and after communion reflect concern for a sacrament instituted by Christ (9-10). But the opening instruction (1-6) has no traces of actual christological language in a New Testament sense. In its treatment of the sacrament and the church, the *Didache* uses Christ

---

[41] In a charming metaphor, Streeter (*The Primitive Church, studied with special reference to the origins of the Christian ministry* [New York: The Macmillan Co., 1929], p. 209) called *Hermas* the "white rabbit" of the Apostolic Fathers; thinking of his Christology, I would rather call him the "black sheep." As Joly puts it, one just cannot "save" this Christology (*op. cit.* p. 31). When Hermas, for instance, takes the Johannine picture of the vine, as Loewenich observed (*op. cit.,* p. 11), the *Christ* is replaced by the *Christian: he* is the vine, suffocated by weeds, no longer useful to his Lord (*Sim.* IX.26.4). This difference is symptomatic no matter whether *Hermas* ever knew the Fourth Gospel.

language; in its ethical exhortation which precedes it, it ignores it. This dichotomy of communication into a liturgical and a moral sphere destroys the intimate interrelation between ethical and kerygmatic language which belongs to the heart of Pauline and Johannine preaching. We begin to understand the root of the problem in the *Didache* after observing that even in chapters 7-15 the references to Christ are not redemptory but only mandatory or eschatological.

We must next inquire into the relation between apocalyptic language and the communication of the Christ. The whole work of *Hermas* is based on his *horasis,* his apocalyptic vision (*Vis.* III.13.1). Apocalyptic imagery in *Hermas* is lively and colorful, like the black, red, gold, and white colors of the apocalyptic beast (IV.1.10; 3.4-5). If we get behind the surface of this apocalyptic material, which is probably pre-Christian, we discover a direction of thought which is by no means apocalyptic but which proves this style to be a literary device.[42] *Hermas'* concern is moral; he does not preach a second repentance to preach the coming of the Kingdom. Although he believes in the coming of the Kingdom, he does not set out to communicate afresh this coming but to pronounce a penitential exception. In the *Didache,* eschatology is still alive and fervent: "Let this world pass away!" is the prayer of the congregation at the conclusion of the Eucharist (10.6). Its sixteenth chapter is a significant expression of early Christian expectancy of the Kingdom: the coming of the Lord; the trumpet; the clouds of heaven. But in this document the language of eschatology is not the language of redemption; the Eucharistic passages either do not know or do not mention the death of Christ. And suddenly we see a kinship between *Hermas* and the *Didache* despite their apparent disparity because they both have no room for a redemptory language tied in with eschatological language; either by repentance or by the kingdom they miss the language about redemption which is so much a part of early Christian communication of ethics and eschatology.

In post-Apostolic communication the problem of the Christ lies

---

[42] When Hermas uses ἀποκαλύπτω, it is no longer in the sense of Rom. 8:18, Luke 17:30, or I Pet. 1:5, but in the meaning of "to exhort," "to strengthen" (*Vis.* III.12.2), or "to reveal meaning of Scripture" (*Vis.* II.2.1).

in the relation between a language of proclamation and a language of command. In the center of the New Testament stands the four-fold gospel. This gospel presents a story, not as critically sifted evidence, but as a sermon and witness to an event. It is a narrative. "He opened his mouth and taught them." (Matt. 5:2.) "Two robbers were crucified with him." (27:38.) "An angel of the Lord descended from heaven." (28.2.) Language presents something. This presentation demands an answer, either by acceptance or by denial; but in the presentation there is a statement which speaks for itself. We may call this the language of proclamation, or, in a modern term, kerygmatic language.[43] As we move into the situation of the church, there is an increasing need to teach and to exhort people. The Christian preacher and theologian cannot help being didactic, as even Paul used didactic language plentifully and as the authors of I Peter and I John, for instance, did. What is of supreme importance for the transmittance of Christian faith is the relation between kerygmatic and didactic language. When Paul addresses a church, say, in Galatia, all admonition is embedded in proclaiming communication. Before he instructs, he witnesses (Gal. 1:11 ff.), and then tells the story of the Christ (3-4). Already in this story the congregations who are being addressed are included (4:8 ff.), because in the story the existence of the church is comprehended (4:31). When Paul then enters clearly didactic language, demanding, beseeching, urging (4:12 ff.), he comes back to the story (4:22, 5:24, 6:14). And as he instructs, he does not merely say what people should do—which is, of course, part of his message—but what they already are (5:13).

In communicating Christian faith, either the kerygmatic or the didactic language will set the tone.[44] We do not exclude either

---

[43] "Kerygmatic language" is stating a fact (C. H. Dood, *The Apostolic Preaching and its Development* [New York: Willett, Clark & Co., 1949], p. 13) but does so by addressing the hearer; the two are related and should not be split (cf. the study on I Cor. 15:3-8 and Gal. 1:11-17 by William Baird, "What Is the Kerygma?" *Journ. of Bibl. Lit.* 76 [1957], 181 ff.).

[44] Stanislas Giet (*L'Apocalypse et l'Histoire* [Paris: 1957], pp. 231 ff.) has stated that the book of Revelation is above all a prophetic and secondarily a hortatory work. In Hermas this is exactly reversed: the apocalyptic style is above all hortatory. Revelation culminates in the triumph of the lamb, while the main purpose of Hermas lies in preaching *metanoia*.

because in the conveyance of faith the one cannot do without the other. But one of the two will determine the direction of Christian communication. In the post-Apostolic literature we observe the rising importance of the didactic trend until the kerygmatic aspect is practically extinct. Ignatius of Antioch is the great exception. The language of his letters is often powerfully descriptive; when he presents his case to the Ephesians he falls into a hymnic style, expressing his witness to the Christ in forceful antithetic rhythm:

> There is one physician,
> born of flesh and of spirit,
> born and unborn,
>
> God in man,
> in death true life,
> of Mary and of God,
> first passible and then
> impassible,
> Jesus Christ our Lord.
> —Ign. *Eph.* 7.2

This is kerygmatic language at its best, theological witness in poetic concentration, communication in a hymn of adoration. Ignatius can make use of Gnostic patterns in order to achieve his kerygmatic purpose, as in the famous chapters about the Incarnation in Ign. *Eph.* 19-20. With equal ease he falls into creedal formulations (Ign. *Eph.* 20.2; 18.2). The basis for all such proclamation lies in his thanksgiving that by the "concord and harmonious love," of the church at Ephesus, "Jesus Christ is being sung" (4.1). Communication of God's act is creedal (the concentration of the act in a hymn 7.2), is witness (the description of what God has done to us: 9.1), but at the same time it is praise, transmitting the song of heaven and sharing in the unison of a choir (4.2). Part of the captivating quality of Ignatius' language lies in the way it communicates the music of Incarnation.

The problem in Ignatius appears most markedly in his letter to the Roman community. This famous epistle about his forthcoming martyrdom at the Circus Maximus is one extensive praise of the witness unto death, with the fear that the Roman Christians may attempt to prevent the execution (6.2) by interfering in his behalf out of kindness (4.1). The ecstatic language of this man who wants "to be poured out to God" (2.2) is a remarkable expression of a martyr's exuberance in the early church. The ecstatic fascination with death ("Entice the wild beasts" [4.2]; "I long for the beasts" [5.2]; "The pains of birth are upon me" [6.1]) debilitates the force of the witness because it is so egocentric and because this egocentricity never frees itself from the desire for merit: "It is difficult for me to reach God if you do spare me" (1:2). The man's aspirations dominate the impression which the Roman reader must have received from his letter. This is not witness; it does not transmit judgment and joy for mankind (Ignatius makes an easy but most threatening distinction between himself and the Romans he addresses [1.2], and at this moment the martyr cannot include the Christians in his witness. Between authentic proclamation and his epistle to the Romans stands, not didactic language, but the fatal notion, ἐπιτυγχάνω, "to gain," "to attain."

We cannot say that Clement of Rome does not know the kerygmatic transmittance of faith. "For the sake of love toward us did Jesus Christ give his blood for us, by the will of God, his flesh for our flesh, his life for our lives." (49.6.) Many passages make this same witness and affirmation. The weight of emphasis lies not in these, however, but in the didactic mandates. The letter contains countless verbs of admonition; one could almost call it "The Letter of the Hortatory Subjunctive." The Roman presbyter hammers mandate after mandate, demand after demand, into the ears of his hearers in Corinth. The tenor of this letter is mandatory, and the kerygmatic element is utilized if it serves to grind the ax and produce repentance and peace in Corinth. The use of the Old Testament is didactic in that it underlines and furnishes the basis for the call to repentance and peace. In this mandatory and didactic language, the good news of God in Christ is not absent, but it is not present in the dynamic force of Paul: "Where the Spirit of the Lord is, there is freedom" (II Cor. 3:17).

Apocalyptic language comes closest to what we have called kerygmatic communication because it seeks primarily to present an event between judgment and hope; the demand may be part of —or may follow the depiction of—the vision, but authentic apoc-

114

alyptic imagery implies a change of life on the part of the hearer. The best example of this may be found in the Little Apocalypse of Mark 13. Such implication differs from a blunt demand to do or not to do something. The most kerygmatic passage of the *Didache* appears in its last chapter, in the announcement of the fiery trial (16.5), the signs of the truth (16.6), and the clouds of heaven (16.8). Occasionally, *Hermas* rises to apocalyptic proclamation, as in his opening vision or in the description of the servant *(Sim. V.6)*; but on the whole, the apocalyptic style is obviously meant for a moral purpose; it is no more than a tool for mandatory communication. The problem of apocalyptic language is not the same in the *Didache* as in *Hermas*. In the *Didache* we have an astonishing lack of redemptive communication; Christ is not mentioned in the first six chapters, and the ensuing chapters show as little awareness of the Christian faith as a gospel of grace as does the opening instruction. *Hermas* knows redemptory language in his proclamation of a second forgiveness but his announcement of this second chance contains no organic link with redemption in Christ.[45] The Lord has given to the angel of repentance "power over repentance" *(Mand. IV.3.5)*; the "one more chance" (IV.3.6) arises from the apocalyptic vision. And suddenly the lack of redemptive language in the *Didache* and the lack of kerygmatic communication about Christ in *Hermas* fall into the same category. Apocalyptic communication ceases to be proclamation of *euangelion*, the redemptive gospel about Jesus the Christ, the joyful message of the death and resurrection of the Christ. Apocalyptic language, once it is severed from *euangelion* in Christ, and once the fulfillment of the Apocalyptic hope is delayed, is bound to become either mandatory,[46]

---

[45] This eschatological remnant is not "eschatological nomism" (against Hasler, *op. cit.*, p. 42), but rather what Eggenberger (*op. cit.*, p. 169) called "cosmic optimism." When the primitive Christian address loses its eschatological relation, it turns into legalism (Kamlah, *op. cit.*, p. 74).

[46] The creative contribution by Rudolf Bultmann in this respect is his distinction between apocalyptic and eschatological. In the Gospel of John, the first is absent but not the second: ("Die Eschatologie des Johannesevangeliums," in *Glauben und Vertstehen* [Tübingen: 1933], pp. 134 ff.). The disappearance and the preservation of these two are not identical problems, as it can easily be proved by comparing the apocalypticism of *Hermas* with the millenium in Irenaeus, or the penitential answers in *Hermas* with the penitential answers by Irenaeus. To have confused the two is the grave error of Martin Werner (*Die*

or ecclesiastical, or Gnostic. All three dissolve the tension in Pauline eschatology which communicates an event which has taken place and which will take place.[47]

The post-Apostolic period marks the dilution of the apostolic communication of the Christ. What has been a language of witness, affirming and conveying the most significant event in life, becomes pragmatic, purposeful, moral. Judgment and joy turn into prohibition and command. Affirmative communication of the gospel event is not historical in any modern sense, as if it were void of subject and intention; it is always language with an address, it challenges the hearer to denial or response. It has ethical implication. When the gospel depicts God's act in Christ, it involves the hearer—or rejects him by his own rejection. Whatever the demand of response is, the redemptive force creates a response. The first generation after the apostles begins to lose this characteristic of Christian language. Less and less will they chant the narrative—only Ignatius really knows what this means. They teach. They judge. They command. The Christ is there, but he no longer lives as he does in the exuberant language of Ignatius, with his captivating witness of joy.

The Old Testament

Perhaps in no other period of Christian history has the Old Testament been quoted more abundantly than it has by some of the Apostolic Fathers. *I Clement* and *Barnabas* consist largely of Old Testament citations. Except in Ignatius, who has merely one or two passages in each of his letters, the Old Testament plays a key role in the transmission of faith. It is Holy Writ (*I Clem.* 34.6; *II Clem.*

Entstehung des christlichen Dogmas [Bern. 1941], [2nd ed.; 1954]. To make the retarding factor the basis for the whole dogmatic development (p. 114) represents the procrastination of the dynamic and complex relation of the "yet—not —yet" in early Christian eschatology to a simple academic formula. Concerning the angel Christology which has been connected with the retarding problem, see Wilhelm Michaelis, *Zur Engelchristologie im Urchristentum* (Basel: 1942).

[47] "In Christ" is *indicative;* in the Lord" is *imperative,* claims Fritz Neugebauer, *New Test. Stud.* 4 (1957), 135, and the two are joined together by the Holy Spirit (p. 136). This is a creative synthesis which does not eliminate, however, the issue of the starting point and of the conflict between the indicative and the imperative.

14.1; *Barn.* 6.12). It must have been assumed that this scripture was known to the recipients of these letters, since prophetic sayings are introduced without any explanatory phrase (*Barn.* 13.7) and the stories of Israel are told as a matter of course and not introduced as if they were unknown (*I Clem.* 45.6-7; *Barn.* 8.1 ff.). Numerous Old Testament metaphors, as well as individual terms, proper names with allegorical meanings, liturgical and theological expressions, appear on every page.[48] Clearly the Old Testament means a great deal to these authors, and must be taken seriously as the basis of their communication.

As soon as we examine content and context of these quotations and of the apparent Old Testament allusions, we are surprised to find that the same Old Testament citations may mean one thing for one author and quite a different thing for another. Of the numerous quotations from the Psalms in *I Clement* and *Barnabas,* only three are identical; when they quote the same passage—for example Isaiah 53 on the suffering servant—their interpretations differ. *Barnabas* sees it in relation to the atonement and forgiveness of sins (5.2), while *I Clement* primarily uses the same text to demonstrate the humility of Christ (16.3 ff.). For *Barnabas* the Old Testament is one great *typos.* Words, stories, prophecies are all christological types. The "temple" of the old covenant is interpreted as the "incorruptible temple" into which God leads us (16:10); the serpent of Moses provides the *typos* for the suffering of Jesus (12.5); and the cry of Isaiah means the cry which announces the new covenant (11.3-5). *Barnabas* has thus become the prototype for the christological use of the Old Testament.[49] *I Clement,* on the other hand, uses the Old Testament with moral intent. In example after example, the Old Testament demonstrates how jealousy has always resulted in evil (4), repentance has always been demanded (8), and obedience has always been a blessing (9). Both writers are agreed in their conscious desire to be rooted in

---

[48] *I Clem.* 4; 31; 36; *II Clem.* 16.3 and 17.5; *Barn.* 4; 7; and 12 would be some examples. Cf. Eggenberger, *op. cit.,* pp. 42 ff.

[49] Christological interpretation and the use of *typos* may not necessarily mean typological interpretation because *typos* may create an unhistorical parallelism which is not the Pauline typology. Bartsch, *op. cit.,* p. 44: the absolute unity between the prophets and Christ prevents a real understanding of a history of salvation—which is vital for the typology of Rom. 4 or Gal. 4.

the holy scriptures of Israel, but a quotation from the Old Testament has little meaning in itself before its use is determined.

The Old Testament is for Clement of Rome moral paradigm. It is very useful to him because he can demonstrate forcefully to Corinth the seriousness of the need for penitential acts and the promise of repentance. Humility (17), the blessed path of life (31), reward (34) —look at the Old Testament and you will find it everywhere! The Old Testament is an ethical code, and because it is holy scripture and therefore the criterion of faith for both writer and hearer (53:1), its command must have made a decisive impact upon Corinth. The problem is that the Old Testament is seldom more than ethical code.[50] In an extensive quotation from a letter intended perhaps to be read in the service at Corinth, Clement quotes the famous passage from Isa. 53 about the suffering servant. This is an example of the humble-mindedness of Christ (16.17). He does the same with Ps. 22:6-8, another of the church's christological texts; again it is only a moral paradigm for the humility of Christ (16.15). There is no indication of the good news *about* Jesus, as in the Old Testament quotation in Acts 8:32-35. What the Old Testament illuminates is the New—but as moral example.

Barnabas sees this text from Isaiah in the framework of past, present, and future (5.3). The Old Testament as *typos* points toward Christ and looks for revelation in the cross of Christ (9:8). Paradigm does not need history but *typos* presupposes it because it means precisely the pointing of an earlier event toward a later one within a historical continuity. Exegesis as Christocentric *typos* represents the salient contribution of this unknown theologian to the history of Christian interpretation. But upon closer examination, the typos in *Barnabas* approaches the interpretative principle of Clement of Rome; we look in vain for any understanding of development, let alone of conflict, between Sinai and Golgotha. Christianity is a "new law" (2.6); this dialectical Pauline phrase becomes a naïve elimination of the very history toward which the *typos* is meant to lead. The polemic of this letter is directed against

---

[50] The replacement of the historical meaning of the OT by spiritualization of revelation and law has been one of the main themes of Diaspora Judaism; cf. Peter Dahlberg, *Die Theologie der Hellenistisch-Jüdischen Missionsliteratur* [Hamburg: 1954], pp. 130 ff.

idol worship (2:4 ff.), but there is nowhere any understanding of the collision between law and freedom, not even as in Matt. 12. The Christian understands "how well Moses legislated" (10.11). In this extirpation of the historical development lies the root for *Barnabas'* legalism and his theology of merit.[51] Upon the identification of old law and new law, of Moses and the Cross, the Old Testament becomes again paradigm, a detour by way of the cross; and the whole emphasis of the later prophets—so beloved in the Diaspora—the spiritualizing the cultus (16.8 ff.) as well as the book of Leviticus (10) (never mentioned in *I Clement*) can be accepted as Christian instruction. The covenant is ours, says *Barnabas* (4.7). Certainly, for the self-understanding of the church in the year 135. But to say this *with* using *typos* and *without* opening the path for Gnosticism would mean to take much more seriously the fact that the covenant has been "theirs." Paul was not grappling with trivialities when he wrote Rom. 9-11.[52] In the step from Judaism to Christianity more is involved than merely seeing "how well Moses legislated." [53]

Here Ignatius comes into the picture. The christological language of the martyr of Antioch portrays the newness in Christ in every breath. This literature does not use the Mosaic code to show how well Moses legislated. His union with Christ, the charismatic touch in his description of martyrdom, the awe and joy in his description of the Savior's arrival—all this impresses the reader by its vibrating sense of newness. In Barnabas and Clement, though in different ways, one always has the feeling that the Christian faith says exactly what the Old Testament says; in Ignatius nobody could come away with such an impression. There is "new hope" in Christ,

---

[51] In a keen formulation, Goodenough (*op. cit.*, p. 47) contrasts the Hellenistic Philonic subordination of "typology to metaphysics" with the Christian subordination of "metaphysics to typology." *Barnabas* comes close to this typology, but he has not freed himself from a metaphysical Christology.

[52] P. Meinhold, "Geschichte und Exegese im Barnabasbrief," *Zeitschr. f. Kirchengesch.* 60 (1941), 255 ff.

[53] G. Bardy (*The Church at the End of the First Century* [London: Sands & Co., 1938], pp. 93 ff.) pointed out that heretical Judaism is the problem for the post-Apostolic age; such heretical Judaism, however, exists right within Christian circles, with a double trend: (Judaistic-) Hellenistic Gnosticism and (Judaistic-) Hellenistic nomism. I am not at all convinced that one should call this nomistic threat "harmless" (Goppelt, *op. cit.*, p. 244); Marcion knew better!

and in contrast to *Barnabas* and Clement, this "new hope" is set in antithesis and no longer merely in juxtaposition to the old; in the new hope the Christians no longer keep the Sabbath but the Lord's Day (Ign. *Magn.* 9.1). The newness in Christ does not deny the prophets. They waited for him (9.2). Now, once he has come, it would be absurd "to talk of Jesus Christ and to practice Judaism" (10.3).

Ignatius paves the way and exhibits the dilemma. His Christocentric proclamation represents the alternative to the moralistic christology of the Apostolic Fathers. Christ is not merely another Moses. The Day of Resurrection succeeded the Day of Sabbath (9.1). But the focus on Christ's newness does not deny the first covenant; the creeds which Ignatius quotes give him roots in the Old Testament because Christ *is* "of the family of David according to the flesh" (*Smyrn.* 1.1). A Davidic Christ who was truly born and ate and drank (*Tral.* 9.1) separates his faith from any Gnostic dualism. Here is a language about Christ which does not refute the Old Testament. Or does it? This is the dilemma! Prophet—Law —Gospel, Ignatius knows this sequence (*Smyrn.* 5.1). In the overall picture, however, it plays a remarkably slight role. Ignatius knows that there is a conflict and he knows that despite the conflict the Old Testament is present in Christian faith; but he makes exceedingly little use of it. Ignatius does not want to forget the Old Testament—he only tends to forget it. But this shows what the problem is in any Christian use of the Old Testament. Compare, for instance, *Barnabas* and *Clement* or *Barnabas* and the Gnostics. To communicate Christ in all his newness, yet as part of the divine plan; as involved in history, yet in collision with it—this is the dilemma of Christian exegesis in any given day. The Old Testament cannot be either the paradigm of Clement or the eschatological example of *Barnabas;* we shall always have to reject Marcion's emphatic no and the genial denial of Sophia; we must seek for the *typos* of *Barnabas* in the newness of Ignatius.

By such a conclusion, however, we have brought the Christian use of the Old Testament into an explosive tension. To grasp history-*typos*-newness simultaneously, by serious consideration of the Old Testament, without ending in the moralism of Clement or in the eschatological symbolism of *Barnabas,* is a matter of creative subtlety. Yet here lies one of the paramount conflicts in the long history of Christian language. Almost anybody can preach to men what they should do; almost anybody can be attracted by Gnostic speculations about heaven and redemption. Communicating the Christ in continuity with Israel yet with the breach from it; using exhortation as a part of and not as as substitute for the gospel— there is the challenge to formulate Christian ethical communication. Proclamation that breathes response; New Testament language in continuity with and freedom from the Old Testament—all this can only be solved concretely in each attempt at exegesis, in preaching and in education. The New Testament relation between history, type, and newness must safeguard Christian faith from Gnostic or paradigmatic abuse of the Old Testament. The common denominator in both is that they have ceased to speak about the living Father and the sovereign grace of the incarnate Christ.

These bonds or conflicts with the Old Testament lead us farther in our discussion of the Gnostic language of salvation. We have spoken of a barrier against dualism and ontology provided by what we called the Hebraic roots of authentic Christian communication. The language which we have observed has preserved on certain levels these Hebraic connotations considerably better than any Gnostic fragment because a language void of ethical significance is unthinkable in prophetic proclamation. To be sure, it is much less attractive than Gnostic speech; the nagging language of command loses all the plastic meaning it had for Israel; spiritualization replaces God's direct address to the land and people, and in the case of *metanoia* the promise is merely one of individual reward. Yet the roots of Hebraic speech are still discernible,[54] only they have been removed from the dynamic stage of Jerusalem, Babylon, and Bethel to the bourgeois setting of a Roman villa.

[54] Christine Mohrmann ("Linguistic Problems in the Early Church," *Vig. Christ.* 11 [1957], 11 ff.) has shown that the Hebraic uniqueness in Greek and Latin language takes its starting point from the LXX (see especially her examples σωτήρ p. 22 and ἐξομολογέομαι p. 25; the double meaning of the latter, "to confess sin" and "to glorify God" is one of the best examples for the presence of "Hebraic roots" in early Christian language). Christine Mohrmann has demonstrated further how a concept (e.g. δόξα—*gloria*, p. 31) can lose its Hebraic root.

The preceding analysis, however, demonstrates that when we speak of Hebraic speech we are not talking about the language used by the Jews before and after the lifetime of Jesus of Nazareth. Already in Hellenistic Judaism which provides the background for post-Apostolic language [55] we find one cause for the failure to communicate biblical faith in its fullness. Apocalyptic language seems to contain in itself Hebraic roots; however, Gnostic apocalyptic speech is as alien from the Hebraic encounter between God and man as anything could be at this period. Likewise the language of ethical command is not *eo ipso* Hebraic. In this period Stoic and Hermetic teaching is used in its ethical exhortation (sadness as a vice,[56] moderate use of food,[57] cycles of virtues [58]) whereby Hellenistic and Hebraic elements flow together.[59] We see a similar syncretistic movement in Clement of Rome's use of Hellenistic natural concepts: God as the sustainer of the universe (20) and the Phoenix as an analogy of resurrection (24-25), both in Hel-

[55] It is, of course, not a matter of contrasting "Hellenistic" with "Jewish" language, which would be utterly naïve, nor of "Hellenistic" with "Palestinian" (against Daniélou, *op. cit.*, p. 335), nor of "apocalyptic" with "Gnostic" (against Daniélou, *op. cit.*, p. 337; cf. Robert M. Grant, *Gnosticim and Early Christianity* pp. 54 ff.), all of which are missing the manifold ties between Jewish and Hellenistic realms; we do not even contrast "Hellenistic" with "rabbinic" (see Rengsdorf, *ThWNT*, IV, 406, n. 110). We speak about the Old Hebraic roots of Mosaic-prophetic thinking in the Hellenistic language; nowhere are these roots void of Hellenistic infiltrations (cf. Goodenough, *op. cit.*, e.g., pp. 72 ff. on Torah in Philo, or p. 253 on the dilemma between "normative" and "Hellenistic" Judaism). The crucial question is the one concerning *presence* and *extent* of these roots in Hellenistic Judaism. There is a further problem to be faced: on one hand, the Jewish mode of writing shines through in the Greek and Latin languages (Christine Mohrmann, "Problèmes stylistiques dans la littérature Latine Chrétienne," *Vig. Christ.* 9 [1955], 222 ff.) ; on the other hand, in a more precise analysis, the Hellenistic literary style which can be traced in Latin literature (pp. 223, 225) is not *eo ipso* Hebraic.

[56] Herm. *Mand.* X.1.1 ff. Richard Reitzenstein (*Das Iranische Elösungsmysterium* [Bonn: 1921], p. 159) sees here Persian influence; cf. *Corp. Herm.* XIII.7.

[57] Herm. *Vis.* III. 9.3; cf. also *Sim.* X.4.3; VI.5.5; *Mand.* XIII.3.5; *I Clem.* 41.3 (τὸ καθῆκον; cf. Eggenberger, *op. cit.*, p. 142).

[58] Herm. *Vis.* III.8.2; *Sim.* IX.15. ff. (*Corp. Herm.* XIII.8-9) ; cf. Sanders, *op. cit.*, pp. 74 ff.

[59] Being the language of the Synagogue (O. J. F. Seitz, "Antecedents and Signification of the term δίψυχος," *Jorn. of Bibl. Lit.* 66 [1947], 211 ff. and Torrance, *op. cit.*, pp. 120 ff.), it has of course Semitic nuances (Ernst Zahn, *Apostolische Väter* [Leipzig: 1906], pp. 485 ff.).

lenistic fashion. The language of a Jewish Diaspora which formed part of the background for this period already permits the infiltration of cosmological and naturalistic notions into the speech of the Greek Old Testament and its users.[60] Moreover, the analysis reveals that we must clearly distinguish between the Hebraic roots and Old Testament language as such. We are speaking about a Hebraic basis, but not about the Hebrew language. The language of the New Testament is not only not Hebrew; [61] it uses the prophetic pattern of speech concerning God and man in terms of time and event, but it focuses this pattern anew on the Christ, the Incarnation, and the new being. Christian language is not merely Old Testament language. There is more to it than just the barrier we have spoken of. The language of God and man is most vital in the communication of the gospel; but the language of law and promise has passed through the conflict and

[60] Stoic language had widely infiltrated Jewish Hellenistic circles (Hans Lietzmann, *An die Römer* [Tübingen: 1933], p. 36). W. C. Van Unnick argued in an article ("Is I Clement 20 purely Stoic?" *Vig. Christ.* 4 [1950], 181 ff.) against Rudolf Knopf *(Die Lehre der Zwölf Apostel, die zwei Klemensbriefe* [Tübingen: 1920]) that this chapter is much less Stoic than usually assumed. The mistake of Knopf was to have called *I Clem. 20 "unjüdisch"* (p. 42) ; the presence of Stoic notions could hardly be denied, not only because of convincing material offered by Sanders *(op. cit.,* pp. 109 ff.) but because *I Clem.* 24-25 shows how Clement does possess a *theologia naturalis;* otherwise, why would he resort to the Phoenix for demonstrating the Resurrection? Of course, this *"Umsetzung der christlichen Auferstehungshoffnung in die naturhaften Kategorien der heidnischen Philosophie"* (Eggenberger, *op. cit.,* p. 140) takes place in Jewish-Hellenistic literary fashion (E. Peterson, "Das Praescriptum des I Clemens-Briefes," in *Pro Regno Pro Sanctuario* [Nijkerk: 1950], pp. 351 ff.), but this does not deny Stoic or Platonic understanding of terms (G. Bardy, "Expressions stoiciennes dans la Ia Clementis," *Rev. Scien. Rel.* 12 [1922], 73 ff. and Michel Spanneut, *Le Stoicisme des pères de l'Eglise de Clément de Rome à Clément d'Alexandrie* [Paris: 1948], p. 373). Further discussions on this topic should consider the comparison between *I Clem.* 20 and *Dio Prus.* XL 38-40 apart from Eggenberger's conclusions *(op. cit.,* pp. 76 ff.) The letter may still be an authentic one (E. Molland, *RGG,* vol. I, 1838) .

[61] We have made it clear from the outset that we do not merely speak about Greek language vs. Aramaic or Hebrew language. Now, Gustave Bardy *(La Question des langues dans l'Eglise ancienne* [Paris: 1948], I, 11 ff.) has shown that there is indeed a linguistic conflict in primitive Christianity, before the migration to Pella. This conflict, however, is not limited to the one between Aramaic-and Greek-speaking converts but continues within the Greek-speaking church; and therefore, what is exhibited in the language struggle of the Christians—perhaps already in the persecution of Stephen—is only one aspect for a deeper conflict concerning the nature of Christian speech.

victory of grace. There is grace in the Old Testament, and there is mediation, but the specific, historical description of the Incarnation creates not a breach (contrast Marcion), but a tension (contrast Clement). Incarnation, described in a language that reflects speech in the mode of acting and addressing without the limitations of legalism—such is the heart of Christian communication.

This gives a double meaning to "Hebraic roots." One makes them primary, the other subordinates them to the newness of the gospel. In order to express the Incarnation, it is vital for theology to have a clear understanding of the Old Testament connotation of "God encountering man"; otherwise Christ will be replaced by gnosis, mystery, or sacrament. But when it comes to expressing the ethical demand, it is necessary to subordinate the Hebraic roots to the *euangelion,* the gospel of grace; otherwise the gospel loses precisely this characteristic of grace. "Hebraic barricade" in the first case means the denial of anthropological or cosmogonic ontologies; "Hebraic barrier" in the second prevents the law from disappearing in favor of a libertinist mysticism. The Gnostics and the Apostolic Fathers give us precious insights into the unique character of the Christian communication about a Christ in whom "God was . . . reconciling the world to himself . . . not counting their trespasses against them . . . and entrusting to us the message of reconciliation" (II Cor. 5:19). In this Pauline statement, the double barrier of primitive Christian language is perfectly expressed.

THE LANGUAGE ABOUT THE CHURCH

The problem of the language of Hellenistic Judaism, a language of exhortation which misses the kerygmatic stream of the New Testament, is not the only problem which confronts the post-Apostolic church. Neither is it the only extreme in opposition to Marcion and Gnosticism. The language of faith is also a language within the community of faith. As this community develops, it affects the language because the concepts of this language are related to the community. This evolution is a necessity, but it is also a judgment. It reveals to us that the language of faith is always a language between the times. We speak a language neither of revelation itself nor of the kingdom of God itself. We speak a language of faith within a community of faith; the language and the community are in a state between promise and fulfillment and are identical with neither. We take the examples for this analysis from the terminology concerning the church and its ministry.

Apostle and Prophet

The New Testament contains several terms revolving around the authority of its message. There are the *disciples,* called by Jesus into his discipleship, sent out in the great mission to proclaim the kingdom of God. They follow him, yet they also betray him. They are witnesses to the Resurrection, and they receive the command to teach and to baptize. There are the *apostles*—already in the Synoptics a parallel term for disciple—taught by the Holy Spirit; called not by man nor through men, but by God. On them the church is established.[62] There are *presbyters* in the communities of Acts and of the later epistles, formed according to the presbyteral bodies of Judaism.[63] There are *deacons,* even if not so named, in the election of the seven who are to care for the needy of Jerusalem. They exist in Philippi (Phil. 1:1) and in the communities of the later epistles (I Tim. 3:8). There are the *bishops,* a rare term, used in the greetings to Philippi in the plural (Phil. 1:1). Probably they are overseers of the cult in Philippi and in other churches (1 Tim. 3:2; Acts 20:28). There are *teachers*—a name which has been frequently given to Jesus (Mark 10:17)—in Antioch, together with prophets (Acts 13:1); in Corinth, as the third group in the Pauline triad (I Cor. 12:28); in the churches of the Pastorals, together with the apostles (II Tim. 1:11). And finally, there are the *prophets* in the communities of Jerusalem (Acts 15:32) and of Antioch (13:1). In the church of Corinth we know them to have played a prominent part in the life and liturgy of the church (I Cor. 14:29). Paul does not have a special term for those who are bearers of other charismatic gifts: those who perform miracles, those who heal, those who speak in tongues (I Cor. 12:28).

The problems of second-century terminology of the church can best be pursued in the study of the difficult dilemma between Catholic and Protestant concepts of New Testament authority. What

[62] Luke 6:13 (δώδεκα ἀπόστολοι); Mark 6:30; I Cor. 12:28; Eph. 2:20.
[63] Act 11:30, 15:2, I Tim. 5:17, Tit. 1:5, I Pet. 5:1.

is the relation between the institutional and the charismatic in the New Testament concept of authority? [64] It becomes apparent to anyone approaching this problem without prejudice that the New Testament contains both pneumatic and institutional authority. Jesus gives, in one instance to Peter, in another to his disciples, the power of binding and loosing.[65] The authority of the presbyters in Christian circles of Palestine is a natural outgrowth from the Jewish background. The apostle as such is a pneumatic and not a legal representative. Paul stresses repeatedly this pneumatic basis for his apostolate (Gal. 1:1; I Cor. 9:11; 15:9-10). The prophet comes next to the apostolate in Paul's triadic enumeration. The prophet Agabus of Acts is the witness to the importance of the prophetic position throughout the Apostolic period. Yet it is Paul who addresses deacons and bishops in Philippi and who gives some final advice to Ephesus. The latter may be the product of Luke,[66] yet may also preserve things which Paul must have considered toward the end of his traveling ministry. Taking all this into consideration, we cannot reduce the biblical testimony of Christian authority either to a legal or to a pneumatic one. To sever it from the power of the keys or to isolate it from the Pentecost experience is a violation of the biblical ministry. The early Christian community lives in a surprising confluence of charismatic and institutional streams. To be sure, certain missionary outreaches emphasize one or the other; Paul stands distinctly for the pneu-

---

[64] Cf. John Knox, "The Ministry in the Primitive Church," in H. Richard Niebuhr and Daniel D. Williams, *The Ministry in Historical Perspective* (New York: Harper & Brothers, 1956), pp. 1 ff.

[65] In the controversy concerning these passages (Matt. 16:18-19 and 18:18), it is often hard to distinguish between historiography and apologetics. A. M. Farrer ("The Ministry in the New Testament," in Kenneth E. Kirk, *The Apostolic Ministry*, [London: Hodder & Stoughton, 1946], p. 146) dares to claim that Paul places the government of local churches into the hands of episcopoi, not charismatics—obviously the case in I Cor. 14. Some positions *for* the authenticity of the Peter passage: Oscar Cullmann, *Peter; Disciple, Apostle, Martyr* (New York: Meridian, 1958), pp. 184 ff., and A. Oepke. "Der Herrenspruch über die Kirche," *Stud. Theol.* 3 (1950), 110 ff.; *against* the authenticity: Hans von Campenhausen, *Kirchliches Amt und Geistliche Vollmacht in den ersten drei Jahrhunderten* (Tübingen: 1957), pp. 135 ff. and Werner G. Kümmel, *Kirchenbegriff und Geschichtsbewusstsein in der Urgemeinde* (Zürich: 1943), pp. 37 ff.

[66] Martin Dibelius, *Die Reden der Apostelgeschichte und die Antike Geschichtsschreibung* (Heidelberg: 1949), pp. 133 ff.

matic. How is it possible that these communities live within different types of Christian ministry? The ground on which this confluence can occur is the person of Jesus and the reality of the risen Christ, in whom and in whose apostles this unity is possible.[67] Our attempts to establish the exact relationship between Peter and James, and between Paul and the Twelve, lead us into uncertainty. Is this only because the texts are lacking? Or is it not rather because the life of the early communities in the reality of resurrection makes possible a congruity which will never again be achievable for the church in all the various concrete situations. It may well be that the apostolic community within both a pneumatic and a presbyteral authority would not have understood the question of church history: how is one to distinguish the spirit from the office?

In the post-Apostolic church, New Testament terminology is questioned. The concepts concerning authority and ministry cry out for modification. *Apostolos* is the highest stamp of pneumatic authority which the New Testament can offer. "Paul, an apostle, not by men nor through men but through Jesus Christ and God the Father who has raised him from the dead." [68] In the *Didache* this *apostolos* is viewed with suspicion. Although he is to be received "as the Lord," the church manual demands that he be tested. If he stays longer than two days or asks for any money, he is a false prophet. If he leaves the community, no more bread shall be handed to him than will last him until evening (*Did.* 11.4-6). The causes

[67] Hans von Campenhausen ("Tradition und Geist im Urchristentum" *Stud. Gen.*, 1951, pp. 351 ff.) and John Knox (*op. cit.*, p. 10) both reject the wrong alternative of a charismatic versus an institutional ministry; Harnack demanded already that the two be seen together (*op. cit.*, p. 359). This is not a unity of certain church orders (Streeter, *op. cit.*, p. 267), neither presbyterial nor episcopal nor congregational, but it is also not a unity of a "charismatic" ministry. As Streeter has aptly pointed out, χάρισμα is nowhere designation for an office (*op. cit.*, p. 104).

[68] Rengsdorf has called this passage in Gal. 1:1 the classical formulation for the apostolate (*ThWNT*, I, 438). Extensive material is in Olaf Linton, *Das Problem der Urkirche in der neueren Forschung* (Uppsala: 1932), pp. 69 ff. Cf. also Hans von Campenhausen, "Der urchristliche Apostelbegriff," *Stud. Theol.* 1 (1947), 96 ff; Holger Moosbach, "Apostolos in the New Testament," *Stud. Theol.* 2 (1948), 166 ff.; T. W. Manson, *The Church's Ministry* (Philadelphia: The Westminster Press, 1948), pp. 34 ff. Hans Joachim Schoeps, *Urgemeinde, Judenchristentum, Gnosis*, p. 15; Markus Barth, *Der Augenzeuge* (Zollikon: 1946); and Dom Gregory Dix, *The Ministry in the Early Church* (in Kirk, *op. cit.*, pp. 228 ff.).

for the warning of the *Didache* are plain. The church finds itself suddenly in the difficulty of maintaining the *status quo* of the apostolic ministry. Pneumatic freedom is being abused. The charisma becomes a tool for the charlatan. A concept of positive worth takes on gradually negative associations. This process has its origins in the New Testament itself (ψευδαπόστολος as the threat to Paul's ministry [II Cor. 11:13]) ; it soon leads to the extirpation of the term in the church. The "apostle" will, with the exception of rare sectarian movements, no more play a role in the actual life of the churches.

There is a double reason for this extinction. The situation of the church affects its language. A Christian cannot speak the language of faith in separation from the life of the community of faith. As "apostle" becomes a concept open to abuse, its negative associations are the result of actual experience. In the course of the church's history, this terminological shift is the fate of almost every New Testament concept. The church always finds itself on the defensive against the abuse of its own language. In the case of the next term, this process can be studied even more readily because the uniqueness of the apostolic office is not the uniqueness of the prophetic office.

The situation of the church is not alone responsible for the elimination of the *apostolos* concept in its ministry. The extirpation is also due to theological reasons. The second century makes an exclusive distinction between Apostolic and post-Apostolic literature. On this assumption, the canon is composed.[69] The disappearance of the concept of the apostle is necessitated by the concept of the canon. Because Christian faith understands itself as a revealed faith, the apostolic office ceases with the creation of the canon. There is no longer the apostle who is permitted to speak in the normative charismatic uniqueness of the New Testament apostle even though he act according to the demands of the *Didache*. The self-understanding of Christianity may create other charismatic agencies, but it cannot re-create the apostolic uniqueness.

Prophet is one of the important concepts for New Testament life. Jesus is called a prophet; and the Palestinian and Syriac communities have prophets, even as Corinth has them. Paul gives to the prophets the second place in the authority of the church, immediately after the apostles (I Cor. 12:28). As in the case of the apostles, the *Didache* announces its doubts. The validity of the prophet is to be determined from his behavior. If he does not live by what he teaches, if he asks for something to eat in his ecstasy, or if he demands money for himself, he is a false prophet (11.7-12). "Prophet" is no longer an accepted concept. The church manual asks for validation. The warning of the *Didache* is not meant as an elimination of the prophet. On the contrary, the prophet may not be questioned when he speaks in the spirit.[70] Yet the negative association prevails as the second century progresses. At the outset of the century, the prophet is still accepted in love, although clearly subordinate to the authority of the bishop (Ign. *Phil.* 5.2). *Hermas* represents prophetic Christianity, yet his Mandate distinguishes carefully between a true and a false prophet (XI.1 ff.). Half a century later, the *Didascalia* warns against prophecy.[71] The canons of Nicaea do not even mention prophets.

This elimination of the prophet has to be viewed from several aspects. It is due to an abuse of the prophetic office. Apparently prophecy invited vagabonds to leisurely living. But this does not suffice to explain the disappearance of the prophet. Many times in the history of the church an office has been abused without the church's relinquishing the specific concept. What stands behind this abandonment is the moving of the church toward the limitation and finally the extinction of the pneumatic, the carrier of the charisma as an independent, nonsubordinate authority within the church. In the community of Corinth, charismatic freedom belongs to the essence of προσέρχεσθαι (I Cor. 14:26-33). For the *Didascalia*, this type of charismatic freedom is nonexistent. The disappearance of the prophet shows the subordination of the charismatic to the

[69] On the uniqueness of the apostolic office, see Cullmann, *op. cit.*, pp. 215 ff. ("There will never be such a witness again.")

[70] *Did.* 11.7. The following warning is strong, but there is still a priority of the prophet over the bishop (Streeter, *op. cit.*, p. 225).

[71] *Didasc.* IV.6.3; VI.20. An even more radical reversal *Clem. Hom.* II. 17, 23: John the Baptist becomes the false prophet. A most revealing passage in Chrysostom *De Incomprehensibilitate Dei* 702 D: prophecy and speaking in tongues could cease without any damage to the word; ἰδοὺ γοῦν νῦν προφητεία οὐκ ἔστιν, οὐδὲ γλωσσῶν χάρισμα, καὶ ὁ τῆς εὐσεβείας οὐδὲν ἐνεποδίσθη λόγος.

episcopal structure, which allows the charismatic to live only under its established premises.[72]

Because the church of history is no longer identical with the "community of revelation" of the New Testament, the church is coerced into a differentiation of types of charismatic and institutional language in the New Testament. The second-century church employs one specific type of authoritative speech. In distinguishing between concepts of the canon, the church judges—and at the same time puts itself under the judgment of—the canon. It must be asked whether the church has surrendered in its discrimination a salient factor of biblical substance. Christian community is the church between necessity and judgment. Our first duty in the analysis of church history is to understand the necessity; the second is to ask whether the church has kept itself open to the judgment or whether it has subdued the canon by its necessity.

This question must be raised in respect to the prophetic in the early church. Christian faith does not alter one branch of its terminology without affecting a series of others. The renunciation of the prophetic concept has always led the church either into restoration and revival of some sort, or into a schism. In the Montanist movement, the prophet concept lives again in its primitive Christian vividity. Montanus appears as the prophet.[73] The church rejects the Montanist prophetic claim, and the movement is driven to a split. In fanatic fervor Tertullian pleads for his prophetic church in his polemic against the catholic institutionalism (*De Pudicitia* 21.6 ff.). And yet the reaction against the elimination of the prophetic in the church does not lead Tertullian back to the New Testament relationship of apostle-prophet-teacher as one would expect. Although the great African postulates the "priesthood of all believers," his misunderstanding of sin and repentance leads him

[72]Cf. Torrence, *op. cit.*, p. 141, "grace was taken under the wing of the church in an official way"; more was therefore dropped than merely the name "prophet," as Linton (*op. cit.*, p. 103) suggested. "False Christs and lying prophets have appeared" (*Syriac Didasc.* 26). The above quotation by Chrysostom throws light upon this disappearance of the prophetic: I Cor. is bereft of its eschatological meaning and replaced by an ecclesiastical one; *in the church* prophecy *has already* disappeared, claims the Father, without fettering the Word.

[73] Eus. *H. E.* V.16.4; Epiph. *Pan.* XLVIII.2.4. The anti-Montanist fragment sees the issue of prophecy when it closes the canon of the OT prophets and, at the same time, views *Hermas* with suspicion (Streeter, *op. cit.*, pp. 212 ff.).

to Judaistic instead of Christian prophecy. Prophetic nomism in its rigor and ascetic extravagance is as alien to the New Testament as is the institution of his great foe, the *pontifex maximus* (*De Pud.* 1.6). What Tertullian revives is a prophet; but it is not the New Testament prophet in a New Testament community.[74]

Instead of the revival of the term there can be a substitution. The martyr takes the place of the charismatic in the church, until he, too, must disappear into the stream of history. The martyr has been seen as a special Christian category, the blood witness of Christ, since the middle of the second century. He is granted visions before his death (*Mart. Pol.* 5.2),[75] he can forgive sins (Eus. *H. E.* V.2.5), he speaks in charismatic freedom (V.16.20).[76] The martyr, at least for the first century of classical martyriology, furnishes by his death the very proof which the *Didache* demands of the prophet as the guarantee of his authenticity. And the martyr possesses during his whole period of suffering the special revelatory capacity which the ordinary faithful of the second and third centuries have long since lost.[77]

It shows the health of Christian faith when the loss of a concept cries for a substitute. At the same time, however, we ask whether the substitute gives sufficient credit to that which it replaces. Tertullian, aware of the inadequacy, does not equal his prophetic nomism with the martyr doctrine of penance.[78] The martyr concept is not the lineal heir of the prophet because the emphasis lies on the witness characteristic and not on the prophetic; because it assumes functions which neither the New Testament prophet nor the one in the *Didache* maintained; and because it lets the prophetic

[74] Tert. *De Pud.* 1.6. The combination of an extreme sacerdotal priesthood of all believers (*De Baptismo* 17) with an excessive prophetic freedom (*Exhortatio Castitatis* 7) denies the biblical subordination of the prophetic to the apostolic and threatens the theology of the body of Christ.

[75] *Act. Pert. et Fel.* 4:2-6; *Mart. Pion.* 2.2.

[76] "Martyr" practically becomes a new word in the second and third centuries (Ernst Günther, "Zeuge und Märtyrer," *Zeitschr. f. Neut. Wiss.* 47 [1956] 150 ff.).

[77] For the theology of martyrdom see the comprehensive monograph: Hans von Campenhausen, *Die Idee des Martyriums in der Alten Kirche* (Göttingen: 1936).

[78] Tert. *De Ieiun.* 12. The substitute is, however, not only one for the "apocalyptic witness' (Günther, *art. cit.,* p. 152 ff.), but also for the prophetic "office."

be determined by a life situation, the persecution, without which the charismatic cannot grow.

This is one example to show how much is involved in the tapering of biblical terminology. Apostle and prophet become terms for the past, no longer designating present authority. The retraction of the apostle is not the same as the retraction of the prophet. The elimination of the apostle is the consequence of the irrevocability of the New Testament revelation. When the second century maintains uniqueness of the canon, it has to exterminate the office of the apostle. Practical conflicts furnish external justification for a step which is demanded by the essence of Christian faith. The prophet is never on the same level as the apostle because he is not the eyewitness of resurrection nor the custodian of the faith; he never plays the prominent role in the establishment of church and faith as the apostle does. In Paul's view the prophet definitely comes after the apostle.[79] Even a church founded upon the apostles of the New Testament is in need of a prophetic dimension. The prophet is elminated because second-century Christianity develops episcopacy as an institution. The dismissal of the apostolic is the result of the self-understanding of Christianity; the dismissal of the prophetic is the result of one specific ecclesiastical development within Christianity. From Montanism to the priest workers of France, the church has always had movements which became aware of the necessity of prophets within the church. The renunciation of apostle means the maintenance of the revelatory dimension of faith; the renunciation of prophet narrows this revelation to a degree which a living faith cannot endure.

The Bishop

Between the last letters of Paul and Irenaeus, the great bishop of Lyons, the New Testament plurality of pneumatic and institutional authority develops into the authority of monarchical episcopacy.[80] The process cannot be satisfactorily traced as a historical development in detail. We only know a few stones which fit into

[79] Cf. H. Greeven, "Propheten, Lehrer, Vorsteher bei Paulus," *Zeitschr. f. Neut. Wiss.* 43 (1952), 1 ff.

[80] A good survey is presented in the study volume of "Faith and Order," *The Ministry and the Sacraments* (London: S.C.M. Press, 1937).

this historical mosaic: texts which represent a transitional stage, as Clement of Rome, the *Didache, Hermas, II Clement;* and texts which are outspokenly propagandist, such as Ignatius.[81] For a long time presbyteral or collegiate structures are found in Rome as well as in Philippi, while during the same period, monarchical episcopacy is already established in other parts of the empire, as in Asia Minor.[82] The structure of the church is not identical in the different provinces until the second half of the second century. The process in question demonstrates the involvement of Christian language in the life of the church. The rise of the concept *episkopos* from the middle of the first to the middle of the second century is therefore another example in which to study the necessity and the danger of a "language of the church" versus a "language of faith."

The second-century Christian church has both internal and external reasons for filling its concept of "bishop" with the monarchical content. I cannot understand why so much time has been spent in trying to establish one specific factor which should be regarded as responsible for the rise of the monarchic episcopate. *Theological* factors play a role. The apostolic authority of primitive Christianity emphasizes the leading power of a charismatic person. The charismatic force with which Paul addresses his communities comes back to life in the episcopal ideal of Ignatius.[83] The *unity of Christian faith,* in the Johannine christological prayer and in the Christ-church mysterion of Ephesians, can lead to a monarchical structure of the church.[84] Matters of *internal church life* must be considered. Financial conflicts occur; there is discord among the leaders; the church as institution has to be established.[85] *External issues* are also

[81] The only thing one can state with certainty is what Walker-Richardson says in *A History of the Christian Church* (New York: Charles Scribner's Sons, 1959), p. 42; that "the monarchical episcopric must have come into being between the time when Paul summoned the presbyter-bishops to Miletus and that at which Ignatius wrote."

[82] Herm. *Sim.* IX.27.2; *Did.* 15.1; Ign. *Eph.* 4.1; *Magn.* 13.1; *Smyrn.* 8.2; Phil-1.1; Ign. *Pol* 6.1.

[83] Campenhausen, *Geistliches Amt.,* pp. 111, 113.

[84] John 17:10 ff.; 17:21 ff. Cf. Ign. *Magn.* 13.1-2; *Eph.*. 5.1; *Eph.* 5.32; 4.4-6. Cf. Ign. *Smyrn.* 8.2; 7.2; Ign. *Pol.* 1.2.

[85] The problems of youthful leaders (Ign. *Magn.* 3.1), of prophets (*Did.* 11); of financial and other conflicts (Herm. *Sim.* VI.3.5-6; *Vist.* III.11.3; 9:6) make the monarchic episcopate what Alan Richardson called "an urgent practical

at work. Against the empire, the church finds it convenient to be represented by one single representative, who is elected as full-time servant of the congregation.[86] There are also *liturgical reasons* which must be considered. Ignatius emphasizes the one service, the one agape, the one baptism, unified by the one bishop. This can lead to giving the bishop the highest authority in worship and in the whole church.[87] The *schismatic threat* to Christianity, already in its pre-Gnostic stage, must definitely be at work behind the endeavor to establish the oneness of the body of Christ by using some hierarchical means.[88] And thus the *Gnostic* conflict plays a most important role in this historical evolution. The bishop becomes the custodian of true faith against the speculative streams within his own city.[89] This leads us back to theological factors. The unity of creed, the unity of apostolic Christianity toward which the second century strives, creates the unity of the office. All this is at work in the creation of the second-century monarchical bishop. The New Testament itself is already drawn into the process. The post-Pauline epistles know of an office in Asia Minor which points toward the office of the second-century bishop (I Tim. 3:2; Titus 1:7).

When the church develops its terminology to describe the hierarchical bishop, it takes a step beyond the New Testament. It uses peripheral terminology and it uses only a section of the New Testament conception of leadership of the church. The term "bishop" is used in the plural in all the crucial passages of the New Testament during the Apostolic period both in Philippi and in Ephesus; in Rome, as well as in the community of the *Didache*, this custom

---

necessity" (*An Introduction to the Theology of the New Testament* [New York: Harper & Brothers, 1958], p. 328).

[86] In the persecution of Smyrna, Polycarp is sought as the representative of the Christian congregation. πεῖσον τὸν δῆμον, says the Proconsul, *Mart. Polycarp* 10.2 (cf. Bardy, *op. cit.*, p. 75).

[87] Ign. *Magn.* 7.2; *Smyrn.* 8.2; breaking *one* bread: *Eph.* 20.2; having only *one* Eucharist: *Phil.* 4. Cf. K. Müller, "Kleine Beiträge zur Alten Kirchengeschichte," *Zeitschr. f. Neut. Wiss.* 28 (1929), 295.

[88] Ign. *Magn.* 7.2; 13.2; *Tral.* 6.1-2.

[89] At the end of the struggle stands the concept of the bishop in Irenaeus (cf. Lietzmann, *op. cit.*, II, 48.) When Prümm (*op. cit.*, p. 284) claims that such hierarchy must have existed long before Ignatius presupposed it, we must say: It is the other way around. His fight for it indicates that such hierarchy is not an accepted fact but must be enforced in the churches of Asia Minor.

still prevails.[90] Only on the outskirts of the canon the bishop is addressed as one within the community.[91] The presbyteral authority which is more often referred to in the canon is reduced to a subordinate assemblage.[92] The episcopal language of the second century is, from the New Testament perspective, nonessential. One cannot say uncanonical, one cannot say unbiblical. Yet the concept "bishop" receives a meaning which it does not possess in Antioch or in Rome in the Apostolic period.[93]

This shift in terminology is the answer to the canon by the church in its life, faith, and liturgy. The apostolic authority dies with the termination of the apostolic age. Whatever apostles wander around in later decades are not capable, either personally or officially, of continuing the apostolic ministry of the New Testament. They have to disappear. Whatever structural form a church establishes can be only a sector of the structural plurality under the apostles. We simply cannot at the same time be the church of Jerusalem, of Corinth, and of the pastoral "Timothy." The terminological shift is a necessary impoverishment. The language of faith cannot disassociate itself from the concrete situation of

[90] Phil. 1.1; Acts 20.28; *I Clem.* 42.4-5; 44.1; 54.2. Herm. *Sim.* IX.27.2; *Vis.* II. 4.2; *Did.* 15.1; *Pol.* 5.3. It is difficult to decide haw much πρεσβύτερος and ἐπίσκοπος are used interchangeably or may have had *local* specifications, but in no case can you mix up monarchical and collegiate episcopric as Bardy has done (*op. cit.*, pp. 74, 80) in order to prove conveniently apostolic origin of the *monarchic* episcopate. This is no longer history but apologetics.

[91] Tit. 1.7; I Tim. 3.2. Here, perhaps, lies the origin of the monepiscopate, although it is so much easier to start theories than to validate them. There is something like a "monepiscopacy" in Jerusalem under James (Streeter, *op. cit.*, p. 77), but is it by no means certain that there is any direct line to the deutero-Pauline epistles.

[92] In Ignatius, bishop and presbytery are close in authority (Ign. *Tral.* 13.2; 7.1; 3.1; *Phil.* 7.1; Ign. *Pol.* 6.1) but the bishop has higher authority (Ign. *Tral.* 12.2. In *Smyrn.* 8.2 and 9.1, for instance, presbyters are not mentioned. Cf. also *Phil.* 3.2.) Presbyterial structures seem to have lasted longest in Egypt (J. B. Lightfoot, "The Christian Ministry," in *Commentary on Philippians* [London: Macmillan & Co., Ltd., 1900], pp. 225 ff.), and it has been suggested by a French scholar that for a long time Gaul had perhaps only the one bishop of Lyons and Vienne (L. Duchesne, *Fastes épiscopaux de l' ancienne Gaul* [Paris: 1894], I, 38-39).

[93] Apostolic authority is not episcopal authority (Dix, *art. cit.*, pp. 266 ff.). Apostolic, presbyterial, and conciliar authority are not held strictly apart in the primitive church (R. R. Williams, *The Authority in the Apostolic Age* [London: S. C. M. Press, 1950], p. 75).

the church. The early church creates its own theory for this taper-ing of biblical hierarchical forms: the succession. The interesting fact is that this theory is more interpretation than fact. Succession does not exist where the monarchical status is first demanded in full force, and the lists of Roman bishops do not coincide.[94] The theory of apostolic succession is the attempt to recreate the apostolic authority of the New Testament within the monarchic episcopate. There is no monarchical episcopate in the letter of Clement.[95] The *monarchical* succession is a theory of the second century. This fact does not denounce the theory. A church must always find some an-swer to the canonic authority which is pneumatic-apostolic—it in-cludes the Palestinian presbytery, the power of the keys given to Peter and to the disciples, and the instruction to the bishops and deacons in the pastoral letters. We simply maintain that this theory is not a biblical theory.[96]

Ekklesia

The forces of the church which are at work in tooling biblical language for the faith of a period can be examined through the second-century development of the term *ekklesia*. "Church" in the New Testament is the assembly of God called by Jesus Christ, and represents in this sense a unified concept.[97] This unity, however,

[94] Ignatius does not have episcopal succession (Ign. *Rom.* 9.1.), and his view of the ministry has been consequently called a prophetic one (George H. Williams, "The Ministry of the Ante-Nicaean Church," in *The Ministry in Hist. Persp.*, p. 30), since it is a ministry in the presence of the living Christ (David C. Lusk in *Scottish Journ. of Theol.* (1950), p. 276-77).

[95] Despite Dix (*op. cit.*, pp. 258 ff.). In his famous passage, Clement does not talk about a monarchic episcopate (cf. Massey Shepherd, "The Development of the Early Ministry," *Angl. Theol. Rev.* 26 (1944), 135 ff.) It seems evident to me, however, that *I Clem.* 42-44 speaks about a succession (against Eduard Schweizer, *Gemeinde und Gemeindeordnung im Neuen Testament* [Zürich: 1959], pp. 133-34). Why else would he deny the right to replace those instituted by apostles, appealing to OT "order," if he did not have in mind some kind of succession of order?

[96] Neither Matt. 16:17 ff. nor any other NT text speaks about a succession of Peter (Richardson, *op. cit.*, p. 310); there is no "transfer" of authority (Cull-mann, *op. cit.*, pp. 225 ff.), and succession and continuation are not the same (*op. cit.*, p. 219). When Dix states "The apostolic succession of bishops was a fact before it was doctrine" (*op. cit.*, p. 274), his sentence must be turned around: The apostolic succession was theory before it was fact.

[97] Karl Ludwig Schmit, art. ἐκκλησία in *ThWNT*, III,510.

exists with an emphasis on charismatic freedom and an emphasis on established office.[98] This office is never an exclusive institution of faith; the words of the keys stand beside the Pauline kerygma: "Christ did not send me to baptize but to preach the gospel." When the New Testament faith uses the concept of *ekklesia,* it uses it primarily in a christological sense; the important fact is that the *ekklesia* is the community of people assembled by and in Christ. It uses this concept concretely (it is a more secular Greek term than *qahal*) ; it uses it for an individual community and for Jerusalem, for a charismatic assembly and for the church as established by Jesus Christ.[99] In its Christ-center, what Karl Holl calls two conflicting views about the church are ultimately one.

The second century is no longer the church governed and guided by the witnesses of the Resurrection. The term "apostle" is dropped as an institutional term in favor of the normative concept for the apostolic authority. When the second century uses the term *ekklesia,* it is involved in the life and conflict of this *ekklesia.* There are the concrete financial disturbances as in the *Didache,* clashes of generations as in Corinth, and, of course, the deadly threat of schismatic tragedy impending as the Damoclean sword upon the church at the outset of the second century. There are liturgical and administrative consequences which bear upon this term. The result is an obvious change in the New Testament concept of *ekklesia.* Roman Catholics and Protestants are apt to overstress the positive or the negative relation of this development to the New Testament.

The writers of that period live in tangible awareness of the *concreteness* of the church. The "church of Syria," whence Ignatius has been brought in chains, which is now deprived of and in need of Jesus Christ and the prayers of the other churches—this church means his Christian past to him. Here he breathes, here he prays,

[98] Schweizer, *op. cit.,* p. 153: the unity of the NT congregation consists in its capability of maintaining the tension between charisma and institution without breaking asunder. Cf. J. Leuba, "Le rapport entre l'esprit et la tradition selon le Nouveau Testament, *Verbum Caro* (1959), pp. 133 ff.

[99] See Karl Holl, "Der Kirchenbegriff des Paulus in seinem Verhältnis zu dem der Urgemeinde," in *Gesammelte Aufsätze* [Tübingen: 1928], II, 44 ff. The conflict between charisma and office cannot be denied (cf. Linton, *op. cit.,* pp. 49 ff. on Sohm versus Harnack) , but in the proximity of Jesus (Campenhausen, *op. cit.,* p. 10-11, 325) the Apostolic oneness is possible.

here he has his Christian life in episcopate, sacrament, communion of saints.[100] He is the victim of a persecution which sweeps over the Syriac church. It is not astonishing that the Christian speaks with love and awe about his church. It is a place of human strife, in need of purification (Herm. *Sim.* IX.18.3), yet it is rightly called "the beloved" (Ign. *Rom. Inscr.*). The individual knows that he has grown into this church, that he has found in it the "assembly of life." [101] In times of external and internal menace, this personal involvement in the existence of the *ecclesia militans* increases in intensity. When the second-century Christian says "church," his close liaison with the concrete community expresses itself. Ignatius lives in the presence of the churches of Asia Minor (*Tral.* 12.1).

This concrete community understands itself in a specific *established form*. Our literature does not yet present one definite form. It is not permissible to read episcopacy at all costs into Clement of Rome. Yet "church" in Rome, "church" in Smyrna, "church" in Antioch are concretely established units.[102] The type is still in fluctuation, as it has been throughout the New Testament, but the emphasis on the established church is enhanced.[103] How can it have been otherwise in the turmoil of inner development with a host of possibilities and in the excitation caused by schismatic forces? That the church enters into presbyteral or episcopal patterns is only of secondary interest. Clement of Rome defies chaos. The primary development is that toward a more definite emphasis on the established concreteness. The rise of the episcopal and the elimination of the prophetic pattern are possibilities which are open to the church in this process.

"Is Christ divided?" Paul asks the Corinthian community (I Cor. 1:13). He has not given any external formula on which unity can be established, yet he uses rather sharp language against those who threaten this unity in Galatia (Gal. 3:1 ff.) or in Philippi (Phil. 3:2). The post-Apostolic Fathers attempt to fathom this concrete unity. The church is only παροικοῦσα, in Rome (*I Clem.*

---

[100] Ign. *Magn.* 14; *Eph.* 21.2; *Tral.* 13.1; Ign. *Rom.* 9:1; 9:3.

[101] Herm. *Vis.* III.11.2 (*after* Vis. II.4); the church becomes younger as the revelations continue. ἐκκλησία τῆς ζωῆς, *II Clem.* 14.1.

[102] Cf. Williams, *art. cit.,* p. 102.

[103] Cr. Campenhausen, *op. cit.,* pp. 98 ff.

Inscr.) as well as in Asia Minor and in Philippi (*Mart. Pol. Inscr.*).
But the church, as dwelling only in alien territory, is καθολική, one
in its local concreteness (*una*) and one in its universality (*universalis*).[104] The step from the *una* to the *universalis* is one which
the church is forced to take. The church of one city is drawn into
the struggle of the church in another city. The conflicts of Antioch
are the conflicts of Smyrna. The unity of Rome and the unity of
Corinth are one concern.

If *ekklesia* is seen in its involvement in the unity of Christ, the
next step is comprehensible. The church is holy (Ign. *Tral. Inscr.;*
Herm. *Vis.* I.1.6; 3.4), because the church is the body of Christ (*I
Clem.* 46.7, Ign. *Smyrn.* 1.2, Herm. *Sim.* IX.17.5). The church is
steadfast, blessed, beloved (Ign. *Rom. Inscr.*). All these adjectives
in the Ignatian addresses reveal the deep sense of veneration this
faith contains for the church. The Ephesian passage concerning the
holiness of the church has a wide resonance among the post-Pauline
writers. This holiness is christologically understood. Based on the
blood of Christ, the church is placed into relation with Christ; the
unity of the Christian with his bishop is the unity of the church
with Christ (Ign. *Eph.* 5.1; *Phil.* 4.1).

At this point, however, the decisive question must be raised. Has
not this Ephesian metaphor tempted the post-Pauline church into
consequences which menace the essence of the New Testament
ekklesia? Hermas speaks about the eternity of the church. The world
is created for her sake. *II Clement* makes this even clearer: Before
the sun and moon, the church was created. And he attempts a
speculative explanation which reminds us of the Valentinian
ekklesia: the male-female and the spirit-flesh principles are realized
in the Christ-church relation.[105] At first sight this appears like a

---

[104] Ign. *Smyrn.* 8.2; *Mart. Pol.* 8.1; 19.2. The step from the local oneness which
καθολική designated in Ignatius (see Ferdinand Kattenbusch, *Das Apostolische
Symbol* [Leipzig: 1900], p. 922) to the *universalis* was a natural one, as one sees
in *Mart. Pol.* Because of the shifted emphasis, however, the "catholic oneness"
of the primitive church (Richardson, *op. cit.*, p. 289) and the *"universalis
ecclesia"* of the second century are not identical with each other.

[105] *II Clem.* 14. Richardson (*op. cit.*, p. 288) has contrasted this Platonic concept of the church with the Hebrew one which is "bodily, visible, tangible."
II Clem. 14 means a *hypostatic nature* of the pre-existent church, exactly as in
the opening paragraphs of *Hermas,* and not merely *"préexistence intentionelle
dans le dessin de Dieu"* (Daniélou, *op. cit.*, p. 338).

simple prolongation of thoughts which are present in Eph. 5. But this is deceptive. The New Testament makes no speculations concerning the pre-existence of the church. There is no eternity of the *ekklesia*. The metaphor of Eph. 5 is robbed of its one analogy and forced into a second analogy which Eph. 5 never meant.

The result of this shift in meaning is of great consequence. "Church" receives an accentuation which may threaten or even annul the whole *ekklesia* concept in the New Testament.[106] The church may usurp the place of the living Christ. He is in danger of becoming subordinated to authority, to canon law, to the external institution. It is a great injustice to see merely this in the second-century church. The possibility, however, is created. The church as an external entity, as identical with the Holy Spirit, has suddenly gained a different place from the one it holds in the New Testament. We have shown that some process is a necessity. Only in apostolic times can the unity of pneumatic freedom and corporate institution be undefiled. The step from the *ekklesia* of the New Testament to the *ekklesia* of the early church is the step from apostolicity to the era between the times.

The language of faith in the New Testament is the language of faith within a concrete community. This language reflects the status of this community. Institutional types are different. Luke, who is influenced by Paul, expresses his material differently from the Pauline letters, because the community of faith which he describes is in its structure different from the Pauline. The language of faith in the New Testament transcends at the same time the language of the community. Kingdom of God, repentance, grace, Christ, resurrection, love—this language spans the entire New Testament, whereas "presbyter," "bishop," "teacher" appear sporadically and are not identical with the totality of faith.

The language of the post-Apostolic period shifts its emphasis. The plural institutional streams narrow down, the fluctuating institutional abundance is depleted. By itself, this cannot be held against the church because every church, from highest episcopacy to freest Anabaptism, is an impoverishment of the New Testament situa-

---

[106] Daniélou understands the crucial difference when he remarks that what Paul says about the Christ *II Clem.* says about the church (*op. cit.*, p. 336). "Office" begins to become a static phenomenon (Schweizer, *op. cit.*, p. 138).

tion. What is of real concern is the second step. The impoverished institutional language tends to take over the primacy.[107] Ignatius presents the episcopate as practically his first concern. The emphasis on obeying the bishop, being subordinate, heeding him, is a keynote of his epistles. We understand the historical situation. This episcopate is only in its early stages, and therefore must be stressed with intensity. The question rises, however, whether the language of concrete church life does not here begin to overpower the language of the gospel. Concern for the kingdom of God becomes concern for the episcopate.

One cannot reduce the problem to the simple statement: the church replaces the New Testament. This dichotomy is as erroneous as the view sometimes presented that sees in the community of the New Testament a model for the church of Rome. The deviation is much more subtle. The New Testament language of faith is not *ex opere ecclesiae operato*. It is not conditioned by one type of hierarchial or presbyteral structure. The language of New Testament faith is in the first place christological. The language of faith in the post-Apostolic period increases the weight on the specific language of the church to a degree which obscures the christological primacy of the biblical kerygma. Not that the christological kerygma is absent in this period! It is, nevertheless, becoming subservient to the ecclesiological concern.[108]

THE LANGUAGE OF NONTHEOLOGICAL CHRISTIANITY

Christianity in its process of formation evidences one more complex of problems which the language of faith within any church and in any era is bound to face. Christian faith is not merely a faith as maintained by one apostle—Paul, or John—or by a few—the writers of the canon. Christian faith is meant to reach the believer. Jesus assembles disciples who hear his message and pass it on. Paul writes to churches which discuss his letters and even answer them. We do not possess these answers, but we can assume

[107] I agree with Campenhausen (*op. cit.*, pp. 76, 113) that this has not taken place in Ignatius, but the trend begins here.

[108] This shift is parallel to the legalistic transformation. Cf. Goppelt, *op. cit.* p. 311 ff., and 298 ff. Schweizer (*op. cit.*, pp. 134-35) underlines the fatal role of the OT *"Amtsordnung"* for the concept of ἐκκλησία in *I Clem.*

that the language of these answers is not the language of the Pauline letters! The degree of difference may have been moderate; one suspects that the discrepancy is already considerable.

The church grows in numbers. The church becomes popular. Christianity becomes a movement. The second century indicates what awaits the language of faith if a popular development is undisputedly accepted.

The Lack of Precision

Many of the Apostolic Fathers often use their Christian language inexactly. *Hermas* gives us a typical picture of loose speech. Not only is his art of composition poor, but the pictures do not fit; the allegories are often a *tour de force*. His introductory theme is feeble. *Hermas* never quite makes up his mind what the woman in his opening paragraph stands for. Sometimes she is an interpreter, sometimes she is the church.[109] The allegory of the tower is not coherent.[110] Imitating apocalyptic imagery, the author speaks from remote places (*Vis.* I.1.3; II.1.1). And after the woman represents the instrument of revelation, suddenly another conveyer of revelation is introduced (V.1). This confusion may be due to the fact that *Hermas* transforms a pre-Christian novel into a Christian apocalypse.[111] If the former work is also his creation, its inexactitude reveals even poorer authorship.

The lack of precision has fatal consequences in the sphere of baptism and repentance. The looseness of language is the reflection of indecision within this Christian period concerning the meaning of both baptism and repentance. *Hermas* and *Clement* both know the uniqueness of Christian baptism. It comes to the Christian once, and to keep it "undefiled" is therefore of absolute necessity (*II Clem.* 6.9, Herm. *Mand.* IV.3.1). The same is true concerning repentance. In accordance with biblical preaching, the post-Apostolic

[109] Herm. *Vis.* I.2.2; III.13.1-2. Cf. Dibelius, *op. cit.,* pp. 451, 487.

[110] Herm. *Sim.* IX.2-4. Cf. Dibelius, *op. cit.,* p. 605.

[111] Daniel Völter, *Die Apostolischen Väter, neu untersucht* (Leyden: 1904), I, 173 ff. and Dibelius, *op. cit.,* pp. 420 ff. Concerning the argument for and against the "Tauftheorie" (P. Galtier, *Aux origines de la pénitance* [Paris: 1951], pp. 132 ff.) this author shares the position by Joly (*op. cit.,* p. 26) that Hermas' post-baptismal μετάνοια is his innovation, both exceptional and opposed to rigorism.

church proclaims that there is one chance only for men: repentance through baptism (IV.3.1; *Vis.* II.2.4). However, *Hermas* suddenly introduces his famous second chance: μίαν μετάνοιαν (*Mand.* IV.1.8).[112] Penitence becomes post-baptismal act. It is involved in a critical contradiction. It is on one side the primitive Christian "reversal" of thought, life, deed—the change of man into the new being.[113] Yet on the other hand it has also become Judaistic work, the fulfillment of a command in order to receive the mercy of God —the piety of man which achieves salvation.[114] And now "baptism" and "repentance" are in conflict. The result is well known, but beyond our scope: the term "baptism" will be forced into a reinterpretation by the term "repentance." What interests us is this first stage. The lack of precision is partly due to the didactic emphasis which repentance has been given.[115] The change of man into the new being with all its theological and ethical implications becomes deed, piety, *opus*. All *Hermas'* good intention of preventing his revelation of one post-baptismal penitence from becoming a repeated one (*Mand.* IV.3; *Vis.* II.2.5) is doomed to fail from the outset.

Deficiency in precision is noted in the whole post-Apostolic theological and christological terminology. The harsh judgment that "*Hermas* has no theology" is justified in view of his terminology.[116] The church is the Holy Spirit which is the pre-existent Son of God. Suddenly this Christ is the highest of the angels but at the same time the Spirit dwells in each Christian.[117] The "binitarian monotheism" of *Hermas* is typical for his epoch. *Kyrios* for Christ stands beside *kyrios* for God, and often it is hard to decide satisfactorily whether, in a particular case, it means Christ or God.[118] The church

---

[112] Herm. *Mand.* IV.1.8. J. Hoh (*Die kirchliche Busse im zweiten Jahrhundert* [Breslau: 1932]) suggests two conflicting wings in the Roman church, one advocating and one denying a second repentance. A similar conclusion in Benoit, *op. cit.*, p. 135.

[113] *Barn.* 16.9; *I Clem.* 7.4; Herm. *Sim.* IX.22.3.

[114] Herm. *Mand.* II.7; *Sim.* VII.6; *Vis.* V.6-7; *I Clem.* 62.2; 57.1; *II Clem.* 9.8; *Did.* 15.3.

[115] Behm (*ThWNT*, IV, 1003) calls this rightly "*Rückfall . . . in jüdisches Gesetzestum.*"

[116] Dibelius, *op. cit.*, p. 423.

[117] Herm. *Sim.* V.6.7; IX.1.1; V.5.3 (Lat.) .

[118] *Did.* 14.1; 14.3; *Barn.* 16.7; 10.11. Hans Windisch (*Der Barnabasbrief*

uses christological formulations but even its leaders sometimes do not quite know what to do with them; there are triadic formulas, yet what they really mean has not been thought through in any way.[119]

The two examples mentioned point to two different problems behind the inexact language of the church at the turn of the first century. Wide circles do not understand the newness of Christian faith. Christianity is a modulation of Judastic and Hellenistic moralism with all degrees of kinship with Gnosticism. Emotionally many of these people are Christians; many may undergo conversions of different kinds, yet the content which follows their conversion does not differ from that experienced in the synagogue. The language is not precise because these Christians fall easily into Hellenistic and/or Judaistic patterns as commonly preached and believed. The looseness of language reveals the factual insecurity behind the emotional change. It proves the necessity of a self-understanding of faith within the Christian community, a self-understanding which asks for the essential reality behind the experience. The essential, the coming of God to man in the Christ, is not merely a purely rational phenomenon. The kingdom of God is not in word but in power. However, this essential in the Christian faith is inseparable from the *kerygma* of Christ, which is not simply the person (as a mystical union) or the sacrament, but the word. Faith comes through hearing.[120] Lack of precision in the Christian language reflects the lack of hearing the kerygma. The convert accepts the emotional connotation, but does not perceive the kerygmatic structure. The story of the second century may be the story of pagan conversion to Christian

[Tübingen: 1920], p. 374) warned against the certainty with which Wilhelm Bousset (*Kyrios Christos* [Göttingen: 1913], pp. 272 ff.) felt competent to decide which meant God and which meant Christ.

[119] *I Clem.* 36.1; 42.3. This is what made Prümm give the title of his work, Christianity as "experience of newness." L. P. Edwards (*The Transformation of Early Christianity from an Eschatological to a Socialized Movement* [Menasha, Wisc.: George Banta Publishing Co., 1919], p. 53) observed that it takes a generation until a religion is well established. (Actually, it takes more than one.) The problem which we face here is not merely one of "establishment." The conflict between authentic and nonauthentic Christianity is not merely a sociological problem. This does not deny, however, that the social aspect of Christianity played an important role (cf. A. D. Nock, *Conversion* [London: Oxford University Press, 1933], pp. 193 ff.) .

[120] Rom. 10:17; 11 Cor. 3:6; Gal. 3:2; I Cor. 4:20.

144

faith.[121] Augustine will repeat it in his own personal development. Second-century Christianity has to come to the point where the kerygmatic content begins to move across the preliminary emotions into the authentic center of Christian thought and life.

The christological indecision seems at first sight to lie on a similar level. Many writers of our period use vague terminology which demands clarification. The origin of this looseness, however, does not lie only in moralistic misunderstanding of Christian faith. This hindrance plays a role, as the moral concern interferes with the christology of *Hermas* (*Sim.* VII.1 ff.), and the phoenix considerably obscures *Clement's* resurrection allegory (25). The problem lies deeper than this. The New Testament does not present us with a systematic view on every cardinal aspect of faith. Paul writes to the Romans an outline of faith, yet even here countless questions remain open. The New Testament is itself aware that questions will be raised in the times to come and it promises to the disciples the paraclete as support (John 14:26). The naïveté of the Apostolic Fathers in christological language, most of all in Hermas, demonstrates the demand of faith for self-clarification. In the New Testament itself *kyrios* is used about God and about Christ. The church which will argue in the coming centuries concerning the relation of Christ and God will only perform the necessity implied in faith. Among all later attempts to establish a satisfactory expression of the Trinity, the triadic statements of the Apostolic Fathers represent a theological stage which stands between the New Testament and the historical solutions of theology. In this puerile innocence, theological language is needed. One cannot build a faith upon the equations of *Hermas.* Yet this innocence also reminds the theologian of the distinction between the faith of the New Testament and the theological answers of history. The pagan world which is converted to Christ passes through a stage in which the biblical word on Christ and on God is repeated with unsophisticated simplicity.

Ignatius of Antioch, in his christological language, demonstrates the problems which are raised by the lack of precision within post-Apostolic literature. He uses parallel formulas with reference to God and Christ. "To attain God," stands beside "to attain Christ";

[121] Cf. Campbell N. Moody, *The Mind of the Early Converts* (London: Hodder & Stoughton, 1920).

"to live according to God," beside "to live according to Christ." The Christian is both a temple of God and a temple of Christ, an imitator of God and an imitator of Christ.[122] Even his unique word creations represent both πατρώνυμος beside Χριστόνομος.[123] His passages on Christ show that some day the church will have to determine what a Christian actually means when he uses simultaneously Θεός for the Father and Son.[124] As we have already seen, the christological language of Ignatius is often biblical. "By the cross in his passion he calls you who are his members." This is biblical language: the cross, of the synoptics and the Pauline epistles; the passion, as a rarer Pauline term; the μέλη of the famous chapters on the body of Christ; and προσκαλέομαι as a frequent synoptic word of Christ's calling together of his disciples.[125] The christological designations which we have noticed—Savior, Son, Lord, Christ the Shepherd, Christ, our Life and Hope—are primitive Christian concepts. Found already in the quotations from the creeds of Antioch, his terminology on the birth of Christ; on pre-existence, death, and resurrection is Christian tradition. Ignatius augments and embellishes this tradition, as theology, exegesis, Christian literature in the broad

[122] ἐπιτυγχάνω Θεοῦ Ign. Rom. 1.2; 2.1; 4.1; 9.2; Ign. Pol. 2.3; 7.1.
ἐπιτυγχάνω Χριστοῦ Ign. Rom. 5.3 (twice)

ζῶ κατὰ Θεόν Ign. Eph. 18.1 (cf. Ign. Phil. 4.1).
ζῶ κατὰ Χριστόν Ign. Tral. 2.1; Phil. 3.2.

ναὸς Θεοῦ Ign. Phil. 7.2.
ναὸς Χριστοῦ Ign. Eph. 15.3.

μιμητὴς Θεοῦ Ign. Tral. 1.2.
μιμητὴς Χριστοῦ Ign. Rom. 6.3; Phil. 7.2. (In Eph. 1.1, either of the two could be meant.)

[123] The first (Ign. Eph. 3.14-15) appears once in a third-century A.D. document (Quarterly of Dept. of Ant. in Palest., 1 [1931], 155), the second exists only in the Inscr. to Rom.

[124] Lietzmann, op. cit., I, 259.

[125] Ign. Tral. 11.2. Biblical is σταυρός in this meaning (Matt. 10:38; 16:24; I Cor. 1.17-18; Gal. 6:12; Col. 1:20). μέλη Χριστοῦ (Rom. 12:4-5; I Cor. 12:12; Eph. 4:25 and 5:30; προσκαλέομαι Matt. 10:1; Luke 7:18; Mark 3:13; Acts 13:2 and 16:10. Instead of πάθος, which is primarily used for our suffering (Col. 3:5; Rom. 1:26), the NT has πάθημα (Phil. 3:10; Rom. 8:18; II Cor. 1:5). The NT metaphor of the head and of the members is used in both directions (Tral. 11.2), a consequence which Augustine later will emphatically deny (Sermo 391, 9.11).

sense always must. In speaking of "branches of the Cross," he uses a demonstrative Gnostic metaphor for the Christian in the church (*Tral.* 11.2).[126] When he takes the Johannine *Logos*, however, a peculiar reference enters his thinking: the Logos has proceeded from silence (*Magn.* 8.2). This σιγή is not tied to the opening of the seventh seal in Revelation but to a hypostatic concept of silence in the Gnostic sense.[127] The poetic passage on the Incarnation of Christ in the Ephesus letter shows an odd mixture of Christian and semi-Gnostic language. Christ "appeared to the aeons." [128] He is a star above all other stars which, together with sun and moon, form a choir around him. This mythology on the pre-existence of Christ is Gnostic. The planning of the Incarnation is threefold: the abolition of magic, of wickedness, and of ignorance. The Gnosticism of this passage is connected with biblical concepts as Gnosticism often is: the "newness of eternal life" is reminiscent of Romans; and the abolition of death (Ign. *Eph.* 19.3) is Pauline, even if not stated in the same words. This Gnostic christological passage leads right into authentic Christology in the following chapter, with faith and love, suffering and resurrection of Jesus Christ. However, even in this chapter, the Davidic Christ and the Eucharist as antidote demonstrate that in Ignatius the primitive Christian words are struggling with alien concepts of different types (20.1-2).

Popular Christian Language

A large amount of literature, which represents a substantial sector of early Christian life, is preserved more comprehensively in

---

[126] For the metaphor of the tree, the root and the branch, cf. Helmer Ringgren, "Der umgekehrte Baum und das Leben als Traum," in *Hommages à Georges Dumézil* (Bruxelles: 1960), pp. 172 ff. This imagery, introduced into Christian literature by Ignatius, will become of great importance in the history of Christian symbolism (an early example in the *Schola Cantorum* of Santa Sabina, Rome).

[127] Corp. *Herm.* X.5; *Sap. Sal.* 18.14-18. Werner Bieder "Zur Deutung des, kirchlichen Schweigens bei Ignatius von Antiochia," *Theol. Zeitschr.* 12 [1956], 28 ff.) has discussed the confluence of mystic-Gnostic and primitive Christian elements in the Ignatian σιγή; cf. also Henry Chadwick, "The Silence of Bishops in Ignatius (*Harv. Theol. Rev.* 43 [1950], 269 ff.

[128] Ign. *Eph.* 19.2 αἰῶνες are therefore not merely "the world" (against Lake's translation, p. 193), but the heavenly, aeonic sphere.

147

the apocryphal literature.[129] Even if some of these writings orig-
inate in the third century, they represent a stream within Christianity which goes back to the early post-Apostolic age. Actually,
there are minimal traces of this current even in the New Testament.[130] What appears as a by-product in the canon is developed
into a whole literature of its own.

The popular language witnesses to the amazing creativity possible within Christianity. We recognize a parallel to the Gnostic
creativity. The rise of Christian faith excites imaginations. The
apocryphal literature is full of fantasy; there is humor, wit, sur-
prise. There are novels with suspense and happy endings.[131] The
creative quality of faith shows forth in the legends about Peter and
John, in the love story of Thecla, and in the fantastic vision of
Paul.[132] In a sense, this is precisely what Christian creativity ought
to engender: wealth of form as the consequence of the newness in
Christ. Had I been a Christian at the turn of the first century, I
would have enjoyed the duel between Simon and Peter much more
than the monotonous instruction of the *Didache!* Toward what is
this creativity directed?

We notice immediately the *miraculous* in this language. The
apocryphal simply cannot tell enough miracles on a single page.
The hands of the guilty who take the Eucharist wither (*Act. Thom.*
51). The infant Jesus heals and brings to life to his heart's content.[133] People are healed en masse and people are raised from the
dead en masse.[134] The language revolving around the miracle, both
of healing and of resurrection, comes easily to these people. There is
apparently a bond between Christian faith and the miracle vocabulary.

[129] Cf. Montague R. James, *Apocrypha Anecdota* (*Texts and Studies* II, 3)
[Cambridge: Cambridge University Press, 1893], p. viii). The apocryphal literature of the NT is the reflection, at least in parts, of the belief of large classes
of ordinary Christians.

[130] The death of Judas in Acts 1:18-19; the resurrection of Tabitha in Acts
9:36-43.

[131] M. Blumenthal, *Formen und Motive in den apokryphen Apostelgeschichten*
(TU 48) (Leipzig: 1933).

[132] Because of their creativity, the Apocryphal Acts have made a considerable
impact on early Christian art (G. Stuhlfaut, *Die apokryphen Petrusgeschichten
in der altchristlichen Kunst* [Berlin: 1925]).

[133] *Inf. Evang. Thom.* 6; 9; 10; 15.

[134] *Abgar* 17; *Prax. Petr.* 130; *Acta Vercelli* 4; *Act. Joh.* 62.

We notice how this miraculous language turns easily into a *visionary* one. *Hermas* is suddenly at quite remote places (*Vis.* II.1.1) ; a vision is not bound to space or matter (I.1.3). There is his cloud of dust, which turns into the obnoxious beast; but suddenly, at a distance of only a few feet, a bride appears (IV.1-2). For Hermas, revelation is epiphany (V.4).[135] The Lord appears in the Apocrypha in the shape of Thomas, of Andrew, and of Paul.[136] On the face of Thaddaeus, Abgar sees a vision, and when Paul appears, he looks like half man and half angel (*Act. Paul* 3). Again, the visionary speech expresses genuine Christian feelings. As the miraculous stands for the astonishing quality of Christian faith, so does the visionary show its transcendental character. Believers of the Christian faith are, in the eyes of many, people who receive visions and revelations—this is a widespread popular notion of post-Apostolic Christianity.

The miraculous and the visionary language frequently turns into a *fantastic* language. The panels of the ceiling lament at the horrible news of the death of Zacharias (*Protevang. Jam.* 24.3). The book which Hermas holds is suddenly snatched from his hands (*Vis.* II.1.4). Where a baptism occurs, a young boy appears (*Act. Verc.* 5). There are streams of fire and fantastic angels, horrible animals and gruesome brutes.[137] The foes of the Christians are described as detestable creatures—they kill and hate and behave like beasts—while the Christians are pictured as the untouchable saints whom legions of beasts cannot destroy in the pagan arena.[138]

The popular language is miraculous for its own sake. The Christian of the second and third centuries loves to hear a sensational story. One has "thrillers" right within the church. Dying lions and risen crowds belong to the normal food of a hackneyed imagination. The fantastic replaces the holy. The "secret things" are what the faithful want to hear. The milk which is sprinkled instead of

---

[135] Cf. also III.13.1; the ὅρασις.

[136] *Act. Thom.* 11; *Act. Andrew* 14; *Act. Paul.* 20.

[137] *Vision of Paul.* 31 ff.; Herm. *Vis.* IV.2.4.

[138] *Act. Paul.* 3.32 ff. Wilhelm Michaelis (*Die Apokryphen Schriften zum Neuen Testament* [Bremen: 1948], p. 218) has called this literature "*erbauliche Unterhaltungsliteratur*," entertainment with occasional "uplift." The best example is the pious conclusion of the fantastic miracle with the bedbugs (*Act. Joh.* 61).

THE LANGUAGE OF FAITH

blood on the clothes of the soldiers at the killing of Paul; the smoked tuna fish that swims away at the word of Peter; the teacher who faints at the spanking of the little boy Jesus[139]—all this is regarded as proof for the divine essence of Christian faith. This is a tragic misunderstanding of the biblical miracle. The grotesque kills the spirit. The apostle of the apocryphal acts becomes a "sorcerer." He acts like one, he is called one by his enemies.[140] The authors of the apocryphal acts present masterpieces of sorcery. But here the apostle has become a hero. People prostrate themselves in front of him to ask for a miracle, they address him as one addresses sublime human dignitaries (*Act. Verc.* 29; *Act. John.* 46). The holy men manipulate their power with sometimes blasphemous arrogance. The preaching of the gospel becomes a "show" (*Act. Verc.* 23). The healing of an old woman in Ephesus reminds one of some second-rate village theater (*Act. Joh.* 30). The child Jesus behaves with a pride that contradicts any serious teaching about the Incarnate Son of God.[141]

The popular quality of these writings lowers Christian literature to the commonplace. The language of faith becomes the language of miracle. The New Testament is filled with miraculous stories, and the historian cannot avoid admitting legendary trends throughout. Yet the miracles of the New Testament are not told for their own sake. This is why Christ refused to perform a miracle on request.[142] Miracles are manifestations of the might of God, τέρας is *always* σημεῖον.[143] The New Testament likewise has a simplicity

[139] *Martyrium Pauli* 5; *Act. Verc.* 13; *Inf. Evang. Thom.* 14.3.

[140] *Act. Thom.* 101; *Act. Paul.* 15, 16. The Christian virgins prevail over tricks by pagan magicans, *Fragm. of Act. Andr.* 10 (Vig. Christ. 10 [1956], 132), Andrew is great because he can perform miracles (*loc. cit.*, 15.23). In Acts 10:26, Peter rejects the reverence offered by Cornelius: "Stand up; I too am a man."

[141] Schlier (*ThWNT*, V, 883) has discussed the change in the παρρησία-concept which becomes demonstration of apostolic truth by miraculous force.

[142] John 4:38. Robert M. Grant, *Miracle and Natural Law* (Amsterdam: 1952), on miracles in the NT (pp. 153 ff.) and in the second century (pp. 182 ff.). The background is presented by Adolf Schlatter (*Das Wunder in der Synagoge* [Gütersloh: 1912]).

[143] Matt. 14:24; Acts 2:22; 15:12; Rom. 15:19; II Cor. 12:12. Origen has already noticed that τέρας does not exist without σημεῖον (*Comm, on John* XIII, 64). The ancient church was not always aware of this issue, and while Irenaeus accepts of course the story of the three men in the furnace (*Adv. Haer.* IV. 20.11), Hippolytus falls for the fantastic episode in *Act. Paul.* 44 (*Comm. in*

of style. The Synoptic story is not "literary" achievement but the product of a folk tradition.[144] The Synoptic simplicity is not the bizarre popularity of the apocryphal acts nor the poor attempt at composition in Hermas. The simplicity of the Synoptics is largely the result of the overwhelming creative force in the language of Jesus of Nazareth himself. The Synoptic pericopae in the parables and teachings of Jesus reflect the capacity of forming in a simplicity which is the opposite from trite. The Synoptic story about Jesus, formed by the kerygma of the primitive church, continues with the same restraint. The artistic power of the word of Jesus infiltrates the church as it creates its tradition about him. This artistic simplicity of primitive Christianity embodies the holiness of its message. The second and third centuries attempt to express this holiness by newfangledness—and lose it thereby. The language of simplicity is not the language of common place popularity. To this day, at work in the substitution of the level of popularity for the biblical simplicity, this misunderstanding leads to the destruction of the holy. The language of the apocryphal acts demonstrates the path from the sublime to the absurd.

The fantastic dimension of this popular language destroys the whole. The apostolic becomes the heroic, which demonstrates the reversal of the biblical kerygma. Nailed to the cross, Andrew smiles (*Act. And.* 21). One can understand the moral quality in this legend; the Christian faith cannot be overthrown by evil. Yet the legend has killed the spirit. There is no laughter at the cross. It is amazing how contemporary "keep-smiling" theology has its predecessor in the second-century popular legend. Thomas plays the

Dan. III.29; cf. Gustave Bardy et Maurice Lefèvre, *Hippolyte, Commentaire sur Daniel*, S. C. vol. 14 [Paris: 1947], p. 161).

[144] Literary (Blumenthal, *op. cit.*, pp. 88 ff.) and theological characteristics are two different matters. Despite Robert M. Grant (*op. cit.*, p. 172-73, arguing against W. Grundmann, *Der Begriff der Kraft in der neutestamentlichen Gedankenwelt* [Stutgart: 1932]) we hold that there is a theological difference between a miracle in the NT and a post-biblical miracle, although some trends do begin in the Canon (Acts 1:18 or 5:15). Acts 9:34 does not glorify Peter— "Jesus Christ heals you"—while in the Apocrypha, the man is glorified as he was in the novel of antiquity (R. Reitzenstein, *Hellenistische Wundererzählungen* [Leipzig: 1906], pp. 35-36, and R. Söder, *Die apokryphen Apostelgeschichten und die romanhafte Literatur der Antike* [Würzburg: 1932]). Blumenthal's conclusion stands, the biblical and the apocryphal miracles are far removed from each other (p. 165).

magician; and as an actor on the stage, he prepares his external appearance with great care before his act.[145] The fear and trembling have departed from the Christian endeavor of these heroes. So different from the agony of Gethsemane, Andrew approaches the cross with unburdened greetings: "Welcome, cross!" [146] The language of the Apocrypha is the speech that has lost the vibration of the holy.

Such popular speech is especially receptive to Gnostic terminology. This is not astonishing since both the Gnostic and the popular have a proneness to the mysterious, the fantastic, and the Docetic-supernatural. When the child Mary is described as taking seven steps at the age of six months, the Gnostic and the bizarre appear together in one and the same sentence. Popular imagination appears with the Gnostic cosmological and dualistic concern: the divine child shall not walk on the earth.[147] If the apocryphal and the gospel acts had not been re-edited by the Christians of later epochs, the relation between them and Gnosticism would be much more apparent.[148] Even now, we can trace clear Gnostic, syncretistic, even Iranian elements in many of these writings. The types of Gnostic language of which we have spoken appear in many of these fragments. One example may suffice: the Docetic language. The Jesus on the cross is not the Jesus who speaks to John in the cave. There is no trace of his feet on earth. The Jesus of the cross does not feel any pain.[149] Docetism is the outgrowth of the miraculous told for its own sake. If all reality can be reversed by the heavenly sorcerer, then his earthly reality is questioned. "He is no man at all," says the author of the *Acts of John* (90). The reality of man is dissolved. A Docetic divine being acts as it pleases.

[145] *Act. Thom.* 5.

[146] *Act. Andr.* 19.

[147] *Protevang. Jas.* 6.1. (According to the new text in *Papyrus Bodmer V* of 1958, Mary takes twice seven steps at the age of six months, Michel Testuz, *PAPYRUS BODMER V, Nativité de Marie* [Cologny-Genève, 1958], p. 51.)

[148] *Act. Joh.* 97; 103; 93. *Evang. Petr.* 4.11. Cf. Dibelius, *op. cit.*, p. 495; we have, of course, also Apocrypha untouched by Gnosticism, cf. Michaelis, *op. cit.*, p. 287.

[149] *Act. Andr.* 21. Robert M. Grant, *Gnostic Origins and the Basilidians of Irenaeus* (Vig. Christ. 13 [1959], 124) explains the smiling Lord of Gnosticism as an interpretation of Ps. 2:4: ("He who sits in the heavens laughs"). To understand the smile as a consequence of Docetism and as an expression of the miraculous seems more evident to me.

The popular perversion of language represents a major problem to the rising church. Christian faith starts a movement which comprises large groups of people in different provinces. This movement causes creativity. Suddenly the leaders of the church become aware that this popular literature has distorted the spirit of the primitive church, not simply because literature has been taken over and reworked by the Christian writers, as perhaps in the Thecla novel, but because popular creativity has taken a turn toward the grotesque, the magical, the sorcerous. Christianity finds it hard to rid itself of the ghosts it has called into being. The necessity of theological precision is demanded not only by inexactitude in the Apostolic Fathers but even more by the status of popular Christian speech. In the Apostolic age the church, through oral tradition, maintains and augments the kergyma of Christ and about Christ; in the second century, the church suddenly finds itself confronted with the evolution of oral tradition into the bizarre.

The Ascetic Abuse

The post-Apostolic literature demonstrates what is perhaps its most fatal perversion of the biblical language of faith in ascetic exaggeration. The problem appears already in the command to fast in the post-Apostolic church. The New Testament knows of fasting, but this fasting is by no means a pivotal concept.[150] Paul bears witness to his own frequent fasting, but he never demands it in his letters (II Cor. 11:27; 6:5). The *Didache* requires fasting before baptism (7.4). For Hermas, fasting is quite closely associated with prayer; he fasts for a whole day to strengthen his prayer (*Vis.* III.10.6-7). This terminology on fasting undergoes a development parallel to the supererogatory language of which we have spoken before. "Fast for those that persecute you!" (1.3). This command of the *Didache* uses the term for fasting in a definitely meritorious way. *II Clement* openly declares prayer to be less than fasting (16.4).[151] The Gnostics drive fasting to the extreme; Marcion "fasts like a serpent."[152] To be sure, according to the tendency of Hellenistic Judaism, fasting is sometimes spiritualized. The *Fifth Simili-*

---

[150] Behm, *ThWNT*, V, 932 ff.
[151] Cf. *Tobit* 12.8-9.
[152] Ephraem Syr. *Madr.* I.17.

tude of *Hermas,* perhaps taken from the source which *Hermas* has used in writing his book, does not demand fasting as Hermas elsewhere understands it. "God does not wish such vain fasting." What is given instead is the teaching of Judaistic religion: do no evil, serve the Lord, keep his commandments, walk in his ordinances, believe in God. This is true fasting.[153] The church does not retain this Judaistic spiritualization but demands the *stations* of fasting, Wednesday and Friday.[154]

Fasting, however, does not represent the cardinal problem. This is to be found in the sexual language of this period. The distortion of the biblical narrative is nowhere carried to such extremes as in this realm, principally in the Apocryphal texts. *Hermas* already amplifies the demands for sexual abstinence. "The wife shall live with you in the future as a sister" (*Vis.* II.2.3). This demand does not differ from sayings which Paul occasionally makes in his letters (I Cor. 7). However, other passages reveal that for *Hermas* sexual asceticism represents quite a different problem than it does for Paul. The apostle accepts the sexual continence as one among other charismata. He allows marrying by all means if the Christian cannot live without sexual life (I Cor. 7.28). The language on continence in *Hermas* is never quite free from a moralistic narrowness which contains something which does not exist in Paul—an erotic undertone. This is evident not so much in the prohibition of a second marriage as in *Hermas'* famous adventure with the merry and gracious girls.[155] If this story has been taken over from a pagan source, *Hermas* accepts subconsciously the erotic undertone, although he presents it in a different fashion.[156] He enjoys the night of continence, in reality or in writing. At the same time, we have here not yet the actual practice of Syneisaxis but tendencies within early Christianity that lead later on to this particular practice of

[153] Herm. *Sim.* V.1.4-5. This spiritualization goes back to the source behind Hermas; cf. Dahlberg, *op. cit.,* pp. 136-37.

[154] Herm. *Sim.* V.1.1; *Did.* 8.1; Tert. *De Oratione* 19.

[155] Joly (*op. cit.,* p. 314) finds it a curious phenomenon that Hermas with his austere morals should accept such an erotic story. Once we understand the problem of this asceticism, the phenomenon is not too strange. It takes quite an imagination, however, to see in this story "*kirchliche Busse,*" as Grotz has done (*op. cit.,* pp. 50 ff.) !

[156] Herm. *Sim.* IX.10.7-11.9.

great repute.[157] Already at this early stage we notice the unhealthy tie between frustrated sexuality and high-strung asceticism. Consequently, the language that describes an event like this is fraught with dualistic motives. One understands why in Gnosticism, carried to one extreme or the other, this dualism could lead to extreme asceticism or extreme libertinism. When *Hermas* describes the women with their "shoulders bare and their hair loose," women who "were beautiful" and "rejected from the house of God" (*Sim.* IX.13.7-9), his language reveals an undigested ascetic demand which contradicts by its nature the ascetic language in Paul. The language of *Hermas* does not reflect the "freedom of the glory of the children of God" (Rom. 8:21).

The apocryphal acts are crass examples of language of excessive asceticism. The *Acts of Thecla* make Paul define the content of his kerygma as he enters the house of Onesiphorus; he preaches the "Word of abstinence and resurrection," and this abstinence is sexual continence (*Act. Paul.* 5). This "sexual continence" precedes the word on resurrection! The focus of these Acts does not lie in the biblical preaching of Cross and Resurrection but in ascetic demonstration. The life of virginity comes before the life of prayer (7). Resurrection is made dependent upon chastity: "There is no resurrection for you unless you remain chaste and do not defile your flesh" (12). Undefiled Hebrew maidens with their lanterns appear in the temple story of the child Mary, and the pollution of the virgin makes Joseph cry out in despair.[158] In the beatitudes of the *Acts of Thecla* Paul calls blessed those who are chaste, who live in abstinence, who have renounced the world; and who live with their wives in continence (5). These beatitudes have distorted the biblical message. Yet this sexual renunciation is regarded as the center of Christian faith. The acts preach celibacy, but in the case of the married, a life withdrawn from marriage (12).[159] The story of

---

[157] This does not exclude at all the theory that Hermas took over this anecdote from his source: cf. Paul Wendland, *Die urchristlichen Literaturformen* (Tübingen: 1912), p. 388.

[158] *Protevang. James* 7.2; 8.2; 13 ff. Cf. Blumenthal, *op. cit.*, pp. 113 ff.

[159] Marriage is "filthy desire" (12); Paul does not let the young girls get married (16), yet naked Thecla enters the arena for her execution (22). The less pronounced sexual factor may indicate the greater age of the *Act. Joh.*, according to Michaelis (*op. cit.*, p .227).

Maximilla in the *Acts of Andrew* tells of a woman whose faith prohibits the continuation of her marriage (*Act. And.* 2 ff.), and Mygdonia in the legend of Thomas refuses to share her bed with Charis (*Act. Thom.* 96).

The accent on sexual matters in these acts leads to most unchristian consequences. Aegeates, the husband of Maximilla, kills himself (*Act. And.* 25). There is not the slightest trace of the Pauline view that the non-Christian husband or wife is sanctified by the Christian partner (I Cor. 7:14). On the contrary, the pious Mygdonia addresses her desperate husband in a bedroom dialogue with unkind aggressiveness (*Act. Thom.* 98). The fragment of Euodius shamelessly reveals this attitude: the Christian wife Maximilla dresses her maid in distasteful decor and sends her at night into the bedroom of Aegeates.[160] The apocryphal acts delight in imploring and screaming husbands, in broken marriages, and in dialogues on sex. (*Act. Thom.* 11 ff.). The sadism of this literature divulges a Christian faith which has been twisted into the slavery of the law. This sexual language bears witness to the fanatic consequences of a Christian life which is divested of the kerygma of grace and coerced into iron chains.

The abuse of asceticism summarizes the tremendous threat which Christian faith faces in the second century of its existence. All the negative aspects of postcanonical language are concentrated at this point. This language about the conquest of sex represents an ultimate dualism; the sexual is identified with sin (*Act. Thom.* 32). Marriage is regarded as the outgrowth of obscene desire. At the same time, this sexual language is based on the idea of merit because it makes sexual abstinence the prerequisite for salvation, and moralistic because the preaching on continence has received a prominence which obscures any kerygmatic message. This language is Gnostic because it removes Christian teaching on sex into a speculative syncretistic atmosphere that suffocates the flame of early Christian spirit. It is Gnostic because it is dominated by a dualistic principle, spirit versus sex, the ethical equivalent to the

---

[160] Cf. also *Fragment of Euodius* 1. The dualistic-Gnostic basis of this sexual encratism comes forth in the epicene speculations of *Clem. Hom.* III.15.3 ff. and XX.2.3 (cf. Strecker, *op. cit.* p. 161).

light-darkness motif of cosmology.[161] This language has certain New Testament justifications—Jesus' teaching on sexual life, the Pauline chapter in I Corinthians on marriage and celibacy.[162] But this language destroys the New Testament language on sex by missing its context. To miss the kerygmatic heart of the Gospel means to pervert any New Testament speech. Ascetic language has replaced christological language. For the people who write and for the masses who read or rather hear the Apocryphal stories, Christianity is far removed from its primitive origins. The popular is about to extinguish the light of Christ.

CONCLUSION

The language of the church differs in many respects from that of the Gnostics. The Old Testament plays a vital part in the proclamation of faith (against the denial of Israel); the earth and its creator are taken seriously (against any negation of Yahweh); and faith is set consciously into the framework of a community (salvation being not merely ascent by knowledge). In all three we find present part of what we called "Hebraic barrier" against dualistic ontology and individualistic mysticism. At the same time, however, there is a kinship, sometimes latent, sometimes obvious, between this language and that of the Gnostics. Dualistic Gnostic notions easily permeate the asceticism of popular Christianity. Ignatius' theology of martyrdom at times comes perilously near to a dualistic world view (Ign. *Rom.* 6.1-4). The spiritualizing of the Old Testament (Adam as the fallen soul) and the paradigmatic use of it in exhortations both disregard the historical meaning of the Two Covenants in Christian faith, while the outspoken denial of the Old Testament and the timeless identification of *nomos* and *logos* deny the dialectic juxtaposition of the two by maintaining either the dialectic or the juxtaposition only. We see clearly how important the world of Philo is for both sides. The most profound kinship can be found in the mutual tendency to make absolute

---

[161] Wilhelm Bousset, "Manichäisches in den Thomas-Akten," *Zeitschr. f. Neut. Wiss.* 18 (1917), 1 ff. and Günther Bornkamm, *Mythos und Legende in den apokryphen Thomas-Akten* (Göttingen: 1933), esp. pp. 99-111. For the Jewish dualism behind the Apocrypha, cf. Blumenthal, *op. cit.,* p. 137.

[162] Matt. 19:10-12; 5:17-30; I Cor. 7.

certain types of vocabularies. As in Gnosticism the one great concern for the individual (ascent into the transcendent through the mystery of gnosis) has become an intellectual, experiential *opus operatum,* so the mandate takes the place of the gospel (if you achieve it you will be saved), and the community becomes identified with faith. This is nothing but the lack of a relational language of which we have spoken, only exhibited on different levels—rewards, episcopacy, asceticism. We find on both sides the same tendency: a certain type of speech tends to take over and become absolute; in the moment this is achieved the sovereignty of God over all Christian speech concerning the church, faith, and ethics is ignored. Vital though all three are for the communication of the Christian gospel, they stand under—not above or in the place of—the redemptive act of the Father in Christ.

The earliest adherents of the new faith were called "Christians" (Acts 11:26). The triumphal hymn in the great chapter on resurrection reaches its climax in the victory through Jesus Christ (I Cor. 15:57). In the triumphant newness of the Christ the gospel was carried through the provinces of the Roman Empire. This new proclamation of the Christ contains a whole string of latent problems. Gnosticism severed itself from any Hebraic basis in spite of its possible origins in Judaism; when the cardinal modes of speaking about the Incarnate God in the language of relation were lost the newness can only be communicated in Gnostic (or ecclesiastical or sacramental) fashion. But the biblical faith has Hebraic roots with a new orientation in relation to the grace of God in Christ, the advent of a new age. The newness in Christ will exist in continuity with Israel but only after a collision between them; otherwise it would have become not Hebraic but Judaistic: historicity would have been spiritualized as in the Diaspora. Both Gnosticism and Hellenistic Judaism display the loss of the Hebraic element, one by understanding the newness, the other by missing it. Christian language is rooted in Jerusalem and moves toward Alexandria, and by losing either, it denies its nature.

Such newness is certainly experiential. These people were not following the crowd when they jeopardized or at least risked their lives in adhering to a suspect religion. As the gospel is communicated, however, it suddenly becomes apparent that personal experience does not coincide with authentic New Testament faith. The ego, merit, that which pays, that which offers reward—all these peripheral aspects of the Christian experience tend to rise to the surface. They are perhaps less consciously extant than the texts seem to indicate, yet language betrays popular desires in the wake of a great emotional experience. We observe consequently how the need for critical insight into the Christian's language is no play at all, but urgently needed self-examination in the faith. To verbalize the emotion may betray the gap between what the believer believes and what he thinks he believes.

This newness is exposed from the outset to the mercy of time. We may wish this were not the case, but we cannot help its being so. Eschatological language enfeebles; apocalyptic language becomes empty phrases; the church has to reckon with a concrete situation; and third and fourth generation believers represent a vitality different from the first. The speech of faith will be from then on under tremendous pressure to conform to the laws of this situation. Language will become popular, ecclesiastical, meritorious, mandatory—always accommodating itself to the pragmatic needs of the church. The reason is a compelling one: the gospel must reach people lest it turn into speaking in tongues. Where lies the criterion? Again we are led toward the question of the canon. A second aspect of canonical language demands clarification. Such language must speak not only to the Christians inside the church but even more to those outside. The church begins to use non-canonical language by speaking in Stoic phrases to the Romans and in Gnostic terms to Alexandria. How high a price can the church pay for this venture without losing the essence of its faith? Or to put it another way: what is the measuring rod of Christian speech?

THE CANON

1. The foregoing study has made it clear that the language of the church is in friction with the language of the canon. It cannot be different since the situation of the later church, as it addresses itself or the world, is never identical with what it was in the time of the apostles. In this friction, the church did not mean to become master of the canon; the irrevocability of the apostle and the rejection of the Montanist prophet make this quite clear. Canonical

speech is normative—this is implied in the very use of the word "canon." It is a most important phenomenon that the writing of the period in which the canon (at least in its most important parts) was assembled often betrays remarkably little insight into the nature of the canon; the Apostolic witness is not the product of this period but precedes it.

2. The language of the canon is "kerygmatic," proclaiming judgment and good news (Synoptics), in the triumph and response of the new creature (Paul) and with the double directions of earth and heaven (John) and of advent and love (John). These three types of language do not constitute a philological or linguistic unity, of course; they represent, however, the main stream of the communication and response to the good news. Between Matthew and John stands the freedom of the justified Christian in Paul; what joins the three together, however, is the Christ-centered, evangelistic communication which we called "kerygmatic language." From such canon-center as we may call it, there are other types of speech which represents a counterweight to misrepresentation. II Peter, the Pastorals, and James are hardly normative types of Christian communication. James utters a warning against a libertinistic misunderstanding of Paul, but it could never replace him. If it does, the center of the canon is lost.

3. What the Synoptics, John, and Paul have in common is a field of force rather than a unified mode of expression. When we claim canonical language as the norm for Apostolic and post-Apostolic Christianity, this is no easygoing norm; on the contrary, it leads to trouble. If James were normative language it would be quite easy: Christian communication tells people what to do, pronouncing judgment or mercy. If, as seems to be the desire in some quarters today, the Johannine passages, deprived of their historical and dramatic parts, were normative, a certain type of Gnosticism would be expected in the transmission of faith. Canonical language is perhaps best symbolized by Paul: it is a language which is always oscillating between proclamation and judgment, always vibrating between grace and demand; language that knows of love without becoming moralistic; language of redemption reflecting, breathing, challenging the freedom of the letter to Galatians. Paul stands between Mark and John, and it is within this

triad that canonical language is to be found. It is the opposite of a cheap vocabulary with a few mandatory or mystic concepts. Such canonical verbalizing of faith is meant to lead to the challenge of the Christ: into a mode of speech that comprehends the biblical witness from Mark to Paul and to John; into the drama from Incarnation to death and Resurrection; into the path from law to righteousness to a "new law."

4. Canonical language between Mark and John is eschatological language, i.e., speech aware of the tension between realized eschatology in Christ and the expected end. The constant change between past, present, and future, and between aorist and subjunctive in Rom. 6:3-11 expresses the fluctuation in eschatological language: "If we *have* been united with him in a death like his we *shall* certainly be united with him in a resurrection like his." "We *were* buried . . . with him . . . that. . . . we too *might* walk in newness of life." "If we have died with Christ, we *believe* that we shall also live with him." (Italics mine.) This is the eschatological language of the canon, it oscillates between past and future, and includes in the future belief, hope, and response. The last book of the canon with its beautiful imagery is a powerful warning that such eschatological language cannot maintain a balance without using mythological imagery about heaven and the end.

5. The language of the canon is plastic language, especially in the Synoptics. Concise simplicity denies to Christianity the popular and cheap means of selling a religious article (the parable is a difficult product) ; plastic is not miraculous, not high-strung, not bizarre. Or, as in Paul, canonical language is intellectual in a vivid artistic degree; Paul's speech—antithetic and synthetic, tortuous and peremptory, now depressed, now bursting into exuberant hymns—communicates Christian faith in a unique mastery of expression. And thirdly, canonical language in John expresses the double dimension in understanding and communicating Christ: the horizontal and the perpendicular, history and heaven, knowledge and love. The Gospel of John is both drama and theology. In all three examples the language that communicates faith unites highly artistic and lively with thoroughly theological modes of proclamation.

As we examine the varied writings of the post-Apostolic period we can see how the center of canonical language may be lost. The transmission of faith may become boring theology. Instead of Paul's vividness we get monotonous instruction, undoubtedly sincere. Or the language of faith turns into a handy whip for theologians who have to assert authority; but the whip cannot promote joy and love for the redeemed church. Even the strong language of II Corinthians and Galatians had that. Theological language is threatened by cheap popularity conquered by the desires of a Christian mob, which wanted to be spoon fed or entertained with the fantastic. Or the language of faith deteriorates into a mere device: words are still there, but they have lost their life. Apocalyptic terminology degenerates into empty phrases; theological language is stored in the closet of liturgical formulas where it becomes harmless. And thus, the pragmatic use of speech, for the individual as well as for the church, determines what can be of value and what must be forgotten—all this, of course, never in conscious planning but in the subtle process of history.

What stands behind this impoverishment and transmutation is nothing other than the presence or absence of the reality of Christ. The second century is by no means *saeculum obscurum*. It radiates the excitement of the apostolic event in its missionary movement and in its clash with Gnosticism; at the same time, it shows tendencies which may lead to the loss of this event, through its alliance with non-Christian language, Hellenistic, Jewish, Gnostic, popular, and ecclesiastical. The Christ is no longer expressed by the unique speech of the canon. At this moment we turn to the great theologian of the second century and examine his contribution.

Chapter 3

The Language of Christian Theology

The rudimentary texts of the extensive work of
Irenaeus offer an excellent example for studying the tenor of early
theological language within the Christian church. Here are exhibited the achievements of the first theological strivings as well
as the failures of theological semantics. The pivotal importance
of Irenaeus, as is well known, does not lie in his systematic presentation—his book against the heretics is despairingly unsystematic—
but in his outlining the basis on which, and the limitation within
which, Christian theology is capable of developing.[1]

THE NECESSITY OF A CHRISTIAN LANGUAGE

Monotheistic Moralism Versus the Mysterion of Christ
In violent protest Marcion clamors against the status and faith
of the church of Rome. The concern about "one more repentance"
replaces grace. There exists an inner threat to the church of which
she is unaware in her sleep: the nomism of Clement, the instruction of faith as reflected in the first manual of Christian church
life. The presence of Marcion betrays a healthy fermentation of
Christian thought where we hardly expect it; here is theology in
evangelistic urgency, theological concern in dauntless intensity
capturing the minds of those who inquire, in refreshing contrast to
the boring religion of works in Hermas. The Christian who is involved in the quest for eternal life and a living faith, and the pagan

---

[1] For extensive literature on Irenaeus see Johannes Quasten, *Patrology*
([Utrecht: 1950], I, 287-313). I quote Irenaeus in the traditional numbering of
Massuet (with the important new volume of *Adv. Haer.* III by F. Sagnard,
Irénée de Lyon, Contre les Hérésies, vol. III, S.C. vol. 34 [Paris: 1952]) and
not from W. Wigan Harvey *(Sancti Irenaei Libros Quinque* [2 vol.; Cambridge:
University Press, 1857]). Unless *Epideixis* is mentioned, the quotations pertain
to *Adv. Haer.*

with the courage to expose himself to a new revolutionary religion are not going to be satisfied with a rehash in popular Christianity of the nomistic diatribe of wandering philosophers or initiations of Oriental priestesses. We can hardly blame any individual who, grappling with the choice between the *Didache* and Marcion, chooses the latter. Alas, the Gnostic affinities, dualism and the breach of the covenant, doom this desperate outcry before it is voiced.

The dilemma of the Christian content is displayed by Aristides' little apology. What he writes is supposed to be a defense of Christian faith, written by a "philosopher," exaggerated though this designation may be. Underneath this little opus lies a Christian conviction and a Christian rule of faith.[2] A slight disillusionment is awaiting us, however, as we analyze the substance of this defense. It begins with an emphatic plea for monotheism; a purely spiritual God, without anger or wrath (1), incorruptible and immutable (4), is one and at the same time in all (13). This is obviously the language of pre-Christian Judaism, with coloring familiar to the Jew of the Diaspora in his conception of the Mosaic faith. After repudiating, not always very originally, the idolatry of barbarians and the errors of Greeks and Egyptians, he approaches the climax: now, the Christians have found the truth (15). This truth is the religion of the Diaspora, in the language of the Diaspora—honor thy father and thy mother, do good to one's enemies, walk in humility (15)—framed by monotheistic assertions and statements about a service of praise, with an ultimate eschatological hope in connection with "recompense of reward" (16). Compared to Mark, to Paul, and to John, it is a poverty-stricken faith indeed. The language of monotheistic nomism displays little distinctively Christian substance other than a repetition of fragments from a rule of faith, and the mention of "people imprisoned or oppressed for the name of their Messiah" (15). Aristides reproaches the Jews—they too have gone astray (14)—but he surely speaks their language without the dimensions added by the New Testament language about the life and work of Christ, a language of incarnation and redemption, a

---

[2] The rule of faith behind Aristides' work has been reconstructed by J. J. Rendel Harris, *The Apology of Aristides* ([Cambridge: University Press, 1893], p. 25).

language of grace and justification. As often in the future history of the church, what claims to be philosophical argument for theology is both poor philosophy and poor theology.

There is one aspect in *Theophilus of Antioch* which is pertinent to Aristides' failure to formulate the Christian content. Here, too, we have monotheistic nomism although on a somewhat higher level (III.9-15). In a disputed chapter, Theophilus explains the term "Christian" by a play on the words χρηστός (brave) and χρίω (to anoint) without even mentioning the name of Christ (I.12). This fact seems so strange that one is inclined to take refuge in the *disciplina arcani* to explain its absence.[3] The fact is, however, that Theophilus is not willing to witness to the Christ when it comes to explaining the name of the Christians. Whatever the reason for this may be, here lies the first grave problem of Christian apologetic language. Does language which is void of the Christ-*mysterion* ever suffice to present Christian faith? After all, Theophilus is dealing with the Trinity (II.15), Adam (II.28), and the cycles of the world (III.28). Can the Christian ever forget the origin and basis of his name if this is what he is willing to die for?[4] He claims to offer truth, the most perfect truth (III.16). If he pretends, in the interests of apologetics, however, that Christian faith is nomistic monotheism, why should the pagan not as well be converted to Diaspora Judaism?[5] "This is my God," exclaims Theophilus (I.14),

[3] G. Bardy (in *Théophile d'Antioche, Trois Livres à Autolycus,* S.C. vol. 20 [Paris: 1948], p. 70) rejects the arcanum theory. However, Bardy's remark (*"l'évêque d'Antioche n'a pas à parler du Sauveur"*) fails to see the problem behind the play with words in *An Aut.* I.12. Why should he not have to talk about Christ when he talks in definite terms about his God (I.14)?

[4] Bardy (*op. cit.,* p. 45), in defending Theophilus' right not to mention the "mystery of Christian faith" in an apology, denies our right to judge the apologists on the ground that our mentality is different from theirs. We have to protest against this principle of historical research. Judgment *ad rem* and judgment *ad hominem* are two very different matters. While the second has to be rejected, the first belongs to the essentials of historical theology since it creates the dialogue with history which alone makes this history alive. Alfred Bengsch (*Heilsgeschichte und Heilswissen,* eine Untersuchung zur Struktur und Entfaltung des theologischen Denkens im Werk *Adversus Haereses* des Hl. Irenäus von Lyon [Leipzig: 1957], p. 164) has rightly spoken about a "fruitful analytic view of a man's mistakes." Such a dialogue does not at all disparage the apologists in their seriousness of faith.

[5] Robert M. Grant (*"Theophilus of Antioch to Autolycus,"* Harv. Theol. Rev. 40 [1947], 256) concludes that because Theophilus of Antioch did not un-

but with this plea for monotheism and with the spiritualization of the law the Jew of the dispersion would have heartily agreed! [6]

As perhaps his main contribution to the history of Christian thought, Irenaeus of Lyons presents a *theological language of Christian proclamation*. This language is first speech of proclamation, not merely because Irenaeus uses the terminology of "proclaiming the good news" (κηρύττω and ἀγγέλλω), [7] but because in the crucial chapters he proffers, often with a simplicity typical for his faith, the message of Christianity. "God became man, and it was the Lord himself who saved us" (III.21.1); this is the language of affirmative proclamation, saying not merely: "Believe in this God"; "You must do this"; or "Let us not do that"; but "God became." Biblical quotation belongs to the realm of positive proclamation; while Clement of Rome always hears in the text a command (humility), instruction (consequence of jealousy), or a foreshadowing of what the Christian is destined to experience (resurrection), for Irenaeus the text presents God's *oikonomia*, the salvific act toward man of the one "who works salvation on earth." [8] Such language permeates the theological argument: Christian communication is affirmation. "The Lord redeemed us by his blood and gave his life for our life" (V.1.1). This "for us," "for our sake" in the theological context (III.16.6) turns language of proclamation at once into affirmation of witness and by a witness. It cannot be severed from the person who bears the witness, from his past and hope, his failures and his joy. To proclaim means to deal with the despair and promise of life; when such language therefore witnesses to an event that not only occurred but in whose occurrence the proclaimer is existentially involved, it ceases to be merely argument, demand, or information. The *fact* ("He took the flesh," III.9.2; "The Father revealed the Son," IV.6.5) is accepted and lived—or denied.[9] Be-

---

derstand the Christian faith his work has been so unsuccessful, but that part of his failure lies in the apologetic method employed.

[6] Dalbert, *op. cit.*, pp. 130 ff.

[7] IV.33.12, οἱ τὸν ἐκ τῆς παρθένου Ἐμμανουὴλ κηρύττοντες; IV.18.5. ἕνωσιν ἀπαγγέλλοντες; III.12.5, τὸν Χριστὸν κατήγγελλον, III.18.3=I Cor. 15:12. Revealing is the trifold expression in III.17.4.

[8] IV.33:4; III.18.7.

[9] Erich Auerbach (*Mimesis, The Representation of Reality in Western Literature* [Princeton: Princeton University Press, 1953]) compares Homer with the OT and finds in the biblical story the unique demand for truth, the woe

166

tween his (sometimes tedious) polemic and (sometimes feeble) argumentation Irenaeus finds the pivot of authentic Christian communication: the affirmative verbal re-creation of the message in which his whole life shares.

Second, proclaiming language seeks to re-create the center. Unlike the case for ethical monotheism, the mind of Irenaeus revolves around the heart of the Christian message without any conscious or unconscious split between a *regula fidei* and an argument without this *regula fidei: homo factus est* (V.18.2) ; in the mystery of Incarnation lies the center of proclamatory speech. To grasp and convey this pivot is the ultimate goal of theological thinking: atonement expressing the work of Christ,[10] resurrection as the Incarnate's victory for man,[11] the concept of man that leads back to the Atonement.[12] The one theme, that Christ "became what we are in order to make us what he himself is" (V *Praef.*), shines in different degrees of radiance through the whole argument against the Gnostics, no longer as monotheistic demand, but as atoning praise. While for Hermas all christological passages are part of his mandatory concern, for Irenaeus all ethical exhortations are part of the proclamation of the *Christus Victor.*

Third, "theological language" is consequently always a language related to the specific Christian center, Incarnation and Atonement.[13] Irenaeus' most famous phrases express the mystery of God in Christ: the God and man who made salvation possible for us (III.18.7), the Son as the visible of the Father (IV.6.5),[14] the Father who is declared through the Son (III.6.2). There is, of

in case there is no response (ch. I on Odysseus' scar) ; the biblical story in its absolute seriousness is set over against the sensory quality of pagan literature (ch. II on Fortunata) .

[10] *Oikonomia* (God's saving plan for humanity) and Incarnation belong together (IV.33.7; III.17.4; Οἰκονομία leads to the advent of Christ (IV.26.1) who became real man (III.18.1) , suffered (II.26.1) , and gave us his patience and his mercy (III.18.5). See the extensive material in Albert Houssiau, *La christologie de Saint Irénée* (Louvain: 1955) .

[11] III.18.3; 11.8; 22.1-2 and *Epid.* 30.

[12] III.22.1; cf. Houssiau, *op. cit.,* pp. 26 ff.

[13] Bengsch (*op. cit.,* p. 15) put it in a nutshell: *"Die Theologie des Irenäus ist ein Kommentar zur Fleischwerdung des Wortes."*

[14] For the Greek τὸ ἀόρατον γὰρ τοῦ Υἱοῦ Πατήρ ι τὸ δὲ ὁρατὸν τοῦ Πατρὸς Υἱός I follow the translation of Henry Bettenson, *The Early Christian Fathers* (London: Oxford University Press, 1956) , p. 105.

course, speculative theology regarding God as metaphysical being, as we shall see later; nevertheless, theological language in ever new affirmations revolves around the Incarnate Event (III.21.1). Irenaeus is aware of forcing Christian theological language into its center when "it is not our duty to indulge in conjecture and make guesses about infinite things which concern God" (II.28.6). We are not speculating about the eternity of God, but we are confronted with the first Christian axiom: "How shall man pass into God unless God has passed into Man?" (IV.33.4). Theological language does not take place within a metaphysical quest but within a response to an act.

Fourth, this theological language is response to "faith demanding theological form." Already creedal language is a dramatic recital of the climax of faith, a form found throughout the Irenaean argument.[15] Moreover, the theologian is compelled to form the center in order to relive and convey the object of his faith, and in order to let the center permeate Christian life, law, love, and church. Faith demanding theological form is not merely *Wissenschaft* [16] as a coherent system of thought but the search for the *cardo*, for the hinge of Christan existence, the re-enactment of that which has, and can, and will create Christian faith. What gives weight to Irenaeus' attempt is precisely the nonspeculative basis upon which it is built. His admission that he lacks "persuasiveness of style" without being capable of excellent composition[17] must stand exactly as it sounds. To read nineteenth-century *Wissenschaft* into this theological enterprise is therefore misleading; the goal is not primarily co-ordination of knowledge in rational precision; it is not inquiry into the scientific process—although such co-ordination and process do take place while the argument occurs; but it is a restatement of faith as response to God, both for the use of the church and in the service of the individual.[18] Despite all the dissection of

---

[15] I shall deal with the artistic form of the creed in a later study.

[16] Here lies the failure in Harnack's criticism of Irenaeus, *Dogmengeschichte*, I, 565-67, which is due to the nineteenth-century concept of *Wissenschaft* from which the second century is viewed.

[17] I *Praef.* 3; II.26.1. Cf. G. L. Prestige, *Fathers and Heretics* (London: Macmillan & Co. Ltd., 1940), pp. 32 ff.

[18] Bengsch (*op. cit.*, p. 57) speaks about an "ethic of the theological inquiry."

Gnosticism and pseudo rationalism which we find throughout his work, its theological form in the crucial realm is much more affirmative and witnessing than analytic or argumentative.

Fifth, Irenaeus is fully aware that theological formulation, though necessary for faith, cannot be a substitute for faith itself. Knowledge cannot rise above God (II.25.4) —one chapter praises the value of simplicity as over against puffed up knowledge about hair-splitting issues (II.26.1-3). This limitation of theological language as a servant but never as a master of *pistis* does not prevent Irenaeus from writing five volumes of theological argumentation. The limitation which Irenaeus forces on himself is not one of a negative mystical theology, "not to know anything," but the one of Paul which he paraphrases in II.26.1: "not to know anything except Jesus Christ, crucified for us" (I Cor. 2:2). This nuclear hermeneutic phrase of Paul necessarily leads the Christian to a theological language which is limited by the subordination of knowledge to faith, to the "knowledge in hope" of God's merciful act towards man (Rom. 8:24).

The Syncretistic and the Polemic

The language of primitive Christian faith, as we have stated, occupies a unique position between the Old Testament and the Hellenistic world. Rooted in the Hebraic, touched by the Greek, the language of the New Testament faith exists in a delicate borderline situation. One is tempted to call it syncretistic, yet this generalization does not catch the essential which lies in the combination of Hebraic primacy plus Hellenistic infiltration, in the transformation of the concept of the old covenant into the christological fulfillment, and in the transmutation of the Greek concept into a biblical theological concept. By its nature this language is susceptible to misconception, almost doomed to lose its singularity. The fascinating history of Christian thought to this day results in part from the fact that the axis of the gospel lies on a razor's edge between conflicting worlds.

Athenagoras offers an example of second-century Christianity's use of theological language in a total unawareness of this conflict. His theological language is *Greek,* and he makes use of his beloved Attic speech in a refined sense. His frame of thought is the language of the "poets and philosophers" (*Supplicatio* 24) —as one quickly realizes, of Greek poets and philosophers.[19] The terminology about God is thoroughly philosophical and Greek: God is a unity (μονάς and εἷς) in the Pythagorean sense (6), the uncreated and eternal being of Plato (19), the nous of Thales (23).[20] When Logos, Nous, Sophia are used for the Son, all three are understood in the Greek meaning of the terms (24). God is seen in the Greek dichotomy of spirit versus matter; He is ὁ ὤν, the Being, as distinct from Hyle, the "perishable."[21] Using the Stoic pneuma and the Aristotelian ζῷον, Athenagoras is not aware of the latent conflict in this use of language. He therefore can quote Stoic polytheism for his montheistic plea: "They multiply the Deity in name, yet in reality, they consider God to be one" (6).[22] Greek is his concept of "virtue," and "inequality," of the "rational life" and the "rational argument."[23] Between the artificer and the harmony (16), universal and general providence (24), judgment and merit (*De Res* 22) lies the rational realm of this Greek mind. Now Athenagoras is aware of the specificity of Christian faith. Christianity is for him absolute, revealed truth (*Suppl.* 9). Yet in his language this does not appear. Why not? The *Supplicatio* itself presents the answer; uniqueness for Athenagoras is expressed in different ways (the chapter on the Trinity [10]; the refusal to sacrifice [13]; above all the Resurrection [36]) but most forcefully in asceticism. The praise of perpetual chastity; the second marriage as "specious adultery"; the quotation of the warning against a brotherly kiss which gives pleasure (32-33) —all this points toward what, for Athenagoras, is a signal part of Christian uniqueness. The unique

[19] Aristotelian influence has been shown by Luigi Alfonsi ("Motivi Traditionali del Giovane Aristotele in Clemente Alessandrino e in Atenagora," *Vig. Christ.* 7 [1953], 129 ff.) .

[20] Illuminating is *Suppl.* 24: ". . . since we employ language which makes a distinction between God and matter, and the natures of the two."

[21] *Suppl.* 4 and 15. Arno Pommrich, *Des Apologeten Theophilus von Antiochien Gottes- und Logoslehre, dargestellt unter Berücksichtigung der gleichen Lehre des Athenagoras von Athen* (Leipzig: 1904) The philosophic background is presented by H. A. Lucks, *The Philosophy of Athenagoras, Its Sources and Value* (Washington: Catholic University of America, 1936) .

[22] ζῷον in *Plato*, Tim. 77 B.

[23] ἀρετή *De Res*. 19; 22; *Suppl*. 31. ἀνωμαλία *De Res*. 17. βίος καὶ ζωὴ λογική 13. ζωὴ ἔμφορος καὶ λογική 25. The rational argument in *Suppl*. 25.

element in faith is not found in a specifically theological language —the Greeks have one God and have reason, soul, matter as the Christians do—but in the language of life, practice, ethos, asceticism. The emotional undertone of this uniqueness leads now and then into differentiations from paganism, the strongest instance being the emphasis on the resurrection of the body (*De Resurrectione* 14-17). There is nowhere developed, however, a theological language which safeguards this faith from the syncretism of its age.

The language of Athenagoras reveals the entangled situation of a second-century believer living between faith and the defense of faith. Two forces struggle within his mind, one seeking to establish a contact with the world, the other trying to bring the newness of his faith to this same world. He wants a span of communication, but at the same time he means to witness firmly to the uniqueness of his faith. He is torn in two directions, the identification creating a bridge of syncretism, the uniqueness producing polemical speech. No Christian rooted in his faith, however superficially, would claim total identification without Christian uniqueness in some way; otherwise his adherence to the Christian faith would be senseless— or pretense. On the other hand, the Christian speaks to the world and will have to discover where his language must be polemical in order to defend the uniqueness of Christian faith. The polemical speech of Christianity is language taking issue with the world. The New Testament is an aggressive book, as was the Old Testament, quite unlike oriental syncretism. We find polemics all through the Gospels—to the dismay of our popular preachers who expound Jesus' faith as a "religion of acceptance." "You hypocrites! You know how to interpret the appearance of earth and sky; but why do you not know how to interpret the present time?" (Luke 12:56.) The Pauline epistles are filled to the brim with disputatious passages against man's breaking the law of God (Rom. 2:12 ff.), against Judaistic foes in Philippi (Phil. 1:15; 3:2 ff.), or against Colossian heretics (Col. 2:20 ff.). Christ's sayings against the Jews in the Gospel of John are controversial: "You do not believe, because you do not belong to my sheep" (John 10:26). And yet such polemical speech by itself is neither Christian nor unchristian; the second century teaches us where and how much Christian language can be—or must be—polemical.

The literature of the apologists makes use of traditional rationalistic polemics, especially in the service of the argument for monotheism. Already Elijah scoffed: "Cry aloud, for he is a god; either he is musing, or he has gone aside, or he is on a journey, or perhaps he is asleep and must be awakened." (I Kings 18:27.) The attack against polytheism with its unjust, jealous, and indecent gods was a commonplace in the rationalist critique of Homeric religion.[24]

The mission of the Jewish Diaspora made use of both prophetic and Hellenistic techniques; and so the apologists, often rooted in the traditions of the Hellenistic Diaspora, share in this assault: Theophilus, Athenagoras, Justin, and Tatian.[25] However, by using contentious language against the polytheism of the pagan world, they are fighting a different battleground from early Christianity. Acts 17 is forcefully monotheistic, but not even 17:29 can be called polemical in comparison with the attacks of the apologists. This is not to say that a Christian writer should not join the battle against polytheism; but to join this front does not make him represent a major Christian concern. The battle of the Academy against Homer is only a prolegomenon to the decisive encounter between Christian and pagan.

A second battlefield, more familiar to the New Testament, lies in the field of ethics. Paul has extensive catalogues of vices (Rom. 1:26 ff.; Gal. 5:19-20; Eph. 5:3-4); Jesus makes biting remarks about Jewish religion (Matt. 23); and the book of Revelation violently condemns Rome (17-18). Ethical polemics are also frequent in pagan literature, especially in Stoic teaching when the Cynic diatribe blasts popular customs and Epictetus rebukes the morals of his age.[26] As in the first instance, the apologists rightly pass strictures on people's lives in their confrontation of the pagan

[24] Sext. Emp. *Adv. Math.* IX.178-79; Cicero, *De Nat. Deorum* I.33, 92. Cf. Henry Chadwick, "Origen, Celsus and the Resurrection of the Body," *Harv. Theol. Rev.* 41 (1948), 93-94.

[25] Theoph. *An Aut.* I.5 ff.; III.7-8; Athen. *Suppl.* 8; Tatian *Disc.* 8; 34; Justin, *Apology* I.9.

[26] Diog. Laert. VII.110-14; extensive material can be found in J. von Arnim, *Stoicorum Vet. Fragm.* (Leipzig: 1903-5), III, 377-490), and C. J. de Vogel, *Greek Philosophy* (Leiden: 1959), III, 127-83.

THE LANGUAGE OF CHRISTIAN THEOLOGY

world;[27] but again, ethical polemics as such do not proffer the gospel, although they often seem to do so. They cannot represent "defense of faith" because the apologists are not content to put their faith simply beside Epictetus but do so apart from him.[28] Precisely because of this inadequacy of rationalism and ethical polemics to express the heart of faith, the apologists resort to emotional polemics. As a matter of fact, they are forced into this because their ethical monotheism does not suffice as a tool of speech. When the Christian uniqueness of which the believer is convinced cannot be satisfactorily expressed, emotions take over. Since his rebuke of Plato is not strong enough (*An Aut.* II.4; III.18; III.6), Theophilus slanders gods and goddesses right and left (I.9-10), calls Plato mendacious (III.29), and reports with grim delight horror tales of cannibalism (III.5). Tatian's work against the Greeks is nauseating in its denunciations. He disparages Plato, Aristotle, Heraclitus (*Disc.* 2-3), ridicules gods and unbelievers alike (10), derides the customs and habits of philosophers (25-26), only to call his own faith also a "philosophy"—a peculiar anticlimax after all his hostility to the philosophies of the Greeks (31).[29] Here lies the crux of the problem; emotional language must support the argument when it is not distinctive enough.[30]

[27] There is a difference between paganism of the gutter and Christian standards (Athen. *Suppl.* 34); between philosophic (Theoph. *An Aut.* III.6) and Christian (III.13) concepts of love.

[28] Aristides sets out to ask "who is in truth and who is in error" (*Apol.* 3); Athenagoras pleads for a fair examination (*Suppl.* 2); and Theophilus of Antioch judges in a final statement the enemies who "have not found the truth" (*An Aut.* III.30). Harry A. Wolfson (*The Philosophy of the Church Fathers* [Cambridge: Harvard University Press, 1956], pp. 19 ff.) seeks levels by which philosophy and faith can be distinguished rationally and philosophically.

[29] Despite all polemics, Tatian at times simply reproduces a Stoic argument cf. A. Puech, *Les Apologists grecs du 2e siècle de notre ère* [Paris: 1912], pp. 33 ff. Kamlah (*op. cit.,* p. 99) claims that only by becoming a Hellenized philosophy is "*das Christentum*" proper created. This may be so; what we try to show in this study then is the deep conflict between the language of primitive Christian faith and such "*Christentum.*" Despite Kamlah's polemic against Harnack (p. 93), Harnack has understood the problem.

[30] Massaux (*op. cit.,* p. 576) found it "normal" that such polemic language in Tatian does not make use of the scripture. It may be normal but it accounts at the same time for the apologetic failure in Tatian. Mere aggression cannot defend Christian faith.

The slander, commonplace among the attacks on paganism, that the philosophers and poets "stole" from scriptures (31) is on the same level because it seeks to explain why the Greek philosophers have a few things in common with the philosophy of Tatian. Moreover, such polemics reduce the Christian argument to the level and focus of its foes—a deplorable failure in apologetic retaliation. When Tatian slanders Sappho, the "lovesick woman" (33), or takes literally the story of Rhea turning into a tree (10), he is fighting on the same narrow and foolish base from which the pagans attacked Jewish and Christian faith, as for instance, when they accuse the Christians of Thyestean banquets and the Jews of killing every year a Greek in the temple at Jerusalem.[31] The reason for such absurd accusation is on both sides a sense of the unique; the pagan world is afraid of it and expresses its fear in scorn and aggression, while the Christian likewise feels it without finding a strong enough ground to transcend this level of aggression.[32]

The most important limitation of polemical speech as a defense of Christian faith is pointed out by Irenaeus; it has validity only when it does not represent the goal but a means, and it can only be a preface to the gospel (Rom. 1:18-32) or a consequence (I Cor. 6:7-11), but not the center. Without the substance of faith, this tool is worthless; even more, it can become demonic because it will lead to a hostility devoid of grace (Tatian). The criterion and context of polemical language must lie in the content and depth, in the sharing of, and in the living within the central mystery of faith. At the core of Irenaeus' language lies the *epideixis,* the "demonstration" of the "new vocation" (*Epid.* 94) which is the "preaching of the Truth" (98). Baptismal affirmation (3) and recital of the rule of faith (6) open up the message which then consists of Old Testament description and interpretation (the garden, 12; Abraham seeking God in silence, 24; David as type for Christ the King, 36) on the one hand and the Incarnation of the Son on the other (the mystery of his divinity and humanity, 60;

---

[31] Athen. *Suppl.* 3. A. Jacoby, "Der angebliche Eselskult der Juden und Christen," *Arch. f. Rel. Wiss.* 25 (1927), 265 ff. and Robert M. Grant, *The Sword and the Cross* (New York: The Macmillan Company, 1956), pp. 66 ff.

[32] Kamlah's *"geschichtliche Selbstbehauptung"* (*op. cit.,* p. 85) is bound to become emotional or unchristian when it loses sight of the primitive identity.

his passion, 70; and crucifixion, 80; culminating in the Resurrection[33] and Ascension—the disciples saw the heavens opened to receive him, 83). Such a restatement of the plan of Incarnation (*oikonomia*) is not merely an intellectual repetition of a creed or of scripture; it knows of the "change of hearts" brought about by the divine act (94). The speech of faith is rooted and shared in the *oikonomia:* "our hearts see God, and become children of Abraham who has been justified by faith" (93). The argument for apostolic faith leads to the triumphant climax, a new life (96), the victory over Satan (97), and the final re-creation of the *imago Dei* (97).

Such is the language of the center. When we turn to the work against Gnosticism the polemical argument is recognizable throughout, entrenched in the demonstrative principle of the *Epideixis.* The struggle against Gnosticism is launched from the *oikonomia* of God in the Old Testament (II.30.9) and from the *incarnation* in Christ (III.10.4). We become aware how vital the debate between Irenaeus and the Gnostic is for the verbalization of Christian faith. This religious battle is fought on the central issues: Docetism or Jesus Christ (IV.33.5); history or dualism (V.36.3); monotheism or emanation (II.13.1-3). Suddenly the Gnostics' contribution acquires immeasurable value because it presents the heart of the matter, mystery and faith; and Irenaeus replies by fighting likewise for the heart of the matter, mystery and faith. No longer are we confronted with a rehash of a controversy which had gone on between Stoa and Academy for centuries; but instead we have a head-on clash of two opposing concepts concerning the center of Christian faith, namely the advent of the Christ.

In this interpenetration of declaratory and aggressive language against the Gnostic lies a most creative element for Christian theology. The feud with Gnostic faith helps Irenaeus formulate his Christology. This represents a realm different from the battle between Tatian and the Greeks; it is rather an "inner-Christian" polemic, i.e., a debate of Christian theology with a faith that calls itself Christian yet that misinterprets the Christian core. Such inner

---

[33] "Resurrection" does not maintain quite a similar importance in the overall scheme of Irenaeus; yet, cf. V.33.1 and 12.3.

confrontation is imperative for creative theological thinking because here, within or at the borders of Christian faith itself, there is a dramatic struggle for a vital truth. What has Plato really in common with the sacrament of the Lord's Supper, which Justin defends against the Roman philosophers? Here, however, between Valentinus' redemption and the Irenaean *oikonomia*, lies the battleground of theology. This "inner polemic" [34] is so creative because it takes place between two forces that have a similar concern about a similar theological center, although the resultant interpretations of this center are diametrically opposed. When Quadratus addresses Hadrian, their purposes of life and goals of action are so far apart that the language of one can hardly infiltrate the mind of the other; but when Irenaeus curses Valentinus he remains on one and the same axis—the redemption of man in Christ. The church can learn from Irenaeus the value of a struggle for the center of the faith.

To be sure, theology must be willing to pay a price for such inner aggression. Already in Irenaeus the controversy is fought with a good many emotions that enfeeble the argument. There is no academic detachment here, nor could there be any. Conflicts over matters of life and death are always intertwined with the feelings of personalities involved; here is no longer academic pursuit but drama played out in flesh and blood—subjective, offensive, violent. Were it not so it would not be a matter of life and death. We are here on the second level of emotional language, that within faith itself. This, in time, can become demonic when the subject of controversy fought over is no longer issues but persons; when the fight continues generations after the issues have been solved or have changed; or when aggression becomes tied to the struggle for power. The failure of human personality is the price creative theological polemics must pay; when the price becomes too high demonic forces take over.

Such inner contention in the service of constructive theology is in danger of neglecting the aspect with which we started, namely

---

[34] Cf. the distinction between *eversio* and *detectio* in the chapter on polemic speech in Bengsch (*op. cit.*, pp. 16 ff.) and the article by C. B. Reynders, "La polémique d' Irénée," *Rech. de théol. anc. et méd.* 7 (1935), 5 ff.

cultural polemics.[35] The apologists had seized a salient dimension in Christian communication which does not come through in Irenaeus.[36] Jesus' attack on the Jewish religion and the denunciation of Rome in the book of Revelation are both directed against cultures as well as a religious way of life. The theological front cannot be merely "religious"; it must become cultural. Not to speak concretely to the cultural situation would reduce Christianity to the irrelevance of a faith in the midst of the desert. When Tertullian seeks for the bearing of Christian faith upon patterns of life, such as the theater (*De Spectaculis* 27) or military service (*De Idolatria* 19), he seeks for relevant consequences. What Irenaeus does indicate, however, is the place of such cultural polemics. Criticism of environment does not make this front a Christian front; it is not aggression which makes it Christian but only the context of redemption. Tertullian's travesty of pagan life and thinking, though refreshing, has no promise in the Christian faith unless it follows and serves, instead of dominates, Irenaeus' axiom of love: "In the beginning God created Adam, not because he was in need of a man but in order to have a being on whom to bestow his mercy" (IV.14.1).

Christian aggression against an outside world has been part of the gospel ever since the prologue of Jesus' mission, when John the Baptist assailed Jews and soldiers alike (Luke 3:7 ff.). The problems of the second century show us that the attack against the outside world must be rooted in the affirmation of hope; we are not merely to parallel one or the other cultural or theological critiques (the Stoics have often done a superb job in this respect), but we are to proclaim the advent of redemption and love. Unless

[35] The danger is therefore not only apologetic narrowness or unconscious dependence (Bengsch, *op. cit.*, p. 48), but this lack of cultural relevance which we do not find in Tertullian. To be sure, as Gustav Winggren (*Man and the Incarnation, a study in the Biblical Theology of Irenaeus* [Philadelphia: Muhlenberg Press, 1959], p. 10) pointed out, Irenaeus does speak concretely about Rome; but there is no concise cultural issue in his work in the sense of the apologists.

[36] This is the problem with the irenic quality in Irenaeus which Morton Scott Enslin ("Irenaeus, mostly Prolemgomena," *Harvard Theological Review* 40 [1947], 165) sees not only in distinction from Tatian but also from Justin Martyr.

we herald the center, we weaken our address. There is a creative theological polemic beside such external criticism which takes place right within the church itself—an inner contention that may produce pain and discord, yet an endeavor indispensable for the formulation of Christian truth. Theology must be polemic in order to proceed. Yet after this the church must become aware of the first; it cannot make its witness without some assault on the cultural situation of its age, even though the front lines must change from one generation to the next. Jerusalem has something to do with Athens, or rather with Alexandria; but when Christian faith takes itself seriously Jerusalem ceases to be Alexandria's suburb.

Conversion and Its Understanding

Justin Martyr is the classical instance of the semantic conflict arising from a Christian conversion. The basis of this great martyr's Christian existence is his acceptance of the Christian faith. "A flame was kindled in my soul" (*Dial. Tr.* 8) ; this is the sincere expression of the faith which entered his life (30). With this faith Justin boldly declares at the end of his life, before the prefect Rusticus: "Yes, I am a Christian" (*Act. Just. Mart.* III.4). The historian and the theologian who set out to analyze the thought and speech of the martyr must be aware that there is a faith willing to die (V.6) ; by the blood of such faith the church suffers and grows in her superhuman battle with the emperor. Our judgment of the martyr's language must never become anathema against the man; the language of Justin is an index of the church's need for theological precision and biblical authenticity.

Justin was converted to the Christian faith as he learned it in the second quarter of the second century. He knows Christian language and uses it frequently. One layer of this thought is biblical. In many instances he speaks about Jesus Christ as an historical figure. He was born (*Apol.* I.13)—the virgin birth plays a considerably larger role in his work than in the canon (*Dial. Tr.* 66). He lived under Cyrenius (*Apol.* I.34; 46), suffered and was crucified under Pilate (I.13; II.6), was raised from the dead (I.67). The "words of the Savior" (*Dial. Tr.* 8) mean a great deal to him. He is familiar with the teaching of the gospel (*Apol.* I.15); and he knows the *basileia* (I.11), the Resurrection (I.18-19), and the

Parousia (*Dial. Tr.* 31) as three pillars of Christian belief. The liturgical language of the church is familiar to him: baptism, Eucharist, the Sunday gathering for worship (*Apol.* I.61-67). The ethical language of the church is part of his faith: his quotations from Matthew (I.15-17) and his ascetic emphasis (I.29) reveal the influence of Christian ethical tradition in the post-Apostolic communities. This is the faith which receives him, teaches him, and baptizes him, giving him the language of the church in which he can worship, praise, and commune with God.

But then, Justin argues with Trypho and with the Roman senate in defense of the Christian faith. And as Justin undertakes his defense, another language interferes with the Christian language. He sees the emotional accusations of paganism, inaccurate and senseless, the exposure and eating of children; promiscuous concubinage as they are at the Christian gatherings. His defense of faith is purposely on a *rational level*. The basic assumption of Justin's languages lies in the short phrase: ὁ νουνεχὴς καταλαβεῖν δυνήσεται, the man of intelligence is capable of understanding Christian faith (*Apol.* I.46). Philosophical proof plays a pivotal role in the argument against Trypho; *apodeixis* is the rational argument which leads the hearer into faith.[37] At the end of his exposé Justin has "proved at length that Christ is called God" (*Dial. Tr.* 124). Persuasion and understanding designate the process which leads to Christianity.[38] Even those of scanty intelligence can be persuaded to accept it (*Dial. Tr.* 29). The criterion which Justin lays before the pagan reader is that of rationality. If this faith is "according to reason and truth," honor it; otherwise, despise it! [39]

[37] ἀπόδειξις *Dial. Tr.* 55 (Pl. *Phaed.* 73 A; Arist. *Apol.* 71 ᵇ17); ἀποδείκνυμι *Dial. Tr.* 59 (Pl. *Rep.* 472 D; Arist. *Apol.* 75 ᵇ37); δείκνυμι *Dial. Tr.* 63 (Pl. *Leg.* 896 B; Arist. *Apol.* 90 ᵇ34). The rationalistic frame of thought shows up best in Justin's definition of philosophy as ἐπιστήμη τοῦ ὄντος and ἐπίγνωσις τοῦ ἀληθοῦ *Dial. Tr.* 3.

[38] *Apol.* I.10; 55; 36. The prophetic was not "understood" until Jesus (I.32). The argument from fulfilled prophecy (*Dial. Tr.* 33-53) although originating elsewhere fits the rationalistic scheme extremely well; you can prove that Christ is the truth.

[39] *Apol.* I.68; I.53. Justin is not aware of the deep conflict between this sentence and the concluding remark of *Dial. Tr.* 7: "These things cannot be perceived or understood by all, unless God and his Christ give it to him to

179

Christian faith is explained in the language of Hellenistic philosophy. Justin reports what attracted him to Platonic philosophy after his search for truth: *knowledge* of what exists in reality; clear *perception* of truth; *reward,* a happy life *(Dial. Tr.* 2). When Justin sets the Christian faith of the Old Man beside this platonic faith, the terms reappear: *wisdom, truth, knowledge,* a *happy life (Dial. Tr.* 7-8). The antithesis between truth and error is rational and philosophical; truth is taught, it is parallel with reason *(Apol.* I.12); knowledge is parallel to the philosophic consideration (θεωρία) *(Apol.* II.8).[40] The Greek concept of free will is tied up with Christian truth; "choice and knowledge" become the opposite of "necessity and ignorance" *(Apol.* I.61).[41]

As a consequence terms connected with *teaching* maintain their well-known importance in this literature. The prophet is understood as teacher *(Apol.* I.31), Jesus has many primitive Christian features, yet it is as a teacher that Jesus is of first importance *(Apol.* II.8).[42] The Incarnation occurs for the purpose of teaching, which is the conversion and restoration of the human race *(Apol.* I.23). Truth is taught by God *(Dial. Tr.* 38). What the catechumen receives is teaching, as the Christian has received teaching from Christ *(Apol.* I.8; I.10).

Justin continues to speak the language of his pre-Christian philosophy after his conversion. Not only does he call Christian faith a philosophy which is "safe and profitable" *(Dial. Tr.* 8), and the enemy of the church, Crescens, not worthy to be called "philosopher" *(Apol.* II.3), but he also speaks in the framework of Stoic and Platonic thought. This is most visible in his famous Logos

---

understand." This remark, on the other hand, shows that Justin is not merely an apologist. He is talking on two different levels.

[40] The philosophic θεωρία in Plato *Phileb.* 38 B; Arist. *Metaph.* 989 ᵇ25; Epic. *Ep.* I, p. 3. Christ is worthy to be called Son of God because of his wisdom, *Apol.* I.22 (cf. also *Apol.* II.8; I.56 and *Dial. Tr.* 8). Michel Spanneut *(Le Stoicisme des Pères de l'église de Clément de Rome à Clément d'Alexandrie* [Louvain: 1957], p. 434) makes the Stoic influence ultimately responsible for the rationalist tendency in the early Fathers. This holds true especially for Justin Martyr despite his anti-Stoic polemic (cf. *Apol.* II.7).

[41] See especially *Apol.* I.43 and II.9; also II.7 and *Dial. Tr.* 141.

[42] *Apol.* I.21: Jesus Christ, our teacher, was crucified. I.13: Our teacher of all this is Jesus Christ. In both places, Justin puts his διδάσκαλος beside creedal formulations about Christ (also I.46).

concept. Ever since *dabar yahweh* crossed the borders into the Hellenic, its semitic concreteness and actuality, almost a material quality, could no longer be maintained. The hypostatic tendency in the Wisdom literature, the Word in the Johannine prologue, the Philonic "second God," are on different levels, and it is a grave mistake not to distinguish minutely the nuances which the Logos contains in different writings. In Justin the biblical Logos is not altogether absent. God's word to the prophet redeems and judges (*Apol.* I.33).[43] The Logos of Justin is on the whole, however, remote from the biblical Word of God. It is the power of God (I.14), the spirit of God (I.23), the first-born of God (I.33),[44] but it is at the same time rational principle (*Apol.* II.10). Logos means a hypostatic fruit (γέννημα), brought forth from God without sexual union (I.21), but at the same time it is the seminal logos of the Stoics, the logos in every man which, according to Justin, the philosophers did not know in its entirety (*Apol.* II.8).[45] And therefore, Logos is reason, according to which man lives, parallel to truth, conceivable in knowledge and contemplation; and the world as well as the individual man participates in it.[46] The opposite of Logos is the irrational and unreasonable: τὸ ἄλογον (*Apol.* I.12). The identity of word and reason, the hypostatic quality, suggestive of Stoic pantheism, all this distinguishes the Logos in Justin's vocabulary.

What happens in these examples is the equation of Christian and

[43] Harnack observed already that the Logos in Justin is not merely divine reason but the word of revelation (*op. cit.*, I, 531). For the semantic problem in hearing John 1:1 see Jules Laurence Moreau, *Language and Religious Language* (Philadelphia: The Westminster Press, 1961), pp. 41-42.

[44] The Logos can be a second God (*Dial. Tr.* 56; 128); cf. Turner's observation that "for the Apologists the emphasis lies rather upon the Discarnate God," *op. cit.*, p. 38.

[45] Also *Apol.* II.10. λόγοι σπερματικοί in Stoa, *Diog. Laert.* VII.136; Galen, *Def. Med.* 29; cf. Gustave Bardy, "Saint Justin et la philosophie stoicienne," *Rech. de sc. rel.* 13 (1923), pp. 491 ff.

[46] The human race participates in it, μετέσχε, Apol. I.46; II.8; I.6; 46; 59. There are again two levels when Justin puts beside this participation of the world in the Logos an inspiration of the world by the Logos, *Apol.* I.5; cf. Harnack, *op. cit.*, p. 509. It is utterly misleading to present simply the biblical pattern of the two as a neatly "orthodox" theologian, as Vivian A. C. Little (*The Christology of the Apologists* [London: 1934], p. 175) has done; cf. Lietzmann, *op. cit.*, II, 180-82; and Wolfson, *op. cit.*, pp. 192 ff.

philosophical terms. When Justin accepts Christian faith, he accepts a "philosophy" (*Dial. Tr.* 8). Piety and philosophy belong together (*Apol.* I.12).[47] For Justin, Socrates and Christ are related because the former knew Christ, i.e., the Logos (*Apol.* II.10).[48] As Christ is crucified, the sons of Jupiter suffer (I.22); as Heraclitus is persecuted because of the Logos, Christ is persecuted (II.8); Noah and Deucalion go back to one and the same event (II.7). The philosophical terminology is employed because Justin is insensitive to the discrepancy between the Johannine Logos as Word and the Platonic logos as reason.[49] God is discernible only to the nous (*Dial. Tr.* 3). In this Platonic phrase, Justin uses the non-Hebraic substance of biblical language. In his preference for the LXX (*Apol.* I.31), he remains true to his basic understanding of Christian language; he reads Greek thoughts into the LXX concepts (*Dial. Tr.* 71). And he reads these concepts into the New Testament. The step from Logos to *sperma* is for him a natural one (*Apol.* II.13), whereas the leap from biblical Logos to Stoic *sperma* is in reality one of greatest consequence.[50] His equation of Plato's symbolism of

[47] The right philosophy must be found; this is the starting point in *Dial. Tr.* 3. *Apol.* I.3 quotes Plato *Rep.* V.18 on the importance of philosophizing for the state. As Turner (*op. cit.*, pp. 77 ff.) remarked, mysticism and metaphysics belong together in the attempt to change Christian faith into a Greek religion. Kamlah (*op. cit.*, p. 93) does not see anything strange in Justin's equation because he does not want to admit the consequences in the conflict of two languages. For him, *Pauline* language is merely speech that has not yet come into contact with the "tradition of actual reason" (*Tradition der eigentlichen Vernunft*); Kamlah does not reckon with the fact that primitive Christian speech has a pattern in its own right which cannot be judged from the "superior" level of Greek reason. What the German scholar means with "*Eigentliche Vernunft*" is reason in the Greek tradition, metaphysically phrased by Greek tradition. To be sure, we may speak about a "functional harmony between Christian religion and philosophy" (Jules Gross, *La divinisation du Chrétien d'après les pères Grecs* [Paris: 1938], p. 134) but what creates the harmony is emotional desire plus cultural existence but not the tools by which this harmony is expressed.

[48] *Apol.* II.13; I.46; cf. J. M. Pfättisch, "Christus und Sokrates bei Justin," *Theol. Quart.* 90 (1908), 503 ff.

[49] Even if a notion of a principle is implied in the prologue of John, "Logos" for him means primarily a person and not a power (see A. H. Armstrong and R. A. Markus, *Christian Faith and Greek Philosophy* [London: Darton, Longman & Todd, 1960], p. 19). Of course, it is "primarily" and not "exclusively," as we have concluded in the chapter on Gnosticism.

[50] This conflict is not understood by Spanneut, *op. cit.*, pp. 295-323. Spanneut does not see in primitive Christian faith what we have called its "Hebraic roots."

the cross with the biblical cross can occur because he pushes the Johannine Logos into the realm of the seminal logos and thus opens the way of symbolic toying with biblical terminology within a symbolic world view conceived after the Greek manner (I.60).

The Greek view of Logos has its consequences in Justin's use of "virtue" and "vice." Heracles' famous choice is quoted as an example for the human decision between virtue and vice (II.11). The nature of the world lies between these two alternatives (II.7), and the "wicked" and the "virtuous" are Hellenistic types taken over into the Christian faith (I.12). Hellenistic moralism affects biblical language; injustice and righteousness are understood within the moral framework of Stoa and Academy and are equated with temperance and reasonable decision.[51] "Those are deified who lived near to God in holiness and virtue" (I.21). Consequently, merit and reward are openly promoted (I.43-44).

Justin Martyr speaks a double language, using on one hand the terminology of the church (sacrament, theology, Christian ethics); on the other the concepts of his philosophical past and of those whom he addresses (rational terminology, Hellenistic ethics).[52] The problem is not the existence of two languages[53]—there will always be two in the genuine exegetical endeavor—but that there is no real clash. We naïvely educe two languages side by side as if they were harmonious while in reality they are antipodal. Because the conflict between the two is neither understood nor felt, the "new language" to which Justin has converted is not strong enough to infiltrate the language of his past to its roots. The liturgical and ethical sphere of speech is overpowered by the rationalistic structure of thought; the biblical Word can never be more than a

---

[51] *Apol.* I.6 and I.68. The Stoic background of Justin's ethics has been presented by C. Clemen, *Die religionsphilosophische Bedeutung des stoisch-christlichen Eudämonismus in Justins Apologie* (Leipzig: 1890), pp. 145 ff.

[52] Not only for Justin but for this whole period the language taught in Stoic schools (Spanneut, *op. cit.*, p. 431) naturally infiltrated Christian communication. We are confronted with the same problem as in Gnosticism: when does it begin to take over primacy?

[53] Armstrong and Markus have formulated the problem well; on the one hand theology must use relevant and available language (*op. cit.*, p. 147); on the other hand, as in the example of the λόγος σπερματικός, by trying to bridge the gulf between Christian and pagan thought, such language eliminates the gulf (p. 144).

marionette for the Stoic logos. When the logoi are called rational forces, full of divine power and grace (I.55), this runs counter to all Hebraic-Christian axioms. In the emotional realm, there is an authentic conversion; in the rational, the philosopher remains a tyrant over the Christian.[54]

The schizophrenia in this linguistic situation is a serious problem for all apologetic communication. We may seek an apologetic language as a "method" versus a biblical language as "substance"; or we may strive to express the Christian truth more or less in the idiom of the time. If this occurs without any consciousness of the clash, the endeavor fails, and apologetics turns into surrender. Justin's main problem, however, is not an apologetic one, despite the traditional designation of this type of Christian literature. The problem exists whether we address the world or not. What is lacking is the bridge from the emotional acceptance of biblical faith to the intellectual acceptance of its roots.[55] The premise of identifying the biblical Word with the philosophical seminal logos bars him from expressing his faith in the language of Christian theology. It threatens to surrender the intellectual content of faith to the non-Christian philosophy which he tries to convince of the Christian truth! No wonder Marcus Aurelius slashes the stubbornness of the Christians in disgust (*Med.* XI.3); if their underlying faith is homogeneous with philosophical beliefs to such an extent, why on earth do they need to die for it? From the *Apology* the Stoic emperor could not have really perceived that the faith to which Justin was converted rose from another way of thinking about God and man, claiming divine sovereignty and human response—unlike the rationalistic philosopher, unlike Rome, and unlike Athens.

In this dilemma Irenaeus makes his contribution to the problem of theological language. The argument about God cannot be severed from the revelatory basis of faith. The knowledge of God is the knowledge which God reveals to man in Christ, and the knowledge which the Son reveals to whom he chooses (IV.6.1-7).[56]

[54] *Dial. Tr.* 2; cf. P. Keseling, *Justin's "Dialog gegen Trypho"* c. 1-10 und Platon's "Protagoras," *Rheinisch. Mus. f. Phil.* 75 (1926), 223 ff.

[55] The conflict can be phrased as one of *"Neuheitserlebnis"* versus *"Neuheitsbewusstsein"* (Prümm, *op. cit.,* p. 467).

[56] The fragment by John of Damascus in IV.6.4 is especially illuminating.

The knowledge of God, which is the speech of God, is inseparable from the revelation of God. This knowledge comes from the Father. The Father announces himself through the Son (III.6.2). The consequence of this self-communication of God is the "recapitulation" of man (III.16.6). On this basis Irenaeus points to the main issues which Christian speech has to consider between Apologetics and Gnosticism.

1. The language of faith is *apostolic*. The voice with which the church of the present speaks is the voice of the apostles and the voice of the disciples (III.5.1).[57] Apostolicity in the language of faith is the consequence of the uniqueness of revelation. When God is himself the teacher of truth,[58] the speech of the man who stands within this truth must be related to the historic speech. Apostolicity is for Irenaeus not simply a matter of church polity. To call it an attempt to save the unity of Christianity in a moment of alarming drift towards schism mistakes the inner necessity of this theology. Apostolic speech is demanded because this faith understands itself as part of the redemptive act of God. The voice of the church testifying to this act is the voice which was spoken during this act itself. What is truth? That which Peter and Paul have seen (III.13.1). "Seen!" (*Deum viderunt.*) Apostolicity in the speech of faith is demanded because "truth" for this theology is not merely an abstraction but incarnate reality. What is knowledge? What Christ imparted to his disciples, which led to the healing acts (III.5.2). Because faith revolves around "recapitulation" in its historic, physical concreteness, apostolic speech is the consequent verbalization of this faith.

Irenaeus adds to apostolicity another concept—that of *tradition*. Again the language of the church in contrast to the language of speculation is not merely the self-preservation of Christianity but the expression of his theological presuppositions. Faith for him is faith within a community of faith, the *ecclesia* (IV.26.2). The voice of faith is the voice of the church (III.1 ff.). The creedal expression is an expression by the church (IV.33.8).[59] The individual Christian needs the support of faith in the church (IV.21.3). Tra-

---

[57] Prophets and apostles are named in III.8.1.

[58] IV.5.1; *quoniam impossibile erat sine Deo discere Deum.*

[59] For this passage see Harvey, *op. cit.*, II, 262, n. 6.

dition brought apostolic faith to Irenaeus. The Christian's faith is involved in the life of a church, and it is tradition which ties both the believer and the church to the apostolic age.

2. Tradition and apostolicity are vague concepts. They can explain the anti-Gnostic emphasis of Irenaeus, but they cannot in themselves explain why the apologetic schizophrenia or nomistic poverty is transcended in the thought of Irenaeus. Justin as well as Clement means to be apostolic and ecclesiastical. Irenaeus sees Christian faith in a specific *chain of language*. The moralistic fathers grasp only a sector of the language of faith, its hortatory aspect. Justin, speaking at different levels in his attempt to address the pagan world, dissects this language. Irenaeus strives to bring Christian terminology into a relation with the whole and into a relation with the center. To use his own plastic metaphor: Irenaeus seeks for an authentic theological mosaic (I.8.1).

We use a Greek fragment to demonstrate the basic chain of revelatory language: the Spirit descends—the only-begotten Son of God becomes incarnate—the *oikonomia* of salvation is achieved by Jesus Christ, as the Lord in the canon and as the apostles and the prophets confess (III.17.4). This statement contains in a comprehensive unit the chain of faith: *oikonomia* (the divine plan, the rebuke of dualism) [60]—Incarnation (σαρκωθέντος ἐν ἀνθρώπῳ) — Jesus Christ (in the unity of God and man: ἑνὸς καὶ τοῦ αὐτοῦ ὄντος) —witness (the biblical testimony in the unity of Old and New Testaments).[61] Theological argument is understood as an endeavor to present the essential concepts and to grasp their essential relations. Irenaeus learns from the Gnostics that a gospel of truth can be written with many primitive Christian expressions. The duty of theology in an era of apologetics and speculative confusion is to demonstrate the Christian language of faith as a whole, as a chain of concepts which are related to each other. The first book against the heretics makes use of this method. The Gnostics have a faith

[60] An interesting modern definition for the Greek οἰκονομία is given by Hans Urs von Balthasar (*Theologie der Geschichte* [Einsiedeln: 1959], p. 54: "*konkrete Gestalt des Heils,*" the concrete form of salvation.

[61] We have here a good example for constructive polemics; οἰκονομία affirms the historical plan of Incarnation; the oneness of the Christ denies Docetism; the "apostles and prophets" stand for the unity of the Old and the New Testament.

which "neither the prophets proclaimed nor the Lord taught nor the apostles delivered" (I.8.1). The argument of faith is the argument from proclamation—teaching—transmittance. The argument for the unity of God is the argument from scripture—prophets—Christ—the church—and the world which manifests him (II.9.1). It is the argument from prophecy, from the scriptures, from Abraham, Moses, and Paul; but at the same time it is the argument from the theological self-understanding of Christ, the incarnation of the Word of God, the unity with the Father, which includes at the end the church which is linked to the Incarnation by the apostles (IV.20.1-12). In these paragraphs of Book IV, Irenaeus uses a whole chain of concepts to demonstrate apostolic faith in the unity of God. When he distinguishes Christian "knowledge" from the Gnostic type he explains the chain which surrounds it: promise—revelation—advent—grace—liberty (IV.11.4).

The chain of such language does not always have the same individual links, of course. The terms used depend upon the occasion of the argument. However, the main links of the chain are clear: God—Christ—the Holy Spirit—the prophets—the apostles—the canon—the church. The spirit is often lacking, and church/tradition by no means figures on every occasion. The chain of speech is not an impoverished one-sidedness which allows only one circumscribed development of thought; it changes its expressions and width from a mere double frame to an extensive demonstration. The whole book against the heretics is a far-reaching application of this principle, developing against the Gnostics Christian faith as understood from its center.

3. The language of Irenaeus revolves around two poles: the one God and the Incarnate Son (III.20.2).[62] The terminology of *man* (Adam) is directed toward God's becoming man (the second Adam; V.16.3). Knowledge is the knowledge which Christ has imparted; only through Christ do we receive knowledge about the Father (IV.6.7). *Law* is directed toward Christ as its end and final

[62] As F. Loofs (*Theophilus von Antiochien, Adversus Marcionem und die andern theologischen Quellen bei Irenaeus,* TU 46 [Leipzig: 1930], pp. 355-56) saw here lies the center of the thought of Irenaeus, *invisibilis visibilis factus est,* III.16.6; cf. also Harnack, *op. cit.* I, 582.

cause (IV.12.1-4) .[63] The *ethical* terminology is christological—obedience, love, judgment (V.8.1 ff.) . The christological centrality is monotheistic; Gnostic language has been at times Christocentric to a degree that completely annuls God as Father. Hence the language about "good" and "just," flesh and immortality, generation and aeons, circles around the one God. Because there is no knowledge of the Father apart from Christ, the unity of the monotheistic and Christocentric language is one of inner necessity (III.21.3) .[64] Whether Irenaeus succeeds or not in maintaining this unity throughout is another matter.[65] It is enough for the moment to see where for him the center of language lies.

This center represents the axiom for the theological communication of Christian faith. As the fascinating history of the trinitarian controversy proves, this axis of Christian self-understanding contains an immense tension. How can the Christian maintain the concept of the biblical Father (Isa. 64:8) with the incarnate (John 1:14) and redemptive (II Cor. 5:18) act of God? Irenaeus introduces into Christian thought the central tension from which theology can no longer withdraw; the Christian center consists of two poles, the one God and the Incarnate God.[66] For all its history, this conflict, arising right from within the New Testament, though with different terminologies, cannot be evaded by Christian theology (unless the core is surrendered to Judaism or to Gnosticism) , just as it can never rid itself of the tension between creation and redemption.[67]

We have observed that the apologists speak a double language, intertwined with their defense. The difference between their speech and the polar language just envisaged can be studied in their relation to the creed. Justin Martyr knows the creed (*Dial. Tr.* 85) and

[63] *Quomodo finis legis Christus si non et initium eius esset?* (IV.12.4) .

[64] *Praeparavit et praeformavit* (with Sagnard, *op. cit.,* p. 356; the MSS have *reformavit,* Harvey, *op. cit.,* p. 114) *Deus fidem nostram quae in filium eius est* (III.21.3) .

[65] One example suffices for the moment: in III.25.5 ethical language does not stand completely within such a circle.

[66] IV.6.2: *Neque enim Patrem cognoscere quis potest nisi verbo Dei est id est nisi Filio revelante; neque Filium nisi Patris beneplacito* (cf. Houssiau, *op. cit.,* p. 78) .

[67] For the christological problems and their relations to monotheism see Houssiau, *op. cit.,* pp. 163 ff.

undoubtedly it means for him what it says; this great convert does not merely die for an emotional attachment but for a conviction. Unlike Justin, however, the monotheistic and christological creed becomes a part of Irenaeus himself. It is not mere quotation (I. 10.1). He does resort to creedal speech from time to time (III.16.3), paraphrasing (I.22.1), arguing with it (II.30.9), or merely falling into creedal language at random (III.18.3). The central theme of the early creed, the *Deus-homo*, becomes the center of the verbalization of faith. Such language seeks to express the monumental Christian drama: promise-advent-redemption rather than to produce the rational coherence of theological systematization. Not that the creedal language of the *Deus-homo* would create irrationality in communication (it points throughout toward a *fides quaerens intellectum*), but the argument is response. Language of the center means less a metaphysical quest than a dramatic recital.

4. The theological language of Irenaeus that centers upon the apostolic faith in the one God in Christ is a language which reflects and expresses the Christian's involvement in the object of his faith. "Involved" language means communication by a man wrapped up in what he believes, and determined by the forces that re-created his life. Induced neither by an autonomous natural process nor by rational detachment, this language is the product of faith which for the Christian is the origin of all things (Theoph. *An Aut.* I.8). The argument *adversus haereses* claims to be and tries to be rational—rightly so; but its determinant is the existential involvement of the Christian in the object of his faith.

Such involvement is twofold. In the argument about the unity of God a Greek fragment from John Damascene has been preserved which states the Irenaean position precisely. Those who see the light partake in the light; those who see God are in God (ἐντός εἰσι τοῦ θεοῦ) and partake (μετέχοντες) in his splendor. God gives life (ζωοποιήσῃ) to those who hold him and see him in faith. Participation in God is the knowledge of God and the enjoyment of his goodness (IV.20.5). The Christian who speaks about God is in his presence and therefore aims to praise God with his language; thus Irenaeus resorts to a hymn in the middle of Book III (III.6.4). Theology turns into praise. What the Gnostic knew, Irenaeus practices; after all, this happened to Paul, to the poets of the

Psalms, to Job, to the unknown Israelite who wrote the battle hymn of Judg. 5. The words of scripture, in a harmonious melody, praise the Creator God (II.28.3).[68] Irenaeus does not reach the artistic level of some Gnostic hymns. "There is only one and the same God and Father who has been proclaimed by the Prophets and handed down by the Gospel whom we Christians worship and love with our whole heart" (III.10.5). Worship and love.

This involvement, however, also concerns the human aspect of the canon of faith, the Incarnation. In the life of reasoning in III.17.4 the argument rests on the prophetic and apostolic witness which is at the same time the witness of the Lord himself.[69] The three verbs of that passage voice the earthly dimension of the Christian involvement: "to witness," "to confess," "to proclaim." Christ, the prophets, and the apostles are to be taken seriously; so is the community of faith, the believers; and so is the history of faith, the Old Testament. "To proclaim," "to teach," "to transmit" [70]— such combinations envisage Christian truth within history, revealed and not merely deduced. Seeking to express the mystery of Incarnation means to share in it; [71] here lies one of the decisive factors in the anti-Gnostic front. Irenaeus understands his argument against the heretics as a rational endeavor to correct their errors (I Praef. 2), but in reality his argument (reasonable, to be sure, as much as possible) flows from involved response to the grace of the Incarnation.

---

[68] The text is not fully certain (cf. Harvey, op. cit., I, 352). The polyphony of scripture creates the symphony in us which turns into the praise of God— Laudantem hymnis Deum qui fecit omnia.

[69] 1.) ὁ Κύριος μαρτυρεῖ.
2.) οἱ ἀπόστολοι ὁμολογοῦσιν.
3.) οἱ προφῆται κηρύττουσιν.

[70] οἱ προφῆται ἐκήρυξαν, ὁ Κύριος ἐδίδαξεν, οἱ ἀπόστολοι παρέδωκαν I.8.1. A comparison with the combination in III.17.4 (preceding footnote) shows that the distribution of the verbs in relation to the three (prophets, apostles, Christ) is not essential, except for the transmittance by apostles.

[71] Irenaeus' argument against the Gnostics and Athanasius' argument against Arius have this basic denominator of an "involved language of redemption" (Samuel Laeuchli, "The Case of Athanasius Against Arius, Concordia Theol. Month. 30 [1959], 416 ff.) but the emphasis is quite different; for Irenaeus involvement lies in the historical event and in the community of believers (the humanity of Incarnation), while for Athanasius involvement lies in praising and adoring the subject of redemption (the divinity of Incarnation).

The Christocentric and monotheistic speech of Irenaeus represents the redress of the semantic failure of the post-Apostolic generation.[72] Instead of moral exhortation Irenaeus proclaims hope; but unlike dualistic metaphysics the christological hope is comprehended by the paradox of two covenants and the paradox of a unity of God with Christ. *Una salus* is the axis of theological speech; metaphysical speculation and nomism are replaced by the theme of God-becoming-man. The language of Christian theology has reached its center, both as the product of the self-understanding process in faith and as a continuation and response to the axiomatic forces in Pauline and Johannine Christianity.

Irenaeus is neither Mark nor Paul nor John. He quotes them all, yet he speaks his own language. How does this attempt to convey faith compare with the New Testament? We seek first the biblical substance of his speech and then try to outline some of the problems in the tools he uses for his theological thinking.

THE LANGUAGE OF BIBLICAL REVELATION

New Testament Language

Unus est Dominus Deus (III.6.3). After all the monotheistic passages in the post-canonical literature of all types, we ought to determine the biblical substance of the language of Irenaeus behind this quotation of the Elijah controversy (I Kings 18:21). Who is this *Deus* for him? Is he the sustainer of Greek cosmology? This concept does exist for him—God is *conditor* and *inventor* (II. 30.9).[73] Is it the cosmic force of Stoic thinking or the demiurge of the Academy? Traces of this type of thought, too, can be detected.[74] Or does Irenaeus represent the Philonian synthesis, a God who is the creator but who creates the Logos and loses thereby a great deal of the personal character he has in the Bible? In certain cases Irenaeus seems to recognize impersonal qualities in God. God can be a philosophical being, not much different from what

---

[72]See F. R. Montgomery Hitchcock, *Irenaeus of Lugunum* (Cambridge: University Press, 1914), pp. 127 ff.

[73] III.6.1: *Qui dominatur omnium*, II.30.9: *Ipse fabricator, ipse conditor, ipse inventor.*

[74] See especially IV.38.2-3: God is the creator of an eurythmic and consistent cosmos (38.2) who creates man in his order, and such order means growth (38.3; II.28.1).

the apologists understood him to be (IV.20.6). Does Irenaeus know the biblical God?

The test can be made when Irenaeus quotes Exodus 3:14. The *qui est* of the translator is obviously ὁ ὤν of the LXX. This might have tempted Irenaeus to make some interesting remarks about the eternity and essence of God. Instead, he immediately turns the phrase from Exodus to the act of God. He is the one who has manifested himself, who has borne witness to the Son, and whom the Son has announced (III.6.2). The God of Irenaeus is a God who *acts*. He created the earth—as Irenaeus constantly insists in repudiation of Gnostic cosmogony.[75] He gave the law of the old covenant (III.10.5). The God of Irenaeus is beyond the necessity of nature and being. God in his sovereign freedom is not in need of man—man is in need of God (IV.16.4).[76] He is not the "slave of necessity and cause" but free to act according to his benevolence (V.4.1).[77] The creation of Adam is creation in freedom *ut haberet in quem collocaret sua beneficia* (IV.14.1). This means the rejection of both necessity and first cause. This rejection does not lead Irenaeus into the mystic realm of negative experience but to the lordship of God, a lordship which is acting and which evokes the response of praise. When Irenaeus discusses the mammon passage in Matt. 6, he contrasts Lord and mammon. *Lord* in this moment does not mean simply divine rule over heaven and earth but more than this. As Lord, God demands service. The disciples who are in the service of the Lord may not submit themselves to the service of mammon (III.8.1). In response, this God is praised by the shepherds (III. 10.4).

The God of Irenaeus is a *Father*. In his lengthy argument in Book III on the unity of God, Irenaeus faces the term Father (III.11.1). In contrast to all Gnostic concepts of nature, mother

---

[75] I.20.3; II.9.1; 16.3; III.25.1. God *sends* his Son (III.12.2) and the Father commands, even though the Son is the *"demiourg"* (IV.38.3; I.12.1). *"Aktivität ist durchaus Gott eigentümlich,"* concludes N. Bonwetsch (*Die Theologie des Irenaeus* [Gütersloh: 1925], p. 55). The same result is expressed by John Lawson (*The Biblical Theology of Saint Irenaeus* [London: The Epworth Press, 1948], pp. 120 ff.).

[76] The difference can be seen by comparing IV.17.1 with Plato's *Tim.* 28 C. For Irenaeus, God is capable of creating life anew as he has created life in the first place (V.3.2).

[77] *Vivunt enim in quantum ea Deus vult vivere*—V.4.1.

principle, fertility, the Father is absolutely unique (III.6.1).
Fatherhood is understood through sonship, an understanding which
distinguishes the Father from all speculations about a cosmic
sustainer. The Father is the one who acts in his Son, who speaks
to his Son, who gives him the heritage of the nations, and who
subdues his foes (III.6.1; 10.6). The Father announces himself to
the world through the Son whom he has anointed (III.6.2).[78] The
Father-Son vocabulary is that of Incarnation and redemption (III.
17.4). The Father reveals the Son to men, the Son leads them to the
Father (III.13.2) —this is the axis for all that Irenaeus has to say
about God and Christ. The Father is a *God of mercy;* the Son is
the herald of the Father, announcing him, leading his people to
the Father (III.10.2). These are the components of Irenaeus'
theology.

This Father-Son concept is a central axis, not simply one angle
in a many-sided theology. The Son and the Spirit are the "two hands
of God" (V.5.1). Not only is this metaphor Hebraic [79] in its core,
but it also shows God as one who acts. The hand is a metaphor for
the incarnate act. The Spirit is likewise connected with the work
of God as the prophetic Spirit speaking in the Old Testament;
and as the Spirit performing the work of Christ *(Epid.* 26), leading men to Christ, or being led to by Christ (IV.19.2 ff.). In the
"two hands of God," the biblical God is meant, in contrast to any
eternal, natural, cosmic deity. Faced with this biblical realism of
the saving act, theistic, seminal-pantheistic, mystic, or natural theology does not altogether disappear but becomes secondary. *Unus
est Dominus Deus* is a statement concerning the God who acts in
his unity. The monotheistic formulas always lead to their christological counterparts (III.13.1); and therefore, *unus est Dominus
Deus* means a God who is witnessed to and praised.[80]

This biblical substance of the theological language in Irenaeus
can be traced in countless chapters. A few examples suffice. ἐπαγγελία

[78] Cf. also III.12.5 and IV.38.7. "Almighty Father" leads to the *oikonomia*
of the Son.

[79] See Lawson, *op. cit.,* pp. 123 ff. Spanneut *(op. cit.,* p. 286) fails to see the
conflict between such basically Hebraic language and the Stoic terminology
about God; his quotation of Rom. 10:12 misses completely the distinction between Christian and Stoic speech about God.

[80] III.25.7; cf. Sagnard's concluding remarks *(op. cit.,* p. 413).

is God's announcement through his Spirit (III.12.1); παραγγέλλω designates the bringing of the apostolic message (III.12.2); καταγγέλλω is the proclamation of the Christ (III.12.4). κηρύττω is used in the authentic apostolic sense: the announcement as the act of the prophets (III.12.5) directed toward Christ (III.12.4), announcing the birth of Immanuel (IV.33.11). This faith itself is understood as that which is proclaimed, yet which God himself gives through his Son to unite man with him (*Epid.* 43).[81] The christological language is likewise biblical. Christ is the one who is born as man, who rises from the dead, who descends and ascends again, who suffers and is crucified, who is made flesh and bears the sin of man in his death.[82] The christological language speaks about the wood of the cross, the "mediator between God and men," and uses the metaphor of the first man and second man, the first Adam and the second Adam.[83] "To cleanse with his own blood" (V.1.1) is a New Testament phrase. The Logos is not the principle of reason within the Godhead but the "Word which became flesh." [84] Not only does the demonstrative Old Testament vocabulary appear—Abraham, Moses, Isaiah—in the perpective of the One God in Christ; not only is the demonstrative New Testament vocabulary frequent—the figures, parables, speeches of the Synoptics, John, epistles—but the specific New Testament terminology reappears with new meaning. *Oikonomia* is the divine plan, applied

---

[81] *Epid.* 43. Even if Lawson (*op. cit.,* pp. 244 ff.) has violently protested against the attacks of Paul Beuzart (*Essai sur la théologie d' Irénée* [Paris: 1908], p. 125) and Joh. Werner (*Der Paulinismus des Irenaeus* [Leipzig: 1889], pp. 202 ff.), all the texts carefully discussed by Lawson still show that the emphasis on the intellectual assent to the *regula fidei* is stronger than on the *fiducia*. As we have to show in the following chapters that the language of Irenaeus is often biblical but contains unbiblical forces in more than a linguistic way, we cannot naïvely conclude that faith in Irenaeus is "surely in accord with Pauline doctrine" (Lawson, *op. cit.,* p. 244).

[82] IV.30.3; III.12.2; 16.6; 18.4; 18.7.

[83] V.17.3; III.18.7; V.5.1; 16.2.

[84] *Epid.* 6.IV.12.4; II.16.4. III.17.6: *Verum est ipse Deus.* IV.11.4 and V.1.1. "Word" expresses what Loofs (*op. cit.,* p. 355) called "identity of revelation" between God and Son. Irenaeus does not reject the Logos doctrine but because God is for him a living personality (Bonwetsch, *op. cit.,* pp. 57 ff.) this Logos doctrine is definitely restricted. Of course we cannot expect a concept of the Logos in the sense of W. J. Phythian-Adams ("The Logos Doctrine of the Fourth Gospel," *Church Quarterly,* 139 [1944], 1 ff.). Cf. Emil Brunner, *The Mediator* (London: The Lutterworth Press, 1934), pp. 249 ff. and 328 ff.

to the Old Testament, concerning the act of God through his Spirit in the prophets, and for its fulfillment in the Incarnation of his Son (*Epid.* 6) ;[85] *kairos* is the significant expression for the fulfillment of the divine *oikonomia* (IV.36.7) ; *koinonia*, in the sense of participation in life and light, is that which God *gives* (V.27.2). The language about the church as the body of Christ and his members, about the sacrament in connection with the Holy Spirit, and the emphatic rejection of schism [86]—these are biblical. And so finally is the language of eschatology, the judgment, the parousia of Christ, the new heaven and the new earth, the resurrection of the body, the realism in the whole eschatological thought of Irenaeus.[87]

This language is biblical not simply because it uses biblical speech. We have seen how this statement does not mean much in the existence of the church apart from the canon. The language of Irenaeus is biblical because it is Hebraic in a theological sense. His God is theocratic, merciful, a God who speaks, and not the nature-god of Gnostic experience or the rational principle of Justin. This language is biblical because its Hebraic substance has not been diluted by the process of Hellenization into a new nomistic diatribe. However, the language of Irenaeus is neither "Hebraic" nor Hebrew; it is Greek. We have to ask: Does this Greek element in the thought of Irenaeus infringe upon the substance of the Gospel? Does the balance between Jerusalem and Athens still comprehend Jesus and the Christ and the totality of the gospel, or does Irenaeus, despite all his efforts, succumb to the Gnostic or apologetic movements which he tries to evade?

Biblical Interpretation

The use of biblical vocabulary in Irenaeus is related to his biblical interpretation. The Gnostic vocabulary is to Gnostic allegory what the nomistic vocabulary is to nomistic allegory. The keryg-

---

[85] III.16.6; cf. Bonwetsch, *op. cit.,* p. 69.

[86] V.2.2; IV.18.6; 33.7. *Epid.* 42. III.12.15 and 17.2.

[87] Judgment, IV.40.1; parousia, IV.26.1; the new heaven and the new earth, V.36.1; σῶμα, V.31.2; the seeing of the Savior, V.36.1. Opposing Harnack, Winggren (*op. cit.,* pp. 54 ff.) has shown in a beautiful chapter the biblical aspect of sin in Irenaeus, with both a "physical" and an "ethical" dimension to it.

matic speech of Irenaeus attempts to transcend all four. His biblical language is the theological answer to nomistic and Gnostic speech and must be understood as part of his attempt to create a "biblical theology." [88]

Nomistic Christianity sees in the Bible primarily a sourcebook for ethical advice. To be sure, the language of redemption shines through here and there. Except in Ignatius this language is not really alive. Apologetic Christianity desires above all to find resurrection and Logos. Gnostic faith seeks in the Bible the dualistic mystery of veiled truth by which the ascent of the soul is explained and achieved. In all these attempts at interpretation, the Bible primarily serves a didactic purpose. Irenaeus takes the Bible as an entity in itself. He is reckoning with a comprehensive whole with which the church must grapple. Scripture is kerygmatic unity. His work against the heretics is one extensive attempt to demonstrate the unity of scripture and of biblical faith. For the Gnostics, this unity is broken. Marcion has a fine sense for the antithesis between the old and the new covenant. Hermas is no answer to Marcion but rather a justification for his view! Irenaeus is the theologian and exegete who begins the herculean and never-ceasing task of showing the unity of Old and New Testament, which is the unity of God and Christ, and which is the unity of creation and redemption. The struggle to overcome nomistic and Gnostic vocabulary is the endeavor of theology to express unity of faith.

The first step in this attempt lies in the demonstration of faith as *biblical argument*. The rejection of speculation does not occur on the level which the Gnostics desire, namely, their syncretistic world view. As a counterargument Irenaeus uses "simply" the biblical word—*"simpliciter et absolute et firme"* (III.10.1). This simplicity, however, is not simple-minded repetition of a biblical phrase or word. The process of biblical argument is considerably more complex—in this lies a thorough misunderstanding of a "biblical theology" for laymen as well as for theologians, approving or hostile. The biblical argument is one of elaborating the central

---

[88] We do not deal with many particular aspects of the biblicism in Irenaeus since the same problems arise from other angles. On the question of the gospel *versus* Paul in Irenaeus, consult Werner (*op. cit.,* pp. 25 ff.), on the "canon," Lawson (*op. cit.,* pp. 46 ff.) .

theme, of discovering the large context of a book, and of demonstrating the thread of faith within the whole. In his demonstration of Christology, Irenaeus takes up certain Pauline christological statements. He quotes from Romans the passages on the death and resurrection of Christ; from Corinthians, the reference to Christ crucified; and from Ephesians and Galatians, the mention of the second Adam, the blood, and curse of Christ. Then he continues, showing the same in the Synoptics: the suffering Christ, the Son of the living God, who carries his cross to his crucifixion (III.18.3-5). Irenaeus is not a systematic thinker who can offer a brilliant example of such biblical argument. The attempt is perspicuous, however. A theme is developed within a large biblical range, transcending individual books, and constantly taking both testaments into account. The Gnostics have often taken one passage and built extensive speculation on it. Irenaeus strives to argue from several views, cutting across books in order to establish a comprehensive biblical argument.

Irenaeus has attempted a second type of the same exegetical device. In Book III, he deals systematically with one Gospel after another to demonstrate the one God. The plurality of the gospel is a special problem for him. He interprets on a large scale the Synoptics and John, and then concludes with his famous suggestion concerning the tetramorphic Gospel (III.11.8). Yet in this demonstration Irenaeus refers unceasingly to other New Testament works and to the Old Testament. Biblical speech has become so much a part of his argument that he cannot present one particular concern without constantly referring to the whole. Biblical interpretation is intended to be interpretation within the total context of the Bible.[89] That the use of the material always involves selection, and a selection depending upon the central concern, has already been shown. For Irenaeus, this central concern is the proclamation of the one God who came to man and redeemed him in Christ.

With this interpretation, Irenaeus opens the path for serious theological exegesis. The argument for faith is steered into a biblical direction which is neither a fundamentalist proof-text method, nor the "discovery of moral values," nor the use of the Bible for the demonstration of ideas. What is anticipated and attempted in the

[89] Cf. Prestige, *op. cit.*, pp. 44-45.

work of Irenaeus is the argument for faith from the plenitude, unity, and extensiveness of scripture. *Oikonomia* flows through the entire argument, from before the first day of creation to the consummation of time. It reaches back into the vast canon of revelation and assembles from all possible sources the fragments required for its structure. The early Christian belief in an inspired canon, a belief which Irenaeus certainly would not have denied if he had had to take issue with it, transcends literalism. By grasping the essentials, Irenaeus points to the way to overcome the literalism of gnosis and allegory and to the way of confrontation with New Testament faith in its very nature, in the tension of the God of Moses who became man in Jesus of Nazareth.[90]

Hebraic Realism

A survey of the use of biblical language in the second century shows two collateral trends, the spiritualization of the *ekklesia* and the materialization of the *mysterion*. For Hermas, the church was created before all else (*Vis.* II.4.1); for the Second Clement, the spiritual church is the archetype for the female (14.2); for the Marcosians *ekklesia* is an emanation parallel to the first man (Iren. *Adv. Haer.* I.14.5). Such speculative language about an archetypal *ekklesia* had been used in Eph. 5:29-32, but nowhere does the author of this letter elaborate on any cosmic level or emanative processes concerning the *ekklesia;* therefore, the spiritualization of the biblical *ekklesia,* even in its closest proximity to "Gnostic" language, is checked by the presence of an earthly body (4.11-12). For Paul, *ekklesia* is always a congregation, as in Corinth or Galatia. As a matter of fact, where he develops the theme of the Body of Christ to its fullest (I Cor. 12), he does so in a way which is ontologically so impossible that it becomes obvious that his focus is not any pre-existent or empirical relation between a spiritual Christ and his body before, during, or after the Incarnation, but quite simply the present situation in Corinth: "If one member suffers, all suffer together; if one member is honored, all rejoice together with him" (I Cor. 12:26). Much of the tedious and hair-

[90] Beside creating such a "new exegesis," Irenaeus is also responsible for binding exegesis to the church (cf. Robert M. Grant, *The Bible in the Church* [New York: The Macmillan Company, 1954], pp. 58 ff.).

splitting attempts to make a coherent system out of I Cor. 12 tend to forget that here is no Gnostic ontology (which would explain metaphysically the relation between Christ and the church), but Hebraic understanding of language, designating not *universalia* but physical reality (the congregation in Corinth with all its problems) in relation to Christ. The language makes use of Stoic phrases, such as the metaphor of the human organism, but even in Eph. 5 it speaks of the mundane duties of man and wife (obedience, love, fear), followed by advice to children and slaves (6:1-8).

In defiance of Gnostic ecclesiologies, such Hebraic realism comes back in Irenaeus. The church has Christ as its head (V.18.1) but it is earthly, everywhere (IV.36.2), embracing the whole world (V.20.1). The church is conceived in historical continuity, prefigured in Israel (*Epid.* 26), whose congregation of faith is the older church (*Epid.* 94). As the church of the martyrs (IV.33.9) it has received the adoption and inheritance promised to Abraham (IV. 8.1). Of course, the church is animated by the Spirit (III.24.1), it is paradise planted in this world (V.20.1), but it is also established (IV.33.8), in Germany, Spain, and Egypt (I.10.2). If this physical aspect is taken seriously, it must lead to some emphasis on tradition. There is no metaphysical speculation about the Body of Christ anywhere in Irenaeus.[91] The Body of Christ is bound to the visible church (IV.33.8) and its unity (IV.33.7).

This nonspeculative use of *ekklesia* has an important consequence in the physical language concerning eschatology. Using extensive quotations from the prophets, Irenaeus expresses himself in the most physical language possible (V.34.1 ff.) when speaking of the kingdom of God. He denies emphatically the demythologized eschatology of Gnosticism by maintaining the terrestrial Jerusalem (V.35.2). The counterpart of this is the plastic language about resurrection in I Cor. 15. The Hellenistic mind could only make use of it either in terms of immortality of the soul, or of reincarnation—the two solutions in Gnosticism; but Irenaeus, defending the resurrection of the flesh (V.31-32) composes striking biblical phrases: "He will Himself renew the inheritance of the earth,"

---

[91] ʾΕκκλησία is earthly, related to succession and tradition. As we shall see in the next section, there is a speculative note to ἐκκλησία, but it does not concern the heavenly body as in Valentinianism.

drinking the wine with his disciples at the great banquet (V.33.1).
Naïve eschatology? Unfortunately, Irenaeus had not read *Kerygma
and Myth*. Yet this naïve language preserves a salient element of
biblical verbalization, the Hebraic quality of the earth in language
about God and his acts. The fall (Gen. 3:15), the day of Yahweh
(Amos 5:18-20), the dance of praise (Ps. 149:1-3) —all infiltrations
of Hellenistic modes of speech have not deprived Irenaeus of such
plastic Old Testament language which is extant from the Gospel
of Matthew ("The kingdom of heaven is like treasure hidden in a
field"—13:44) to the dramatic structure of the book of Revelation
("And I saw the holy city, new Jerusalem, coming down out of
heaven"—21:2). This Hebraic quality of language shines through
the eschatology of Irenaeus even though the plastic form does not
reach the artistic power which it held in the parables of Jesus or
the letters of Paul.

The counteraspect to this down-to-earth language lies in the
sacramental sphere. In the middle of the second century an unknown compiler of the concluding verses of Mark 16 presented a
saying of Jesus which must have been part of an Apocryphal tradition before him: "He who believes and is baptized will be saved;
but he who does not believe will be condemned" (Mark 16:16). In
the first half, faith and baptism, in the second—only faith! The
form of this saying is another masterful example for what we
mean by Hebraic verbalization. If life is conceivable only in relation to a living God, then the earthly language—the land, the
symbol, man—cannot become forces to which God could ever submit, even though God chooses or accepts these forces fully as his
own. "The earth is the Lord's." (Ps. 24:1.) The sacrament is therefore *mysterion*, which may mean offer, promise, presence; but it
cannot turn into an *opus operatum* if understood as subservient to,
not as dominating, the living God. This is the difference between
a Hebraic and a magical sacramental reality. The first type is already in danger at the turn of the first century. The Gnostics believe either in a faith free from baptism (Iren. *Adv. Haer.* I.21.1)
—or enact magical rites.[92] What has cracked is exactly the Hebraic

---

[92] We have mentioned in the first chapter the extensive material collected by
Fendt, *op. cit.*

language about the earth in relation to God. The earth is no longer the Lord's; it has been split in two. In Ignatius of Antioch, the Lord's Supper has become a "Drug of Immortality" (*Eph.* 20.2) ;[93] in the Clementine homilies, baptism is the only condition for salvation (VIII.23). The Lord's Supper has become a sacrament of the Mystery cults; the grace of baptism and the command to baptize are understood magically.

As we shall see in a later section, the Irenaean Eucharist cannot be neatly separated from this second-century trend in sacramental thought. Perhaps baptism cannot be either, in every respect. Yet certain aspects of his baptismal language throw light upon the distinction we try to make. In the third chapter of the *Epideixis* Irenaeus explains baptism as the forgiveness of sins; as the seal of eternal life; and as a new birth, done in the name of the Father, in the name of the Incarnation, Death, and Resurrection of Christ, and in the name of the Holy Spirit (*Epid.* 3). The baffling fact for anyone familiar with second-century Christian thought lies in the complete lack of the concern, first found in Hermas, about the possibility of *metanoia* after baptism. Callistus would certainly not have ended a baptismal instruction where Irenaeus did.[94] Could Irenaeus have been so naïve as to be unaware of the precarious situation of a holy church consisting of large numbers of Christians not transformed by baptism? This is certainly not so. Nor can we assume an exceptionally holy congregation in Lyons and Vienne, even after the intense persecution. If neither Hermas nor Cyprian, neither Callistus nor Novatian is found in Irenaeus in this instance, it is because his baptismal language is partly Hebraic. Baptism is adoption (III.6.1) coming from God as a new generation (V. 18.1) ; [95] this is a transformation of man by God's acceptance. The emphasis is always the fruit of life (III.17.2), the ethical change. The Christian is involved in a promise which for him is fact, hence the first person: *"Our* bodies have received the unity" (*Ibid.*), *"We*

---

[93] Beside φάρμακον ἀθανασίας Ignatius also has, to be sure, a more symbolic view of communion, *Phil.* 5.1 and *Tral.* 8.1.

[94] Hipp. *Ref.* IX.1.20.

[95] III.17.2: *Unde et Dominus pollicitus est mittere se Paraclitum qui nos aptaret Deo;* this is the introduction to the baptismal allegory about flour. On baptism as adoption see Winggren, *op. cit.*, p. 162.

have received the baptism" (*Epid.* 3).[96] This is the difference between metaphysical and "actual" sacramental language. For Irenaeus it is response, fact, and promise—all in relation to God, all in faith—reality to be sure, physical reality, but not reality as a system or a consequent form of initiation, but reality to an acting God. This can be the case because the concept of God in Irenaeus is that of a God who acts rather than of a God who is. This is why baptism and spirit can be connected without the one's denying the other.[97]

THE LANGUAGE OF THEOLOGY AS RESPONSE

The Place of the Ekklesia

Second-century Christianity had to determine the use and place of scripture in Christian faith. The establishment of the canon, the *regula fidei,* and monarchical episcopacy was not the work of Irenaeus but was already an established fact when he became Bishop of Lyons. In his writings, however, we find the theological evaluation of this establishment. The questions we have to put to the language of Irenaeus are questions put to the state of the church at the end of the second century and to the relationship between theology and the church as a whole.

We recall the basic chain of his language. It contains, for instance: *unus Deus—vere Deus, vere homo—recapitulatio—imago Dei—*

[96] Even in III.17.2 the negative expression is made in the first person, about Irenaeus and his fellow Christians: *Sicut enim de arido tritico massa una fieri non potest sine umore neque unus panis, ita nec nos multi unum fieri in Christo Iesu poteramus sine aqua quae de coelo est.* And the introduction to this passage is the statement about adoption quoted in the preceding note. Forgiveness of sins is a unique act (IV.27.2) not to be repeated (Benoit, *op. cit.,* p. 190), as adoption takes place only once.

[97] The work on pre-Nicaean repentance by Joseph Grotz (*Die Entwicklung des Bussstufenwesens in der vornicänischen Kirche,* Freiburg i. Br: 1955) makes it quite clear that Irenaeus does not belong in the history of the development of repentence from Hermas to Nicaea. When Grotz, therefore, claims that behind the penitential conceptions of Hermas there must have been the concepts of the primitive church (*op. cit.,* p. 14), then it is obvious that in this respect Irenaeus does not represent the church. In a crucial text (IV.27) Irenaeus could have mentioned such a discipline had he been in agreement with it; but as Poschman points out, there is no indication for this at all (*op. cit.,* p. 218). Irenaeus can have a penitential attitude without creating a penitential system (IV.40.1; cf. Benoit, *op. cit.,* p. 195) because he has not forced baptismal language into a sacramental principle.

vox apostolorum—ecclesia. This chain maintains the heart of New Testament faith, the fulfillment of the acts of God in his Son. It comprises the Father and Christ; it draws man into both as being bound to the one God and to the act in his Son. The question we have to raise in this paragraph concerns the last two links of Irenaeus' chain; we shall discuss the middle links later. Irenaeus realizes the place of the church and of tradition in his argument against the Gnostics. Scripture is not open to free-lance fantasy but is riveted to *ekklesia*.[98] Bound with the latter is truth.[99] The concept which demonstrates the historic flux is *tradition*.[100] Truth is the authentic understanding of scripture which the church has preserved since apostolic times. The consequence of such argumentation is formulated in the famous phrase of III.24:1: "Where the church is there is the Spirit of God; and where the Spirit of God is, there is also all grace; the Spirit namely is Truth." *Ekklesia—pneuma—aletheia.* What does this trifold equation mean?

1. Let us take three essential designations for the church, used by Irenaeus: Body of Christ, bride of Christ, and mother. "Bride" points toward adoption and purity, won by Christ for her sake (IV.21.3); "body" emphasizes the unity of the church (IV.33.7) and its subordination to the head which is Christ (III.16.6); and "mother" designates the capacity of the congregation to nourish its believers (III.24.1). All three are meaningful and expressive metaphors, representing vital concerns of the Christian community. These concerns are assumed even when the words are not mentioned, such as in the "coaptation of the church to the figure of the image of the Son" (IV.37.7), in the allegory of Hosea's bride (IV. 20.12), and in the distribution of faith to the sons (III *Praef.*).

As we look at these metaphors, the first two already appear to be in conflict with each other, the one illustrating the union with the Christ, the other describing purity of faith by the adoption of Christ. The metaphor of the oneness goes contrary to the metaphor

[98] IV.33.8; Γνῶσις ἀληθὴς ἡ τῶν ἀποστόλων διδαχὴ καὶ τὸ ἀρχαῖον τῆς ἐκκλησίας σύστημα κατὰ παντὸς τοῦ κόσμου. Cf. also IV.32.1.

[99] Alone in *Adv. Haer.* there are over one hundred references (Bonwetsch, *op. cit.*, p. 31). Cf., for instance, III.12.7; IV.2.6; V.33.6.

[100] *Evenit itaque neque Scripturis iam traditione consentire eos*, III.2.2; also in *Praef.* to Book III and in III.3.1. Cf. Turner, *op. cit.*, p. 312, and Beuzart, *op. cit.*, p. 149.

of purity and adoption, because no matter what bridal romanticism may dream about idealistic henosis, a bridegroom and his spouse are still two people. When bride of Christ is used simultaneously with body of Christ in any realistic fashion, then the language about the church is in difficulty. The *bride* of the Christ is the not-Christ, though adopted, wed, purified; while the *body* is the Christ himself, organically. The first contains the relationship of an I to a Thou, while in the second it has disappeared. We have here a classic example for the problem involved in mixing basically Hebraic (bride, adoption) with basically Greek (organism, plurality=one) metaphors. The consequences for the doctrine of the church are of great importance. The combination of the two metaphors taken as realistic language cannot mean, obviously, the totality of baptized people, either ethically or intellectually. It is simply not the case that all baptized Christians live and believe like pure brides; as the bishop of a congregation, Irenaeus must have known this. To use them for the episcopate denies the real significance of the body, in the Pauline sense of the diversity of gifts; to use them for any abstraction like canon, creed, rule of faith deprives bride of its metaphorical meaning. This combination can, however, lead to an emphasis on *Corpus Christi* as an external, hierarchical body to which the attribute of "bride" is pinned even though the church is quite obviously not pure in its entirety; or it leads toward the Donatis and Novatian emphasis on the *communio sanctorum* where unity is sacrificed for the sake of the purity of the bride. In both cases, the coalescence of two human metaphors threatens the balance between two biblical metaphors. The loss of this biblical balance illustrates the split into Catholic and protestant types of Christianity.[101]

The threat is aggravated by the appearance of the mother metaphor, a term not frequently but symptomatically present in the crucial passage on the church in III.24.1. When the land could no longer be the mother in the Diaspora, the mother mythology enters the literature of Judaism. Even though traces of this myth are found

---

[101] Prümm (*op. cit.*, pp. 265 ff.) is not aware that he is dealing with two conflicting metaphors, and reads, therefore, the meaning of the "body" metaphor into the "bride" metaphor, thereby depriving the latter of its Hebraic nature.

in the New Testament (Gal. 4.26),[102] the mother principle could not play a key role—for the reasons outlined in the chapter on Gnostic language. When the mother concept is put side by side with the body and bride language, the I-Thou relation of the bride metaphor, already challenged by the body metaphor, is further weakened. The church as mother is an acting subject,[103] while the church as bride is the object of the bridegroom. She receives the implications which the Gnostics as well as the gentile Christians, the adherents of the Diaspora as well as the worshipers of Isis sought in the principle of womanhood: *magna Mater,* on an earthly plane. We cannot say that the Christian community should not be described by mother and bride as long as these two metaphors are understood in their conflicting pronouncements; but when this is no longer seen, then the bridal or the nourishing body receives an emphasis which is fatal to Christian faith because it has been created into an entity of its own.

Did Irenaeus create such an entity? I do not think he did, although at times he comes close to it.[104] The mother metaphor is cautiously and rarely employed; in the crucial passage of IV.33.8 Irenaeus carefully balances scripture and tradition; and—probably the most important reason—he does not make any allowance for a second repentance. Had he really pressed his metaphors he would have been forced to deal with the question of what happens when the bride's members betray the head of the body. He was certainly not so blind as to be unaware of some sort of *communio permixta:* The disturbing fact that he does not deal with the issues of Hermas,

---

[102] To take Gal. 4:26 and treat it as a vital passage for Pauline theology (Joseph C. Plumpe, *Mater Ecclesia* [Washington: The Catholic University of America, 1943]; see the index on p. 131 with the references on Gal. 4:26!) is doing exactly what the Gnostics have done—namely, to take one biblical phrase that appeals to the theologian, and make an axiom out of it, even though the reference is a single one in the bible. Even though Paul's use of the metaphor of the mother must be acknowledged, Paul's other metaphors concerning the church make it quite clear that he never had any intention of creating an ecclesiology in the sense that Plumpe suggests (p. 127).

[103] *"Fide quam ab apostolis Ecclesia percepit, et distribuit filiis suis,"* III Praef. *"In eius sinu educari et Dominicis scripturis enutriri,"* V.20.2.

[104] Winggren (*op. cit.,* p. 161-62) does not see the conflict between the two metaphors when he claims that they are "wholly in line"; the concept of adoption and the concept of a new birth represent two worlds, and much depends on how they are employed. In no case are they *wholly* in line.

Callistus, and Novatian shows that he still uses his language about the church in some sort of Pauline fashion, proclaiming the message, stating in relation to Christ what the church is, without making theological principles out of his metaphors.[105] The awareness of the acting God in the grace of Christ prevents Irenaeus from letting this triad of images for the church become an independent unit; only at times does he stand on the edge of permitting[106] this, because his anti-Gnostic emphasis forces him into it.[107] And now— as always in borderline situations in the church—one step may break the axis which is essential for Christian faith. This borderline is symptomatic for theological language; once it transgresses this border it ceases to be Christian language, but unless it does stand on this frontier it is not really the Christian language of re-

---

[105] In modern understanding of language the sentence "In the Church the Incarnate is unfailingly present" (Georges Florovsky, "Eschatology in the Patristic Age," *Studia Patristica* TU 64, [1957], p. 238) sounds absurd; the Incarnate is not, and has not always been, present in the Church. Yet, the statement could have been made by Irenaeus, (*a*) for anti-Gnostic purposes (III.5.1), and (*b*) in "kerygmatic" language, proffering the promise of God to the church without using these words as tools for ecclesiastical arrogance or a power struggle for a see. Such is the problem in the use of *omnis gratia* of III.24.1; it may be language of promise, but at the same time it may turn into language of diabolic institutionalism (Th. Rüsch, *Die Entwicklung der Lehre vom Heiligen Geist bei Ignatius von Antiochia, Theophilus von Antiochia, Irenäus von Lyon* [Zürich: 1952], p. 117).

[106] Here lies one of the main difficulties in harmonizing the various trends in the research on Irenaeus because each scholar accepts or criticizes texts which are vital for him. This is obviously the case in our own study; the historian fools himself if he does not see his limitation at this point. An interesting case can be observed in the work by Prümm (*op. cit.*, pp. 235 ff.). On one hand, Prümm claims that the step from the NT to the theology of sacramental deification was an "organic and healthy" development of scriptural language (p. 237); on the other hand, he knows the contradiction between an acting God and such speech of sacramental deification. He tries to solve the dilemma by a Thomistic analogy of being (p. 238). The problem is that such interpretation by the refined frame of Aristotelian-medieval ontology violates what modern scholarship has established: that we are dealing with two modes of thinking and that the Hebraic speech loses its character when it is pressed into Greek categories of thought. Ever since the NT, the clash between the two is inevitable; such an interpretation of the clash by Thomistic ontology, however, does not give sufficient justice to the Hebraic character of NT metaphors.

[107] III.12.13; 24.1; IV.33.7. By comparing the passages in III.6.1 and V.18.1 with the aeonic speculations of the Gnostics and the lady of Hermas we can measure the contribution of Irenaeus toward both a theological and an earthly understanding of *ekklesia*.

sponse. In Cyprian of Carthage or in Tertullian, *mater ecclesia* terminologies are no longer safely checked by language about an acting God in the acting grace of Christ.[108] Our triad has been turned into an ecclesiology; the axis is broken.

2. The combination of *aletheia* and *ekklesia* in Irenaeus shows us the same conflict from a second angle. He claims that the Apostles taught exactly [109] what the church preaches (III.12.13), but earlier writings which we have examined do not verify this affirmation at all. When the church preaches such an astonishingly minute amount of essentially Christian substance by using as many Christian words as the Gnostics have, how can you equate *aletheia* and *ekklesia?* [110] The answer points toward the canon and creed, the "doctrine about the Son of God" (III.1.1) and the "rule of faith" (III.15.1). But in this answer, the church paralleled by truth is not, and cannot be conceived of as, the body of Christ in any Pauline sense, simply because all our documentation from the first half of the second century fails to indicate in any way the veracity of Irenaeus' statements. Many circles within the church have not grasped the essential Christian truth. Certainly this is no accusation at all, for Christian faith had to come into its own gradually; but the equation of Irenaeus cannot be held to designate the church as *aletheia* and as body, bride, and mother on an equal level.

[108] Tert. *De Anim.* 43 (*vera mater viventium figuraretur ecclesia*). *De Monog.* 7 and *De Pud.* 51 (the invocation of the mother!). The classical text, of course, is Cypr. *De Unit.* 6 (*Habere non potest Deum Patrem qui ecclesiam non habet matrem*); it is this chapter with its emphasis on bride and mother which expresses the reversal of all early Christian language on baptism and forces the church into either the sacrament of penance or the Novatian or Donatist split. Prümm (*op. cit.,* pp. 265 ff.) cannot reckon with this, for dogmatic reasons which we fully understand. But we must protest against his simple dichotomy between an "hierarchic" (Roman Catholic) *versus* a "liberal" view of this period. The problem is simply not that easy. When Paul says "body of Christ" he does *not* mean "*Gesamtorganismus des geistigen Christus*" (Prümm, *op cit.,* p. 278).

[109] "Exactly" may be a somewhat strong translations for *sic* (Sagnard, *op. cit.,* p. 243), yet the context makes clear that Stephan did not teach anything else, *Stephanus haec docens,* and therefore *sic* does have definite emphasis.

[110] The dilemma has been excellently formulated by Bengsch (*op. cit.,* p. 71) in his attempt to distinguish between "normative" and "constitutive." As Bengsch realizes himself, this interpretation is in itself subject to being interpreted (p. 72). And here, for Irenaeus, tradition is precisely *not "Ueberlieferung im strengen Begriffe"* (against G. Söhngen, *Die Einheit in der Theologie* [München: 1952], p. 320) whom Bengsch quotes in his conclusions on this issue, p. 74).

207

To compare the language of Irenaeus with the literature of the second century is proof enough that his equation is not an expression of fact, but the theological demand to take seriously the *aletheia* which the *ekklesia* preserves and maintains, i.e., the canon and the creed. To possess a creed and a canon somewhere in the cupboard of tradition does not make this creed and canon a meaningful axis of faith; unless communication utters the Christocentric language, it cannot radiate its faith. Irenaeus draws the conclusion from what lies embedded in the primitive Christian tradition and brings it to life; this is, however, a theological claim rather than a statement of fact concerning the "church as body of Christ." In his language about the axis of faith, Irenaeus represents a prophetic claim within the church by challenging a Christianity which possesses canon and creed to make use of them creatively, to wake up from its Rip van Winkle sleep.[111] This is the voice in the wilderness leading the church back to its origin on the one hand, and pointing, on the other, to the ways in which Christian theology can be creative. The challenge of Irenaeus is not the voice of tradition but a charismatic act.

3. The observation of the creative contribution in such theological language leads us to the third dilemma, namely the one of spirit and *ekklesia*. When the second century establishes its episcopal structure, the biblical concept of the congregation of faith tapers off; without wild violation of the texts one cannot say that the primitive Christan church was always an hierarchically governed body. Such tapering occurs in every structure of the church, and Rome as well as the charismatic sects are but limited representations of the New Testament community. The danger sets in when the limitation is identified with revelation itself. Here lies the problem of Irenaeus.[112] He assumes that the church and truth are

---

[111] This is not the voice of orthodox circles (against Beuzart, *op. cit.*, pp. 5-6) but a "prophecy for the future" (Harnack, *op. cit.*, I, 565, Enslin, *art. cit.*, p. 144). That Irenaeus never claimed any charismatic gift for himself (Eus. *H. E.* V.7) does not exclude, but rather underlines, his possessing such charisma (see Amos 7:14-15). Of course, we do not have pure prophetic charisma because Irenaeus maintains history and apostolicity (Bonwetsch, *op. cit.*, p. 39); because of the death of the "prophet" which we have described in chapter 2, the charisma in the church had to seek new ways.

[112] III.11.9 (cf. Theodor von Zahn, *Geschichte des Neutestamentlichen*

without contradiction (IV.33.8) and that the spirit and the church
are identical (III.24.1) . It is from this inference that the fatal fusion
of bride, body, and mother originates. What happens when controversies arise between the canonical, creedal truth and the church?
Can then the body of Christ remain open to a spirit blowing where
it wills, or is the church dependent upon this equation of spirit
and *ekklesia?* We can ask the question differently. When the church
has chosen one type of apostolic congregation, does it attribute an
identical weight of revelation to an ecclesiastical form which is
only a sector of the apostolic church? Again, for Irenaeus there is
no subordination of faith to the church because in his prophetic
contribution he shows the church what it possesses and how it
should make creative use of its possession.[113] This very contribution, however, can turn against the church; [114] as in all great
prophets of history—Hildebrand, Francis of Assisi, Luther—what
was the charismatic thrust may become the demonic tools of an
institution preserving established religion and killing the spirit in
fanatic zeal. The Irenaean equation may lead to the sterile language of ecclesiasticism in all its frigidity, quenching prophetic
life.[115]

Kanons [Leipzig: 1892], II, 968 ff.) The important text is in V.6.1, πολλῶν
ἀκούομεν ἀδελφῶν ἐν τῇ ἐκκλησίᾳ προφητικὰ χαρίσματα ἐχόντων.

[113] The Holy Spirit is the main force eliminating dualistic metaphysics (Paul
Galtier, *Le Saint Esprit en nous d'après les pères Grecs* [Roma: 1946], pp. 59 ff.) .
The problem is understood indeed by Wolfgang Schmidt (*Die Kirche bei Irenäus*
[Helsingsfors: 1934], p. 31) when he assumes his duty to seek an Irenaean
"Kirchengedanken" but not an Irenaean *"Kirchenbegriff."*

[114] Concerning III.3.2, Schmidt (*op. cit.,* p. 79) is right: the interpretation of
this passage has become a confessional dispute between Protestant and Roman
Catholic scholars. I refuse to contribute to this battle by dealing with the
passage (see the discussion by Sagnard, *op. cit.,* pp. 103 ff. and 414 ff.) . The
very fact that this passage *could* have become the cause for such a dispute shows
dramatically the place of Irenaeus in the church of the second century. III.3.2 is
not merely a problem because the Greek original is missing—to assume this
would be to evade the issue—but because it *can* lead to different interpretations.

[115] Lawson (*op. cit.,* p. 105) speaks about the "gap between what [Irenaeus]
himself takes to be his principles and the way in which a dispassionate onlooker
will find them to work out in practice." Even though there is no church or rule
of faith "standing over against Scripture to interpret it" (*op. cit.,* p. 104) , this
principle may lead toward absolute supremacy of tradition over scripture. III.5.1
may lead to similar consequences (Adolf von Harnack, *Ueber den privaten
Gebrauch der Heiligen Schriften in der Alten Kirche* [Leipzig: 1912], pp. 36 ff.) .
Every contribution to the history of Christian thought threatens that which
it safeguards.

The dilemma in Irenaeus can be illustrated finally by the different processes at work in his focus on ecclesiology and Christology. With regard to both Christ and the church, this second-century theology creates a focus of speech: the Incarnate Christ and the apostolic church. From the viewpoint of biblical language, the two are not on the same level. The christological language of the second century is rooted in the ever-recurring christological language of the New Testament, the Son bringing the kingdom in the Synoptic tradition; the crucified Christ of the Pauline epistles; the Son who is sent from heaven in the Johannine writings. The focus on Christ grows from the central concern of the gospel even though there is a restatement of many points. But the language about *ekklesia* does not maintain the same importance either in extent or concern of one specific form of *ekklesia*. The church cannot exist without both focusing on the Christology by the language of its period, and tapering the plurality of authority; but once the difference between the tapering and focusing of these two concerns is lost from sight, the grace of Christ is strangled by the chains of an institutional principle, episcopal, congregational, or pentecostal. It is symptomatic, however, that Irenaeus, who at times seems to come close to such a threat, can accept without scruples the Montanist charisma.[116] This proves that he never meant the equation of Spirit and *ekklesia* to lead to the consequences which are inherent in his formulations. This, too, is the sign of prophecy. Some call it naïve; some call it authentic. Perhaps it is both.

The Description of the New Life

The immeasurable merit of Irenaeus is that he steered theology into a course which moves toward the core of the New Testament, namely, the theme of God meeting man in Christ. The way in which Irenaeus grasps this theme discloses mercilessly that Christian theology even in its most sublime expression of the event of the Incarnation is never identical with the canonical reflection of this event.

A term which comprehends beautifully the faith of Irenaeus is

[116] III.11.9. Cf. Lietzmann, *op. cit.*, II, 203-4.

recapitulation.[117] In its many shadings *"recapitulatio"* phrases what the Incarnation brought to humanity: the restoration of man through death's being stripped of its power (III.18.7), the consummation of creation in the Son (III.16.6), and the cancellation of the sin committed through the first tree, by obedience exhibited on the second tree (V.19.1). Such restoration of man is the result of a divine plan, *oikonomia* (III.23.1), whereby the Son entered the history of Israel to accomplish God's redeeming will (*Epid.* 37). Here is a good example of a focal term, chosen by theology in order to verbalize in concentrated form a pivotal concern of faith. In order to come to grips with the dynamics of faith, it is highly desirable that theology choose such focal language; the fact, baffling at first sight, that such a focal concept is both copious and complex enhances its value since it expresses the richness of Christian faith and demands that it be understood by correlative concepts.

Recapitulation means the restoration of Adam (*Epid.* 33). As the first man was "chained to death" (*Epid.* 31), the Son performs his saving work by assuming corporal identity with this man of death (*Epid.* 32). At stake is the humanity of the Savior—God becomes real flesh, my flesh (*Epid.* 31), and his victory occurs on an earthly plane (V.21.1). Such is the human situation, between Adam and Christ, not between soul and body, or between pneuma and Hyle, but between lost and recovered humanity, here on this planet. The recapitulating work revolves around the concept of the *imago Dei*. The image that God has created at the beginning of time (*Epid.* 5) has been lost by the man who was meant to live it (III.18.1),[118] what was formed in freedom (IV.20.1) was broken by disobedience (III.22.4). But the image is restored (III.18.1) and can live again (V.2.1), regenerated by the Spirit of God (V.9.2).

[117] For this concept see Reinhold Seeberg, *Dogmengeschichte* (Leipzig: 1908), I, 407; Bonwetsch, *op. cit.,* pp. 98 ff.; Lawson, *op. cit.,* pp. 140 ff.; and Winggren, *op. cit.,* pp. 79 ff., 122 ff., 173 ff. On the problem of translating ἀνακεφαλαίωσις into English see Winggren, *op. cit.,* p. xv. A French interpretation is given by Houssiau (*op. cit.,* p. 227): among other things *recapitulare* is *"ramener vers son chef"* (in III.16.6). Cf. the material in B. Reynders, *Lexique comparé du text grec et des versions latine, arménienne et syriaque de l'Adversus haereses de Saint Irénée* (Louvain: 1954).

[118] As we shall see later, *imago* and *similitudo* are not in the same category in all passages.

Such regeneration is the work of the Spirit (V.8.1). Man is made alive again in Christ. This process is described as vivification, a pithy concept for Irenaeus; in its concreteness lies its great force. "He brings to life" is not an idealistic hope for a nebulous future; the "new life" is a tangible result of prophetic preaching (IV.20.5). "If He does not vivify what is mortal and does not bring back to incorruptibility that which is corruptible, God has no power" (V.3.2). Vivification is the result of the "breath of life" by which man is changed into a new creature (V.12.2). Redeemed man is no mystic escapist from reality but "flesh possessed by pneuma" (V.9.2), vivified by the "Spirit of the remission of sins" (IV.31.2).

It is not the purpose of this study to present the whole theology of Irenaeus.[119] We simply want to show where the conflicts lie in view of the semantic development from the New Testament to the theology of the patristic church.

1. It makes a great difference whether language is the product of Gnostic hope or the reflection of a promise to the whole man. All theological language tends to turn into intellectual toying with ideas, ensuing from the loss of earthly reality. Christian theology faces the plasma, not merely the pneuma, and plasma is the flesh and soil of a created earth. Redemption speaks not merely to my existence but to my body; newness is life, and life is breath and blood. The language of Irenaeus accepts such newness in its paramount urgency; it views redemption not as a hope or a working hypothesis, not as a living possibility, but as a tangible actuality, proclaimed and lived by faith. The devil is jealous of God's creation (IV.40.3), and the Spirit descends into and dwells in the plasma of God (III.17.1). New life is in these creatures which are freed from the serpent, not merely as thought, but as love. Language about redemption must not be severed from the earth by which man has been molded (*Epid.* 32). "He who washed the feet of the disciples sanctified the entire body, and rendered it clean" (IV. 22.1).

Vivification is a comprehensive expression for the challenge of the Kingdom. Contrary to all hopeful admonition for spiritual improvement, it calls for a total change, both existentially and bodily,

[119] For the whole we have to refer the reader to Bengsch and Winggren. Extensive christological material is presented by Houssiau.

and it understands such a change as touching the flesh in which I exist and the breath by which I live. The Christian language of redemption demands a terminology of the now, of the earth, of the whole man; if it lacks this it is not worth being uttered. In vivification the former is the case. The term expresses Christian faith and comprehends the gigantic conflict of death and life and the future hope as a reality, here, in a world of misery and a body of pain. "Vivification" restates the new existence "in Christ."

2. Precisely here the difficulty arises as we penetrate the meaning of vivification in Irenaeus. In one sense, the process of "becoming alive" is an act *in faith*[120] (IV.20.5). Such would be the biblical understanding of a new existence. In other texts, however, a substantial metamorphosis is implied (V.12.1).[121] Vivification is set in close correlation to incorruptibility (V.3.2). That Christ has brought life means: Christ has conferred incorruptibility (II.20.3) of which man partakes (III.18.7). In this moment vivification leads into another sphere of redemptive communication. As certain passages tie God to "substance" (IV.9.1), and as the man whom he formed is *substantia* (IV.39.2), so the vivifying process is understood as a change of man's substance. Because of such language, Irenaeus is driven to distinguish in certain texts (but by no means all) between image and likeness. A substance may be changed but cannot be lost; what is restored is therefore the likeness (V.16.2). The association between vivification and incorruptibility leads the language of Christian redemption inexorably toward a language of deification.[122] The term "deification" itself is not yet present, but hints of such speech can be clearly discerned (III.18.6). To be redeemed is understood to mean: "to have one's nature which God created deified by Incarnation."

Ever since Ignatius of Antioch, forces have been at work which

---

[120] IV.20. 5. ἵνα ζωοποιήσῃ τοὺς χωροῦντας καὶ βλέποντας αὐτὸν διὰ πίστεως.

[121] V.12.1 ff. *Si enim mors mortificavit quare vita adveniens non vivificabit hominem?*

[122] In Irenaeus we find the first theological elaboration of divinization (Jules Gross, *La divinisation du Chrétien d'après les pères Grecs* [Paris: 1938], p. 1959). It is, of course, a divinization by the Spirit (Galtier, *op. cit.*, p. 54; Cf. V.6.2 and V.8.1), but the unity between Christ and the Christian (Paulus Gächter, "Unsere Einheit mit Christus nach dem hl. Irenaeus," *Zeitschr. f. kath. Theol.* 58 [1934], 503 ff.) is not so homogeneous with the Pauline one as Galtier (*op. cit.*, p. 67) had in mind.

contradict the Eucharistic language of primitive Christianity. "Medicine of immortality" (Ign. *Eph.* 20.2) is a concept belonging to the mystery cults and not to the table of the Lord. In Irenaeus the beautiful chapter of Book Five on the Eucharist shows the earthiness of Communion. We are nourished by creation, by "bread which comes from His creation"; and this bread Christ affirms "to be His own body" (V. 2.3). Above all sacramental speech stands the triad of faith, obedience, and righteousness (IV.17.4). This is not Ignatian but biblical language concerning the Eucharist. But then follows the deviation. After our bodies have partaken of the Eucharist "they are no longer corruptible, having the hope of eternal resurrection" (IV.18.5). The bond between the new life and incorruptibility channels the language about the Lord's Supper into a sphere of substantial objectivity. It is symptomatic that the word "hypostasis" is used to describe the result of the Eucharist; "the substance (ὑπόστασις) [123] of our flesh is augmented and sustained" (V.2.3). Our nature is changed. By the grace of the Lord's Supper our substance receives an augmented metamorphosis.

This substantial language of deification leads Christian theology into insurmountable difficulties. The substantial change and the ethical change do not simply coalesce in the life of the Christian believer; yet to make a distinction between the two does not make any sense precisely because "substance" is the total essence of man. Once a man's substance is changed, his life is changed; otherwise the substance is just not changed. When the affirmative and declaratory language of which we have spoken turns into language which makes substantial claims it is driven to make statements which the Christian theologian does not really mean. Here lies the basic dishonesty of all non-Hebraic speech about deification. "They must look more redeemed if I am to believe in their redemption," snapped Nietzsche; this is the justified attack against the language about deification understood in substantial fashion.

3. What is the difference between Hebraic realism and substantial realism? We have seen more of the first type in baptism and more of the second in the Lord's Supper, even though the two cannot neatly be divided, of course. Why should Irenaeus' doctrine

---

[123] This problem is tied to the fact that Irenaeus speaks in V.14.3 about the substance (οὐσία) of Christ's flesh (cf. Houssiau, *op. cit.*, p. 246).

of vivification not be a homogeneous rendering of the Synoptic "kingdom of God" and of the Pauline "new life"? Between the two types of "realism" lie three concepts, all of which deal with the relation of God to man. It would be unfair to deny that grace is present in the work of Irenaeus because he reckons with it (IV.11. 3). The fact is, however, that this concept does not play a key role in his thought. No matter how one presses one text or the other, the thought of Irenaeus does not take grace significantly into account.[124] Grace, however, is definitely a relational concept as Augustine was to discover. In Irenaeus a second biblical concept is lacking, justification by faith. Whatever the reasons for this omission may be,[125] it is again a word which emphatically counterbalances the substantial use of redemptive language. And it is striking that a man who uses so much of the Pauline vocabulary could miss the crucial term of Romans. Apparently here is a word which is not sufficiently alive for Irenaeus to make an impression on him. Justification is the most relational of all biblical concepts. It certainly has substantial consequences because lives are changed and bodies are healed; it is related to the sacrament and to the church. Yet as an act of faith and received through the grace of God, in Christ, justification by faith, more than any other term, removes the desire for a mystery cult in Christian theology.[126] Perhaps the most important aspect lies not in any particular word but in the nature of eschatological language. The Synoptics preach the coming of the Kingdom—this is realism; but the language of the future is already the language of the now. The two are intertwined not by a substantial conception of the Kingdom (a meta-

---

[124] *"Doch dürfte soviel bewiesen sein, dass bei Irenaeus die Gnade sicher nicht zu kurz kommt"* (Klebba, *op. cit.*, p. 149). Such an apologetic statement cannot prevent the observer from concluding that grace is not the main concern of Irenaeus.

[125] Lawson (*op. cit.*, pp. 250-51) understands the absence of the term as the result of its abuse in post-Pauline circles (cf. James 2:19). This argument neither explains nor excuses this lack; although Christology had been abused by the Gnostics, Irenaeus states his own. Moreover, the literature dependent upon Paul did not share in such abuse. We could perhaps say that in some way the absence of the term arises from the reaction to the Gnostic meaning of faith; nevertheless, here again Irenaeus did not hesitate to use Gnostic concepts in order to state his belief (Houssiau, *op. cit.*, p. 207).

[126] Spanneut (*op. cit.*, p. 419) observed that recapitulation receives a more cosmological dimension than it did in Pauline language.

physical entity in action), but by a Christ who proclaims judgment, who commences his redemption, and who assembles the congregation. This Hebraic realism leaves the language in tension between the present and the future,[127] without solving it by means of a dualism, a sacrament, a church or some individual faith. Eschatological realism for Paul is "in Christ," in faith, in living dependence upon the Spirit of God.[128] Once the eschatological dimension wanes, and once justification and grace are misconceived, the "substantial language" used by Paul to describe the new life becomes deification. It is highly symptomatic that Paul uses the verb "to make alive" but never the substantive.[129] Substantial realism in patristic theology is Hebraic realism deprived of its eschatological restraint. It is a reality of grace which is no longer aware that in all speech, sacrament, and community grace begins and ends with the living God; and it is actuality of faith that tends to forget the alien character of this very faith.

One aspect of this mutation of the language about justification and grace into a language about the deified life is apparent in a certain moralistic tendency in the work of Irenaeus. Referring to the renewal of the Spirit he confronts the vocation of the new life with the old prophecy; but when he comes to elaborate on the "old letter" of Rom. 7:6 he merely quotes Jeremiah at length (*Epid.* 90). Apparently he has not understood the text of Romans. The Old Testament is for him a law of love (IV.12.1) but there is no indication of the clash with the law in the advent of Christ. The prophetic and the Pauline *nomos* (*Epid.* 87) are placed in juxtaposition without the collision of which we have spoken earlier.[130]

---

[127] Pauline salvation is always, at the same time, present and future: Maurice Gauguel, "Le caractère, à la fois actuel et future, du salut dans la théologie paulinienne," in *The Background of the New Testament and Its Eschatology*, pp. 322 ff.

[128] Houssiau (*op. cit.*, p. 252) speaks about a certain *"déseschatologisation."* For Paul, the Christ is eschatological reality, a reality that can be extinguished by "divinization" the way it can be extinguished by law, church, gnosis—or faith. Gross (*op. cit.*, p. 106) has seen this when he states: *"dans les épitres pauliniennes la divinisation n'est conçue qu' à travers le Christ."*

[129] II Cor. 3:6; I Cor. 15:22; Gal. 3:21; Rom. 4:17; 8:11. The same holds true for John 5:21; 6:63.

[130] Because Stoic idioms and Stoicism are two different matters, depending upon the use of the Stoic idiom, Irenaeus cannot be neatly placed between Justin and Tertullian, as Spanneut has done (*op. cit.*, p. 253).

This is not merely a "lapse in expression." [131] Irenaeus makes this identification between the Law and the Christ too easily.[132] Such proximity to a new legalism will always occur where theological preaching surrenders the language of faith and eschatology in favor of a language about a new life. When the agony of the collision with the law is not experienced, the language of assurance may turn into another language of the law. Deification and moralism are two spheres in which Christian speech finds shelter once the vibration of living grace begins to slacken, and once the eschatological tension (the *now* versus the *then*) is dissolved.

4. The substantial language of Irenaeus cannot be the last word in a description of his speech. Reading through his argument against the Gnostics, we cannot fail to observe how the language of substance is time after time contradicted or corrected by the presence of Hebraic speech as we have portrayed it. Take a text just mentioned, a sacramental formulation. "Our bodies, after partaking of the Eucharist, are no longer corruptible, having the hope of the eternal resurrection" (IV.18.5); this expounds the link between vivification and incorruptibility. If this link were exclusively understood in terms of deification, the last clause would certainly not contain hope. "Possessing the fruit of eternal resurrection" or something similar would be a much more logical conclusion. "Hope" keeps this statement about an incorruptible body in suspense, despite all. Here lies the reason why Irenaeus nowhere expresses any kind of transubstantiation[133] which invariably results from the loss of Hebraic realism. There is no "medicine of immortality" in Irenaeus. We can see a similar corrective in his language about

[131] "Lapse in expression" Lawson, *op. cit.*, p. 237. Irenaeus makes use of his Greek education and uses even Greek doxographies (Robert M. Grant, "Irenaeus and Hellenistic Culture," Harvard Theological Review, 42 [1949], 41 ff., going back to Herman Diels, *Doxographi Graeci* ([Berlin: 1929], (1879), pp. 171-72).

[132] The excellent work by Bengsch does not see the sharp theological tension between "education in the OT and "sonship" in the NT (*op. cit.*, p. 149). Winggren put his finger on the crucial issue when he remarked that in Paul Adam is set over against Christ, whereas Irenaeus is forced to save the OT and cannot here parallel Paul because of his anti-Gnostic position (*op. cit.*, p. 17). Irenaeus' phrases concerning the difference between OT and NT are as cautious as they can be (*Epid.* 92 and 94).

[133] An extreme sacramental interpretation of Irenaeus, such as presented by L. Spikowski (*La doctrine de l'Église dans s. Irénée* [Strassburg: 1926], p. 51) must be rejected at once.

God; here substantial statements are often unconsciously corrected by parallel statements concerning the freedom and acts of God (III.21.1).[134] Language which speaks of a created order is often subservient to his description of the merciful and loving God (V.16.3), and there is no danger that the limitation of language about God would ever lead to any Areopagite transcendentalism; on the contrary, it leads to a humble Christian *"agnitio"* (II.28.6). The fragments of moralistic theology in Irenaeus are definitely repealed by the merciful *oikonomia* of God.[135] This is neither Clement of Rome nor the *Didache*.

In our discussion about primitive Christian versus Gnostic faith we defined New Testament language as a language between two poles of different strengths. The question was, when does the subordinate pole attain a power by which it annuls the authentic balance? The language of Irenaeus stands within this tension; but in his thought an inferior pole has begun to reach a momentum which may threaten the balance. On the other hand, the balance of Irenaeus is closer to the biblical language than practically the whole of the rest of his century. One reason for his variation from the New Testament is to be sought in the importance he gives to the new life as opposed to faith. All speculation about the deification of man must stand judged by the freedom of God, by the act of faith, and by the ethical consequence.[136] If this does not take place, Christianity is back at the mystery cults. But if this is accepted, then all language about deification which affects faith, church, sacrament, ethics cannot acquire any independence of its own but must remain "open," fluctuating, receptive to correction. Deification in a metaphysical sense marks the end of Christian faith. By using two types of realistic language, one arising from the Old Testament and the other intruding from the mysteries, Irenaeus represents a classical borderline situation in the church's response to Christ. A language of deification is beginning to infiltrate the

---

[134] In Irenaeus, terminology about deification is cautiously employed (Prümm, *op. cit.*, p. 253). Man "is destined to be like God but he has never been destined to be God," concludes Winggren (*op. cit.*, p. 99).

[135] V.8.2. There is a great difference whether the transcendence of the law of which Robert M. Grant speaks (*The Decalogue in Early Christianity*, p. 15) takes place merely in another teaching (by Christ) or in the person of Christ.

[136] Winggren (*op. cit.*, p. 211) concludes that man does not cease to be man.

language of realistic redemption—not conquering it, but on the verge of doing so. No borderline situation can maintain such balance. What Irenaeus phrases will become the threat of the next generation. And thus as the language of deification spreads in the next century the ethical rebellion is already awaiting its turn in the monastic movement in Egypt.

The Concepts of the Greeks

It is the duty of theological language to present the focus and to mark the accents. Since new problems are to be faced in the life of the church in every new generation, the language speaking to such a new situation must have its own specific quality. The cardinal terminology may remain static, but the emphasis given to each of the terms fluctuates, one theological generation counterbalancing the errors of the previous one. The focus never changes but the accents must always shift. They are already shifting in the New Testament.

As the accents are shifted in each new situation, theological communication employs—is compelled to employ and has always employed—non-Christian language. There are two types of such words, one a language transformed by the New Testament (canonical transformation), the other a completely new speech. Whereas we dealt with the first in our chapter on Gnosticism, we are concerned at this stage with the second. Several possibilities are open in the use of such non-Christian concepts.

1. Whenever a dialogue with contemporary society is begun, words of that age must be used. The *Epideixis* is addressed to Marcianus (1) and it is not odd, therefore, that metaphors and words familiar to him appear in Irenaeus' work. Symbolic language describes the final metamorphosis of the earth by Christ (*Epid.* 61). Instead of *ktisma* Irenaeus says plasma (V.12.3); he sets allegory beside the biblical parable (V.26.2), and the Greek term, "incomprehensible" (ἀκατάληπτος), is as good an adjective as any for the hidden character of God (IV.20.5). He knows the Greek tragedies (V.13.2) and quotes a phrase from Plato's Timaeus (III.25.5). As a good theologian he takes the liberty of coining a word of his own.[137] This crossing of the borders of language belongs

---

[137] ἀχαλιναγώγητος, V.8.2.

to the "proclamation of the Truth" (*Epid.* 98), which is the Alpha and Omega of Christian speech. It often has a hidden apologetic purpose, but it is often no more than an attempt to establish a point of contact. Terms familiar to the recipient enter into the proclamation, sometimes deliberately but more often by unconscious assimilation.

It would be absurd to claim that the content of faith is harmed whenever a nonbiblical word is received into Christian speech. The mention of a telephone or a jet plane makes a sermon neither less nor more Christian. The use of non-Christian language for the proclamation of faith, in the service of faith, can be of the highest value since it gives to Christian faith a specific means of addressing a contemporary situation. No preaching is done relevantly without some use of this borrowing technique. The critique of culture; the art forms of faith; the restatement of the Christian axioms—all this takes place with the constant acceptance of a non-Christian vocabulary. The question is not whether or not this can be done but whether the new word leaves or destroys the center of faith.

We may enter the conflict at this point. When Irenaeus describes the law of the Old Testament as *naturalia legis* (IV.13.1),[138] as natural precepts (IV.13.4) which are "noble and common to all" (IV.16.5), he makes an equation which he had never intended to make. The Mosaic law is not a natural precept but an expression of the will of God, and is thereby diametrically opposed to the natural realm of Canaan. The law of Yahweh is not the law of Baal. Had Irenaeus been pressed on this issue he would not for a moment have quibbled with such an objection. Here is the first axiom in any use of contemporary language: every concept is potentially capable of ruining the focus when viewed in the wrong perspective. This does not relieve the Christian from the duty to avail himself of such language; it compels him, however, to be on his guard. A later age may read an identification of Mosaic and Stoic *nomos* into a concept that originally nowhere threatened the uniqueness of God's *oikonomia*.

2. The New Testament does not possess a word for the freedom of the human will. *Eleutheria* in John and Paul means something

---

[138] The concept of "natural law" goes back to Justin *Apol.* II.2 and *Dial. Tr.* 45, Athen. *Disc.* 14 (cf. Spanneut, *op. cit.*, pp. 252 ff.).

distinct from either rational or ethical decision. Freedom, in the famous formulation of I Cor. 9:26, is service, not bondage in a determinative sense but living response. It is not conceived in the framework of possibility or choice but of love; in freedom man answers a call, becomes free from himself and serves. The free will (αὐτεξούσιον) is a concept set in motion by Justin and accepted by Irenaeus (IV.37.3).[139] Freedom becomes a choice which the human being, gifted with reason, is capable of exerting (IV.4.3). *Liberum arbitrium* is a *"potestas"* (IV.37.4), understood within the preparatory and maturing process of education (V.29.1), a test of man's reverence, fear, and love of God (IV.16.5). As the last reference indicates *autexousion* is already, at the outset of its long history in Christian thought, forcing the discussion on Christian faith into a chaos of contradictions from which theology can hardly free itself. *Autexousion* is no longer response but an autonomous anthropological concept. But Irenaeus ties his freedom to faith (IV.37.4), unaware of any conflict with the Hebraic concept of God.[140] Irenaeus would never have waived the heterogeneity of grace to which he witnesses in his work.[141] As a matter of fact, the main anti-Gnostic defense of a Father-God collides with autonomous freedom, the axiom of later Stoic ethics (*Epict.* II.10).

In this instance an important issue is at stake over the infiltration of non-Christian language into the speech of faith. Irenaeus uses a basic philosophical term for the communication of the Chris-

---

[139] The Greek concept of freedom has been introduced by Justin Martyr, *Apol.* I.43; II.7; cf. Tatian *Disc.* 7 and Theoph. *An Aut.* II.27. αὐθαίρετον in Athen. *Suppl.* 24.

[140] Klebba's distinction between freedom of choice (αὐτεξούσιον) and freedom of ethical capacity (αὐτάρκεια) cannot solve the conflict between Greek and Christian ἐλευθερία. There is some truth in his protest against Chr. E. Luthardt (*Die Lehre vom freien Willen und seinem Verhältnis zur Gnade* [Leipzig: 1863], pp. 13 ff.). One cannot claim that fifteen hundred years of church history were wrong until Luther came and discovered it all alone. The fact remains, however, that this infiltration of Greek philosophic ideas (Plato, *Rep.* X.617 E), often in contradiction long before they reach the Christian Era, prevented theology from understanding what Jesus, Paul, and John meant when they spoke about freedom, service, and obedience.

[141] For the contradictions in the concept of ἐλευθερία in Irenaeus see Beuzart (*op. cit.*, pp. 59 ff.) I do not see how Klebba (*op. cit.*, p. 142) could claim that we find the "early Christian doctrine about freedom of the will nowhere better than in Irenaeus." We would have to say: it is nowhere more contradictory.

tian concern. It seems feasible to apply the concept of the freedom of choice in order to express the Christian belief that God has created man in his image and expects man to serve him and love his creation. By this adaptation of a basic Stoic term,[142] a neat trap is laid from which Christian language can hardly extricate itself. Julian of Eclanum and Augustine are both dominated by a Greek phrase forced upon biblical speech. However, this is inevitable because only in retrospect are we aware of which concepts represent a threat and which do not.[143] For this reason the history of Christian thought reveals one constant correction of theological speech in which a later age visualizes the problem laid by an earlier one.

3. A special kind of Hellenistic influence on the semantics of Irenaeus can be seen in his language about progress. Man has not always been in the perfect stage (IV.37.6); "infantile" at first (IV.38.1), he grows through learning (V.3.1), advancing through an intermediate level, "adjection," [144] and maturity (IV.11.2) toward perfection (IV.38.2). Such progress is described in the Greek terminology of education as an intellectual ascent; man ascends "toward the perfect, approximating the Uncreated one" (IV.38.3). The biblical reference which he quotes is, of course, I Cor. 3:2 where Paul reminds the Corinthians that they still need to be nourished with milk since they have not yet grown up. We may, therefore, simply have the continuation of a biblical metaphor, adapted to the life and needs of the Christian community. Another factor may be involved, however.

We have observed that the language of Irenaeus does not seem to reckon with the question that was so urgent for Hermas: What

[142] Christian theology attempts to fight the Stoic "destiny" (Epict. IV.199) with a phrase borrowed from the Stoics (Chrysipp. Stoic. II.284). Bengsch (op. cit., p. 138) claimed that this does not represent a foreign element in the work of Irenaeus because he does not enter the academic problems involved in the employ of the concepts (p. 137) but illustrates simply the choice of good or evil in the Bible. Certainly, Irenaeus avoids the problems inherent in such a concept (Wingren, op. cit., p. 38); but once the concept became part of the theological vocabulary, later theologians could no longer continue to avoid the problem. And therefore, the view a posteriori proves how much of a foreign body this concept really has been in Irenaeus.

[143] Cf. Harnack's critique of Justin Martyr, Dogmengeschichte, I, 547 ff.

[144] The Latin word is adjectio, the unused English word "adjection."

about forgiveness in grace? The proclaiming language about baptism presents one chance in life, no more. In the Eucharist one escape is presented, the offering of the gift of creation and the partaking of the body of Christ; yet this does not reconcile baptismal language with the state of the congregation, viewed soberly and without any highfalutin' pep talk. In the Greek language about educational progress, Irenaeus cannot solve this problem either, but he can soften it, especially since he ties it to the language about the spirit, as he has also done with baptismal language.[145] If man has been created to grow, the imperfection of the saved does not betray baptism as treacherously as it seems at first; the necessity of an enlightened advance of man can at least in part explain the conflict between baptismal promise and the actuality of the congregation. We perceive in this instance that Irenaeus could not free himself sufficiently from some substantial notions even in baptism. The language of education steps in where the language of baptism seems to fail.

We can now see another aspect of the use of non-Christian language in theology. The Christian seeks certain thought forms in order to answer his own problems of faith. A non-Christian concept may step in where the biblical concept has been unsuccessful. By using this device the church usually replaces one set of troubles by another. Moreover, in the long run this escape mechanism will prove unsatisfactory. The language of progress does not hurt the Irenaean system; it is an interesting side line, but there is no principle of a "religious education" which would force the doctrine of grace into the categories of an Athenian school.[146] Still, the application of such Greek language illuminates the weak spot in the Christian's position. The language of baptism could not remain totally unguarded because it was moving toward a sacrament of deification. Baptism could have been channeled into such patterns. By creating a sacrament of penance the church has followed not Irenaeus but Hermas.

[145] Cf. Karl Prümm, "Göttliche Planung und menschliche Entwicklung bei Irenaeus," *Scholastik*, 1938 (13), pp. 206 ff. Benoit (*op. cit.*, pp. 191-92) sees clearly the relation between baptism, divinization, and growth.

[146] Bengsch (*op. cit.*, pp. 120 ff.) : IV.37.7 cannot be taken as an independent statement about "human development." God stands above human evolution (p. 124).

4. A last method of dealing with non-Christian language leads us back into the heart of Irenaeus' faith. In Christology as well as in theology he does not hesitate to express himself in philosophical Gnostic concepts such as unbegotten, an adjective so dear to Gnosticism, or *ousia,* the most important of the words in the Greek quest for being.[147] God the Father is described in philosophical language as *simplex, noncompositus, similimembrius,* completely identical with himself, a God wholly *ennoia* and wholly *nous,*[148] the pure rational being of Athenian thought (II.13.3). When he comes to elaborate on the Incarnation, Irenaeus does not reject Gnostic terminology—which will become so important for neoplatonic ontology: generation, production, emission (II.28.6). And in the description of the Holy Spirit he is not reluctant to accept language of syncretistic mysticism, "to partake in God," "to be within God," [149] "to enjoy his goodness" (IV.20.5). All such language seems to indicate that Irenaeus throws his theology right back into the fire from which he attempted to snatch it.

At certain levels this is the case. Irenaeus, like most great theologians, is no mathematical genius but a life in Christ, lived in the contradiction of speech.[150] To discover in his work the same thought patterns which he attacked is no difficult matter. Ultimately, however, it would not be fair to pin Irenaeus down at these points. Such seemingly contradictory metaphysical language stands in the service of the great mystery, which is the incomprehensible act of God's mercy. The conclusion of the previous passage II.28.6 is revealing; we do not try to create any definite system of emission— in modern language we do not attempt to counteract Gnosticism by creating another type of metaphysical coherence between the substance of God and the substance of Christ. Between vivification and

---

[147] Olof Gigon, *Grundprobleme der antiken Philosophie* (Bern: 1959), p. 20: the first definition of the self-understanding of post-Aristotelian philosophy was *"die Erkenntnis des Seienden als Seiendes."*

[148] *Sensus* is probably the translation for an original νοῦς, Harvey, *op. cit.,* I, 282, n. 3.

[149] This ἐντὸς τοῦ Θεοῦ is not ἐντὸς ὑμῶν of Luke 17:21 (cf. Walter Bauer, *Griechisch-Deutsches Wörterbuch zum Neuen Testament* [Berlin: 1937], p. 446).

[150] The contradictions which H. Koch ("Zur Lehre vom Urstand und von der Erlösung bei Irenäus," in *Theol. Stud. u.Krit.:* [1925], pp. 183 ff.) has emphasized cannot be denied.

the vision of God stands the faith of the believer (IV.20.5) .[151] The trinitarian language of Irenaeus cannot be pressed in all its metaphysical consequences; the metaphors are in collision and discord, the hand of God *versus* the Logos of God, the Son as anointed (III.18.3) *versus* the Son as fulfilling his ministry (IV.20.6), the Holy Spirit as descending upon Christ (III.9.3) *versus* the Holy Spirit as the unction (III.18.3) .[152] All this delineates the one axiom that God was in Christ reconciling the world to himself, in language serving the "salvation of those who were in distress" (IV.12.4), but not in language intending to establish a structure of heavens and intermediate beings.[153] The trinitarian language intends above all to involve the Christian in creation, atonement, and the presence of the Holy Spirit,[154] and the triadic expressions receive meaning and enhancement from the liturgy.[155] "The Father decides and commands," while the Son "carries out the plan of the Father," and the "Holy Spirit supports" (IV.38.3) is not a triad of a heavenly constellation but of the Christian life in relation to the creating and redeeming God.[156]

We are back at the Gnostic problem, only in a different key.

---

[151] Cf. Harvey, *op. cit.*, II, 217 n. 1: διὰ πίστεως is only in the Greek text.

[152] To construct a "theory of ideas" in Irenaeus (Wolfson, *op. cit.*, p. 263) means merely to read Philonic and other patterns into Irenaeus. As Irenaeus emphasizes, he has no answer, for instance, and denies to give an answer, to the metaphysical question concerning God and the devil (II.28.7; cf. Winggren, *op. cit.*, p. 41).

[153] In J. Héring's distinction between biblical, eschatological, and Platonic idealistic language ("Eschatologie biblique et Idéalisme platonicien," in *The Background of the New Testament and Its Eschatology*, pp. 444 ff.), Irenaeus stands closer to the Epistle to the Hebrews than to Origen.

[154] Houssiau (*op. cit.*, p. 23) describes this tenor of speech as an "esthetic conception of the spiritual life" rather than a system of logical deduction; this "harmony" of faith clashes throughout patristic literature with the Greek principle of reflection by which it is compelled to express itself. One has to warn against the remark of Houssiau insofar as it could be misunderstood (contrary to the author's intention, I am certain) as favoring an esthetic irrationalism which would be absolutely alien to Irenaeus.

[155] I am fully aware that I have not dealt in this study with another deep problem in theological communication, namely the conflict between prayer and thought, between theological and liturgical language.

[156] For these reasons, one should not be astonished when Irenaeus confuses anthropological concepts (Winggren, *op. cit.*, p. 153 against Klebba, *op. cit.*, pp. 164-65 and pp. 22-23).

All borrowing of philosophical or other language serves to verbalize and communicate the act of God in Christ; without such a process of assimilation there can be no satisfactory proclamation of faith. When we talk today about encounter, existence, and the I-Thou relationship, we are doing just the same thing. All Christian language belongs to the thought, worship, and life of the believer; but in every one of the non-Christian concepts tendencies are prevalent to become independent and to break the center. The trinitarian formulations in Irenaeus point toward the mystery of the Incarnation in which by the power of the Holy Spirit man participates, sharing in the life of the church, offering the gift of creation. Such language is not intended to make ultimate metaphysical statements about God's essence. It certainly makes metaphysical statements—that cannot be denied. But whatever metaphysical language is employed seeks to describe a mystery rather than to set up a system.[157] The primary concern is response and not metaphysical coherence.[158]

History must go its course. What Athanasius understood in his protest against the Arian metaphysics, the fathers of the fifth and sixth centuries will forget. Trinitarian language is taken as metaphysical rule. What has been a creative contribution in explaining the mystery of the *Deus-homo* is going to kill the spirit of theology by driving it into hairsplitting controversies. They will fight about *homoiotheleuton* because they no longer know that for Irenaeus metaphysical speech is no more than the servant of the response in a life that has responded to the newness of grace. Once more—we may call such language naïve; we may also speak about prophetic simplicity; in such limitation lies the essence of Christian communication.

[157] For these contradictions alone it is a mistake to claim that Irenaeus has a precise view of the whole doctrinal system which he presented (Klebba, *op. cit.*, p. 130). This is exactly what he does not possess.

[158] One of the best examples for this is Sagnard's interpretation of the symbolism of the four Gospels. Irenaeus' imagery and symbolism do not represent a cosmological argument for a philosophy of numeric perfection but a descriptive demonstration ("*une vue esthétique*" rather than "*une démonstration logique*") for the fact of the canon (*op. cit.*, pp. 193 ff.). Again, this does not reduce Irenaeus to irrational estheticism but rather expresses the ontological limitations in his language.

CONCLUSION

The language of Irenaeus is a theological language. It attempts to convey above all the truth about God, what he has done and what he said. Because of the nature of New Testament faith, theological language means communication of what God has done in Christ. Christian language is language about redemption. Such language witnesses, spelling out a drama whose goal is the consummation of the hearer in a new existence. When it fights, it fights for the axis; when it borrows it serves its core. But when it praises it fulfills its *raison-d'être*. Such speech is neither command nor cosmological information but judgment and promise. Responding or rejecting, the church and the world stand addressed by a narrative. But theology must search for the meaning and for the center of the redemptive witness. And thus theological language must analyze and sever, not in the playful mood of word studies but conscious of the fact that it is of vital importance how the axis is phrased. *Lingua quaerens intellectum.* The intellect in turn may break the speech; here lies the threat in all theological language. But the fact that whatever the Christian touches may become demonic does not free him any time from facing this very issue. There is no authentic faith which does not seek theological language.

All of us would like this to have happened in Irenaeus in a more exciting and artistic way. The argument could be more subtlely and less tiringly polemical. The development of thought unfortunately lacks the systematic clarity which would be desirable at such an important stage of Christian history. The speech of Irenaeus, as he himself is aware, is poor language. Yet in many ways Irenaeus has grasped the essence of the language of faith. It is a language which preserves the tension of the gospel. In Irenaeus we find again Christian speech oscillating between Jerusalem and Athens, neither a Greek language of ontology nor a merely Hebraic speech of the Old Testament, but Hebraic speech that uses Greek without being conquered by it. It oscillates between two poles of unequal strength but without being subdued by the weaker of them. It is language in a magnetic field where it remains in movement. Because of this movement we can never fully pin it down. The Hebraic infiltrates the non-Hebraic, correcting the latter, questioning, yet attracted by it because the gospel speaks from the covenant of revelation to the cosmos of darkness, making use of the language of the cosmos for its proclamation. From situation to situation, the proclamation and its correction take place anew. In Irenaeus the language of substance and ontology is always crossed by the language of the theocratic covenant and the free divine act of revelation. As the New Testament lives in the intangible, the language of Christian theology is led by Irenaeus into this realm between two poles.

Theological language of the second century finds its best expression in the small homily, discovered only some years ago, which is the work of Melito, the bishop of Sardes in Lydia.[159] This sermon represents only a minute part of Melito's extensive writings; yet here come to life the linguistic forces we sought in the theology of Irenaeus. In powerful concentration, the paschal homily proclaims the newness of Christian faith (7) as it develops the Exodus theme. It is a personal address to the Christian congregation (2), but in homiletic form. In rich imagery the salvatory work of Christ is told, prefigured by the Exodus, leading to redemption. The language in which all this is phrased reveals a rich creativity of Christianity in Asia Minor. Melito makes use of the Oriental style of asyndetic speech; that is, he juxtaposes parallel expressions in order to repeat and enchance poetically what he originally says:

> Why have you done, Israel, such new wrong?
> You have dishonored the one who honored you,
> You have held in contempt the one who glorified
> you,
> You have denied the one who witnessed for you,
> You have rejected the one who proclaimed to you,
> You have killed the one who brought you to life.
>
> — (73)

Melito uses the Pauline rhetorical antithesis in order to express the alternative of death and life, old and new (32). He falls into

---

[159] The homily is now available in a manuscript of the third century, *Papyrus Bodmer XIII, Méliton de Sardes, Homélie sur la Pâque*, ed. Michel Testuz (Cologny-Genève: 1960). Bibliography in the edition of Bernhard Lohse, *Die Passah-Homilie des Bischofs Meliton von Sardes* (Leiden: 1958), p. 8.

hymnic and poetic style when he praises the triumph of the risen Lord (100); and when he ends his sermon, he lets Christ speak in the first person, creating a captivating hymnic coda (103-4). This is theological language at its best: biblical and creative; solid in content and abundant in form; lively and poetic; a language with one purpose to express the merciful act of God in his Incarnation and to communicate this act to the world. Here theological creativity vibrates as it should, varied and refined, perhaps sometimes bordering on sophistication and a stylized technique, yet the opposite of monotonous instruction or a boring treatise of theology. Here language of Christian theology is alive! It is tragic that the work of this bishop, like so many hymnic and theological works of early Christianity, has not survived. Probably for dogmatic reasons, the church did not dare to sing the early chants about Christ for fear of their inherent modalism, although these works often surpassed other Christian literature in quality. The church kept the dry pages of Clement and Barnabas. This fact, too, belongs to the history of the language of faith. And so we are all the more grateful that a beautiful example of what theological language in the second century could be has come to life once more:

> You, Israel, have not been found,
>   you have not seen God,
>   you have not perceived the
>   Lord,
>   you have not known, O Israel!
> But this is the firstborn of God
>   who was begotten before the
>   morning star,
>   who made light to rise,
>   who made the day shining.
>   — (82)

The Language of Faith

What we have observed in our study is the first great act in the dramatic history of Christian speech after the close of the apostolic age. At the formative stage of the Christian church, conflicts emerge that have not died since, conflicts concerning man's speech about God. The observer might be appalled by the adolescence that is exhibited in the early church's struggling with the verbalization of its message; at the same time, in this impetuous search for the meaning of faith lies freshness. Naïve and bold, this age is uninhibited as yet by a millenium of Christian tradition.

As we stand in the pulpit today, or as we communicate the Christian gospel in a home or a classroom of the twentieth century, we face exactly the same dilemma which we encountered in the fascinating decades after the turn of the first century. And thus, the second century both precedes and follows the twentieth in the research which we have done. The dialogue of history is unthinkable if the viewer is not rooted in the agonies and discoveries of his own age. But as we turn back, attempting to understand the beginnings of the history of our faith, the past raises its voice and the documents begin to speak. Between the document and ourselves, something takes place.

Of course, the past is never as simple as historical research depicts it. But the past would never live unless its drama were outlined by choice and limitation. History does not reproduce reality; it is only a dialogue with reality which tries to delineate those contours that have meaning for the present. It is only through the vision, preceded and followed by the document, that the man of the present enters a few of the countless doors to a shrouded past. Without the vision "history" remains a lethargic mass or scholastic boredom. But after man has entered the past from his own perspective he must learn to see his vision in its proper limitation. Reality transcends all human vision.

With these presuppositions in mind we shall try to summarize the issues involved.

I

When God created the world he brought, in the language of Genesis, the animals to man and asked him to name them (Gen. 2:19). God did not dictate from heaven what human speech ought to be—the creature to whom he gave dominion on earth (Gen. 1: 28) was endowed with the freedom to create his own language. The word is the product of man's free creativity: "whatever the man called every living creature, that was its name." God did not name the animals. As God had created the world in an abundance of color and form, the speech of man arises from an abundance of the human imagination. Speech is form, created with beauty and imagination. In language, man plays and thinks; in language, communication is established and art is created; in language, man becomes man. When God viewed the world, behold it was very good (Gen. 1:31).

The creature to whom God entrusted the dominion on earth rose against the one who alone was to be God. "You will be like God." (Gen. 3:5.) The fall is not merely rebellion as an act of human emotions; it is also thought, conceived and formed into words. The serpent speaks. Pride, idolatry, and self-exaltation are verbalized by the same creative mind which named the animals. When man distorts his relation to God, he perverts his speech at the same time; communication ceases and the tower of Babel dominates mankind (Gen. 11:9). The freedom to create is abused, and with their language men glorify human idols, the kings of the Seleucides and the emperors of Rome. Because men speak different tongues they will hate one another. Nature is pronounced a deity. And thus, the cherubim with his flaming sword guards what could have been the meeting place of human language under the lordship of God had not man's words polluted the garden of human freedom (Gen. 3:

24). The idol has replaced the Creator; the speech of Adam is language in a lost paradise.

In a thousand years of Israel's history a language of revelation arose which we called "Hebraic." It is the speech of man in front of the burning bush and the train of Yahweh's gown, a language between promise and demand, a language addressed to a land and to a people. In Semitic realism this language reproduces life in the terminology of the earth, speaking in verbs, in time, and in event, but all this in relation to a living Lord; above all human speech stands the sovereign God breaking into history with the Sinaitic command and the prophetic message. "Now the word of the Lord came to me." (Jer. 1:4.) This language of the Old Testament is not purely "Hebraic"; already in Israel it is entangled in the turmoil of the civilizations of the Near East. Canaan forces upon Sinai the idolatry of its speech; Baal and the broken cisterns that hold no water (Jer. 2:4-13). The pride of Jerusalem poisons the language that was meant to glorify God in justice and in love; in faithlessness Israel betrays the one who calls (Jer. 3:19-20). And yet, despite all this, we see the existence of the language of revelation from the archaic documents of Old Israel to the magnificent literature of the prophetic age—a language about, and in relation to, the Father of Israel who time and again entered the course of his people with judgment and mercy. Here lies the root for the revelatory self-disclosure of God in the new covenant.

II

When God comes to man in his Son, he employs the Hebraic mode of thinking. Language contains an eschatological tension; it describes the immediacy of the kingdom that has already come with Christ, "in the midst" of Israel. Language is relational—Jesus never gives metaphysical statements about the nature of God and the essence of man; but rather, he always puts man in front of a divine act. "Many are called, but few are chosen" is not a topic for a sermon on predestination, but an address to the people of Galilee who are confronted at this very moment with the challenge of God in Jesus of Nazareth. His language is full of potent imagery. Jesus uses the plows and the foxes to describe a veiled mystery. When this language becomes theological—in Paul and John—it is thoroughly influenced by the theological language of the Old Testament. The speech of redemption is the speech of Israel.

Yet it is more. At the birth of Christ, the kings from the East laid their language at the feet of the child. Paradise lost offered its speech in response to salvation. The child of Epiphany does not reject the gifts of an ancient civilization; the metamorphosis begins. As the child is willing to receive the gifts of kings who bend their knees under a new star, the primitive church accepts the language that Hellenism has employed for centuries. When Paul and John describe the advent of salvation, not only do they not speak Aramaic, but they do not use language in a purely "Hebraic" fashion. The world of the Septuagint; the thought patterns of a confused age; the impact of an empire that brought relative peace to torn civilizations—all this touched the communication of the apostles who were rooted in the prophetic speech of Israel. The "Hebraic" is the stronger of two poles (it never permits a metaphysic principle of any kind to take over); but the stronger pole has accepted a second one —the language of the Greeks—that is not the speech of Sinai or Thekoa.

The language of the new covenant is the language of redemption between Passover and Epiphany, to use once more Ethelbert Stauffer's imagery of the Wise Men. God's self-communication reaches the world in the mystery and in the newness of Advent. Above all, New Testament language intends to verbalize the redemptive act of God in Christ. The language of the prophets is given new dimensions by this intent, "Son of Man" or "Messiah," "servant" or "king," receiving new meaning in the presence of the earthly and the risen Christ. The meaning of a Greek word can only approximately be determined by its history and background, vital though this background be for the study of the Christian concept. Every term, whether or not it comes from the Septuagint, has undergone some slight transmutation in front of the Christ, and therefore we are driven to search for the context which alone can determine the precise meaning of the term. The newness may be almost invisible or it may be significant—but the newness is there. Christian language is speech about Christ and speech in Christ.

233

III

God comes to man in an act which man cannot repeat. This climactic event of salvation is reflected in the canon of the New Testament. The event and its document belong together. The Christ who acted and spoke in the house of Zacchaeus is the Christ who acts and speaks in Luke 19. Because of this interrelation there can no longer be Christian language apart from the canon. Christ has always used the canon to challenge the world and waken his church. The canon is man's word about God's act in Christ, a human word which God accepts and through which he reaches the world. In this human document God addresses the world of darkness by the power of a word as he addressed the people of Israel by a Son born of Mary. In the canon the event receives meaning and becomes "word," in sermons, in parables, but above all in the dramatic story of the gospel. The verbal reflection of Christ's era shapes the speech of the Christian who puts himself under the Christ; this is why Christian preaching or teaching immersed in the language of the New Testament is so necessary for the education of the faithful and for the dialogue with the unbelieving world. The Christian needs the language of the canon, its theological terminology as well as its plastic imagery in order to be confronted with Christ, because the "Hebraic" use of language teaches us the possibilities of speaking about God, and because the form of the New Testament language opens the richness of speech about Christ. Do we not need the score of a symphony in order to reproduce its beauty?

The Christian who imagines he has thereby received a trite and untroubled access to faith is sadly mistaken. Here is no catechism with a few axioms, no simple formula of a conversion experience, no neat set of business rules that solve all problems of life. In a Satanic fashion the church and its believers have always turned the shocking language of the Sermon on the Mount and the drama outside Damascus into bourgeois principles that harm no one. We want to be satisfied with the humanistically understood command of the Golden Rule; the Christian intellectual endorses some phraseology in John 1; and the church is often happy with riding Matt. 16 or Acts 2 to death. The canon always eludes such narrowness. Here is no simple textbook for an evening course, but a complex and rich world of communication. Language of the canon between Jesus, Paul, and John; language both eschatological and didactic, proclaiming and demanding, refuses to be reduced to a single track, despite the fact that laymen protest and preachers sigh in view of contradictions and the lack of uniformity. Indeed, the life of Jesus is contradictory as seen by Mark and John, but the communication about Jesus, the Christ, cannot exist without using both. This is the riddle of the canon as well as its richness, and out of these two it has challenged Christians for two thousand years. The richness, however, is not unlimited; the canon does not accept just any form of speech concerning the Christ. This is why we speak about a canon. It stands over against the banal world behind Hermas and *Didache*, a world of popular moralism, and the high-strung speculations of the Gnostics, a world of metaphysical sophistication. The canonical affirmation of early Christianity represents the creative self-limitation of Christian faith. There is a point where the relation between the person of salvation and the word of salvation ceases to exist. But within this limitation, faith finds its elliptic realm of creativity, between the event of the Christ and the word about the Christ.

Speech about the Christ is not the Christ himself. To assume such an identity renders Christian language idolatrous and suffocates any fire which this language may be able to kindle. The written code may kill (II Cor. 3:6) unless the communication of faith takes place in power (I Cor. 4:20), in Christ who lives in the Christian (Gal. 2:20). As in the event of Incarnation, the word about Christ and the word in Christ belong together, but the first cannot claim to be the second unless this Christ is present himself. All Christian language is therefore penultimate; it can never claim the ultimate, the Christ, unless this Christ gives grace, forgiveness, and joy in his Spirit. This suspense is the chief paradox in Christian language. Between *notitia* and *fiducia* stands always the living God. A moral code seems to be beyond problems. The initiation depicted in the Villa dei Misteri of Pompeii has a progressive routine of conversion leading to the possession of the Dionysian mystery. A book on hermeneutical principles lays out the steps toward discovery. All three concerns are certainly significant for Christian speech: the ethical command, the emotional undertone, and the philosophic search; the language of will, experience, and reason. Yet beyond all this, the question of whether there is real life, abundant and fruitful which creates community and transforms the world, is not merely one of language, ethical or intellectual. The Christ who wants and chooses the church, the sacrament, the command, and the knowledge, is always beyond this. Only in this second limitation of Christian language can we perceive what it means *to say*, in the Christian community, in the reality of daily life: "Christ lives in me."

IV

At the shore of a lake in Gallilee, after an absurd command had sent him out to fish, Peter throws himself on his knees: "Depart from me, for I am a sinful man, O Lord" (Lk. 5:8). Such is the speech of the believer before the reality of revelation. It was a strange message that reached the Jewish people in the eschatological phraseology of Jesus, although they must have been familiar with a good deal of its imagery (Mark 1:22). One assumes wrongly that the disciples understood—although they were expected to do so (Matt. 13:11)—because only after the resurrection of their Lord, with the support of the Paraclete, did they begin to grasp what his words could have meant. The Pauline message of redemption and the Johannine word about grace were either foolishness or scandal. Only "he who is of God hears the words of God" (John 8:47). The alien characteristic of Christian speech, just as clearly present in the Gospels (the Sermon on the Mount with its shocking paradox) as in the Pauline letters, is the one cardinal fact in Christian language which the Gnostic, especially the *Gospel of Truth*, understood. Ultimately it is only in faith that the Christian grasps the nature of Christian language. This does not mean fatalism, but the Christian does have to expose himself to this language in order to grasp its essence. After thinking and speaking in the alien language of the Christ we begin to understand what this language really means. Christian language is speech from faith into faith (Rom. 1:17). By speaking the language of faith, we grow in this very faith and understand, in turn, more deeply what this language contains.

When the authentication of faith lies in this faith itself, it lies in the life of such faith and not merely in its intellectual recognition. As a Christian speaking the language of faith, I belong to the earthly assembly of this faith, the church of Jesus Christ. The word "forgiveness" receives its full meaning when the one who employs it lives in the community to which forgiveness is promised. All language about the Christ contains a relevant urgency concerning daily life (such as marriage, work, and politics) and is not merely an abstraction concerning earthly existence (such as death and life, matter and spirit, chaos and rest). This is where Gnostic language failed. The language of Christian faith arises from the canon, contains the traditions of the Christian churches, and speaks to the present-day congregation; the creed ties the community to the history of faith, and the sacrament uses God's own earth and man's product from this earth. Such language is meant to praise God and to worship him in the corporate adoration of the church no less than in the meditation of the individual, in confession, adoration, and intercession, as well as in the intellectual and ethical deliberations of the Christian mind. But praise in worship must become praise in service. The gospel speaks to the Hellenistic civilization and to the Roman world; here its language grasps people and changes them. The speech about Christ is directed toward the world, from the vineyards of Palestine to the offices of Rockefeller Center and the assembly lines of Detroit. The Christian community that praises God lives in the world.

"You shall love the Lord your God . . . you shall love your neighbor." (Mark 12:30-31.) The language of faith is employed within a double involvement of the believer. The man who has discovered faith is sent into the world. Alien grace creates service in love. Faith and love, praise and communication; the perpendicular and the vertical—between these two dimensions oscillates the language of Christian faith. We hear and we respond; we praise and we serve. The first part of the Lord's Prayer addresses and praises God; the second revolves around man, his guilt, and his bread. The relation between the two in the New Testament is not merely that of command and obedience, although Christian language must frequently resort to this simple didactic method. The story of salvation asks for a response and invites the Christian to imitate and to discover what this story really means. When I see a disciple falling on his knees before the incomprehensible work and word of Christ, I share in this scene and I am called to follow. The vision creates response—or denial. Francis of Assisi or Nietzsche—when response becomes life, the story is understood. The biblical drama can challenge man to decision and courage or to revolt and blasphemy. Between hearing and response stand two persons who give Christian language its tension and its depth: the *ego*, the Christian in his revolt, his failure, and his hope; and the Christ, the inscrutable act of mercy, the Cross, the coming of the Kingdom. Christian language cannot be severed from these two, otherwise it leads into statements which are either nonsensical or untrue; it can only be understood and employed within the relation between the Redeemer and the redeemed. How else can a Christian speak about "Christ, the Light of the World," or the church as the "bride of Christ"? "We love, because he first loved us" (I John 4:19) is not a statistical phrase but a description of man's response when living in the promise of Christ.

V

To be a Christian means to stand in a clash of two languages. The believer in Jesus Christ uses the words, idioms, and imagery of the Bible, such as *freedom and world, saved by grace, prodigal son,* and *mustard seed*. They represent the root of his faith, since they belong to God's unique revelation to us. These words and sentences are translated, which means that they are given another frame of life and of thought. "Freedom" means one thing in the New Testament; another in Greece, Communist Russia, or a Western democracy; and still another in psychology or in art. There may be a relation, close or distant, between Rom. 8:21 and these concepts, yet they are not identical. When we try to communicate to the Christian of a democratic nation or to a psychologist, we must use his language; we employ the speech of the culture in order to speak at all. But at the same time we are to preach not a political theory or a philosophic principle but freedom in the grace of Christ, the freedom of forgiveness and of service. Only when we put ourselves into both the speech of the canon and the idiom of our age can we proclaim relevantly this freedom as grace and forgiveness. The word of freedom and grace is translated and enters the factories and homes of our century, but in order to achieve the translation we need the other language which is used in these factories and homes. Every translation, every sermon and dialogue, every encounter among Christians and between Christians and non-Christians stands within this clash of two languages. To deny the conflict would mean either to speak Greek or Hebrew (and even then our language would never be purely biblical because we would still project ourselves into it!) or not to preach the gospel at all but succumb to modern speech. The canon itself mercilessly throws the believer into the tribulation of speech. Has not Paul become a Jew to the Jews and a Greek to the Greeks (I Cor. 9:20-21)? You cannot relate to the Greeks without using their language. This is the conflict of Christian theology. It receives its highest importance in the Christian sermon and instruction where the word of the gospel is explained, brought to life, and applied by modern speech. The Christian preacher and teacher stands in the middle of the clash.

Christian speech is canonical language at the borders of the world. The relation between the Hebraic roots and the non-Hebraic fragments in New Testament faith repeats itself in the clash between the uniqueness of the canonical word and the relevance of contemporary language that interprets and receives this word. "Border-line situation" designates indeed a mutable element in Christian faith; the church speaking at the border of the world fails and corrects itself. The language of faith needs a constant critical re-evaluation: the earliest theologian overcomes the nomistic paganism in popular Christian speech, the church of Nicaea checks the failures of Origen's Greek phraseology, and the subtle language of Thomas seeks to guard medieval theology from the failures of both realistic and nominalistic concepts. The struggles of Roman Catholicism with modernism and the Protestant clashes with Fascist, Communist, and capitalist distortions of Christian speech show the intensity of the conflict. When a church does not dare to stand at the border, it sacrifices its relevance and dies; but when a church does not accept the language of the gospel, it will similarly die by conforming to the world and by losing the power to speak. What a fascinating oscillation of Christian language! Again, the man who stands in the center of the clash is the man in the pulpit, because he may give his community Christian roots—or he may betray these roots and lead his congregation to betrayal.

When we say "clash" we do not mean apologetics which expresses only inadequately the relation between the two forces. It is an illusion to believe in a Christian language free from apologetics which is the point of contact with the world; but it is also foolish to deny that this very apologetics is bound to fail. Apologetics as a rational argument is effective only as long as the person addressed does not perceive its failure; the man who has read Nietzsche will not be argued into the existence of God. But the language of contact must be used, only the Christian transforms the concept of contact, and by transforming it he is never fair to the concept as it was. This is Paul in Athens. Whether or not he took the approach reported in Acts 17 is somewhat irrelevant because this approach is not Paul's creative contribution to primitive Christianity. One cannot censure him for having gone to Athens (and modern theology is wrong when it seems to do so); but neither can one claim that he made a crucial impact there. Christian theology must go to Athens but it must not be astonished when it finds itself rejected. We try to use the speech of Athens in proclaiming the gospel there —but if this gospel falls on fertile soil, it is despite the method and not because of it. All new concepts which we use to preach Christ are more or less faulty and must be surrendered after they have been employed; but there is no preaching without these concepts. This is the frontier situation of Christian faith. We do not cry because we know of the doom that hangs above the entire history of Christian speech. Failure or no failure, the hope of the Kingdom propels us into the midst of the clash; there is no lasting city (Heb. 13:14). And therefore we shall not be intimidated by the fear of using the wrong language as long as we stand in the biblical word and struggle for relevance in the contemporary one. All the gospel asks of us is the willingness to surrender our speech should it prove detrimental to the biblical word about Christ.

VI

Parallel to the clash with the world goes the clash within faith itself. Here is a basic canonical triad: the language of the Synoptics, the language of Paul, and the language of John. A second level of conflict is dispersed throughout the whole New Testament: keryg-matic speech about the loving act of God and mandatory speech about the command following this act. And, again dispersed throughout the whole, there are various concepts and imageries with different implications: atonement, justification, redemption, and sanctification; or the body of Christ, the new Jerusalem, the vine, and the bride. All this belongs to the word which presents the event of the Christ, but somewhere we must find the center. Our study on the second century has shown us that a great deal de-pends upon the focus, since this focus determines the whole rest of Christian speech. If the center is a "new law" of Christian ethics, then the whole tenor of Christian faith will radiate such legalism. Now when we compare the Gospel of Matthew with the Gospel of John we indeed find a common center, the eschatological proc-lamation of the good news, the redemption of man in Jesus Christ. Yet the delineation of this advent of the gospel has different em-phases—all we need to do is to point to the two different types of eschatological language. There is a unity in the good news of the two which stands out clearly when we set both against the *Gospel of Truth* with its crypto-Docetism, or the salvation by Augustus in the Priene Inscription of Asia Minor, or the philosophy of religion in Philo. This canonical unity between the Gospels demands a search for the center of salvation: what do the words about Christ mean in relation to each other, Matt. 1 versus John 1; the Sermon on the Mount versus the last speeches in the Gospel of John? How do we understand all these christological statements together? We are tempted to paraphrase Anselm of Canterbury: *lingua quaerens intellectum,* the speech of the New Testament demands understand-ing, an understanding which must take place between analysis and response. The clash is bound to arise. The history of Christian language is one desperate struggle for the center of faith. Paul's sharp polemic against the abuse of the elements (Col. 2:8), circum-cision (Phil. 3:3), or law (Rom. 3:20) is nothing other than the beginning of this history. When two apostles disagree as to whether or not they should eat with Gentiles (Gal. 2:11 ff.), they are already in the midst of this conflict that will not come to peace until the coming of the Kingdom. Because of a daring speech the first martyr is stoned to death outside the city of Jerusalem (Acts 7:57).

All Christian language may turn demonic: the imagery of love, of the bride and of heaven, as well as the parables of the prodigal son and the separation of the chaff from the wheat. Faith becomes an idol and the powerful message of justification reverts into a dead orthodoxy; the sacrament becomes *opus operatum* and the church sets itself over against the grace of God; the law strangles the freedom of the Spirit in the legalistic narrowness of humanistic Christianity. What does all this say? The rebellion of Adam returns in the Christian's abuse of his speech. In a correct faith; in the structure of a church, high or low, apostolic or free; in the laws of a discipline which quells the breath of joy; or in the idolatry of experiential religion—in all this man can again be like God, setting himself up as a sovereign Lord. We may shudder at the diabolic consequences which can be contained in Christian speech. The language of adoration itself may turn against God; the liturgical prayer replaces the living Lord; poetry becomes redemption; confessions sound like empty phrases. When the very word about Christ is abused to protect the Christian from the same grace that Christ has promised, and when "kerygmatic" language serves as a means for man's aggression and hostility, then we see how the sublime concepts of faith are reduced to tools for the destructive act of the serpent. Judas Iscariot was a disciple. By the door of the cathedral of Strasburg stands the devil who tempts the virgin; whenever a Christian hears or communicates the faith about Christ, there is a serpent lurking close by.

Christian language has a tendency to become sterile and empty. In the search for the focus there must be a security which the Christian and the church achieve and reach. But when that security is broken, not by iconoclasm but by the spirit that moves mountains, then the grace of God has shaken the church. Blessed is the generaion in which the spirit of grace blows through the barricades of speech. Alas, sometimes the church is no longer able to keep the prophet, and then, as a judgment, comes a split. The tower of Babel comes back in the pride of the church and the arrogance of men. But we cannot eliminate history. As Christians of today we relive, and partake in, the history of Christian speech. The ecumenical movement has driven the churches to share in their common history, in their speech—which means in their concerns and denials.

Every conflict of Christian speech in the past is a part of the conflict of Christian speech today, regarding the church, the world,
reason, or worship. As this study has profited so much from the
brilliant works by Sagnard and Puech, so the Calvinists, the Roman
Catholics, and the Anabaptists can no longer exist without the
other's language whether they like this or not and whether they
admit this or not; otherwise, they deny the judgment and grace of
God. When two churches split, both of them suffer. The Christian
today shares in the history of his language, and it is the demand of
our age that we become aware of this and reckon with it.

VII

The life of the Christian shall abound in the presence of the
Holy Spirit—this is the great promise we receive from the New
Testament. Humanity will be brought to life by the Spirit that
comes to us in Christ (Rom. 8:11); and living under this Spirit,
we shall understand the fullness of the language of faith. To a
world grappling in confusion and fear, agonizing in the opacity of
its speech, the Spirit brings the perspecuity and joy of the word
of God. Living in the Spirit, man becomes immersed in the depth
of the language concerning God, and the speech about Christ and
redemption receives meaning where it seemed full of contradiction
and nonsense. "To you it has been given to know the secrets of the
kingdom of heaven" (Matt. 13:11), believers in Jesus Christ are
told. The mysteries shall be understood where the Spirit is at work.
Life under this Spirit is, on one hand, the Christian's presence before God, with his mind and with his prayer, listening to the word
that reveals mercy in Christ, and adoring the one who is revealed
in this word. The Spirit teaches (Luke 12:12). Life under this
Spirit is, on the other hand, life in the Christian community,
service in the body of Christ, and the dialogue with the world, from
which he learns what forgiveness and sanctification do and do not
mean and begins to realize the significance of words such as "grace"
and "love." The language of faith belongs to such a life in the Spirit.
The "spirit of faith" (II Cor. 4:13) which opens for us the mysteries of the Kingdom is that force in Christian thought and life
which never removes the whole veil of biblical language concerning

God's redeeming act in Christ, but only a portion thereof; even this gives us a foretaste of the holy joy in heavenly adoration.

When the Holy Spirit creates new life in the freedom of Christ (Rom. 8:2), it is bound to affect the speech of one who has been freed to such a life. If a church comes alive, its speech also lives; and the deadly coldness of a written code is replaced by the vividity of speech in the Spirit (II Cor. 3:6). The vivid parables of the Synoptics, transmitted and formulated by the simple Christians of the primitive church, are no less examples of this creativity in the Spirit than is the vivacious style of Paul's theology. As the Spirit is freedom (Rom. 7:6), the language in the Spirit will be language in the freedom of the Lord (II Cor. 3:17), and this freedom appears not merely as emotional freedom, in intellectual content or in ethical behavior, but in the form of this language itself. The Spirit of truth, which teaches (John 14:26), presupposes, as we have seen, adoration before God and life in a Christian community; but it also results in creating afresh the language by which the mysteries of God are understood. The Spirit creates, therefore, in theology the language of "translation," i.e., the terms, idioms, and exegetical imagery by which we preach and grasp the word of God. In this the Spirit also creates new forms of addressing the world and of taking issue with the world, as Paul, full of this Spirit, faced the false prophet in Cyprus (Acts 13:9) and addressed the men of Athens (17:22). In preaching and theology, in life and worship, we receive through the Spirit the power, freedom, and courage to seek incessantly new idioms of response and new means of verbalizing the gospel, new tools in our understanding of biblical faith, and new language by which we can speak to the world. The newness of faith leads to the newness to speech; and the creative power in the freedom in Christ must result in the creativity of Christian language.

What does it mean, this creativity? We may ask concretely, what happens when the man portrayed by Picasso or Rouault, carrying with him the agony and meaninglessness of a century, comes to the light of Christian faith? A hopeless human figure kneeling in front of the cross receives the vision of redemption. There is meaning, there is new life, there is God! And now, faith turns into poetry which overflows with the joy of redemption. Only one who is hopelessly vapid can leave the place of a miracle without raising his hands to commence a song. When the church has been touched by the breath of the Spirit, this Creator Spirit will produce a chant: "Sing to the Lord a new song!" (Ps. 96:1.) The language of response turns into praise, and praise is the triumphant expression of adoration by the man who has been forgiven and who stands in front of the living God. When Simon comes to the final realization of his hopes, he cannot but sing (Luke 2:25 ff.). In its great moments of grace, the church received and created its new song— the Gregorian chant, the Huguenot Psalter, and the Lutheran hymn. Did not Jesus himself rejoice in the Spirit (Luke 10:21)? Around the throne of the eternal God, the triumphant hymn of adoration is chanted: "Holy, holy, holy, is the Lord God Almighty, who was and who is and is to come!" (Rev. 4:8).

The Christian petitions the Holy Spirit for the newness of his speech. "Lord, teach us to pray" (Luke 11:1) —this petition by the disciples becomes the prayer of the church, *Veni Creator Spiritus.* What Jesus gave to the disciples is the Lord's Prayer, in its concise form and architectural structure, a highly creative work; what the Holy Spirit gives to the church is a new verbalization of grace and a new speech of response. Only a miracle can shake the Christian church from its dull *status quo,* and only a miracle can enliven the conventions of speech, be they liberal or orthodox. This is the work of the Spirit which makes us free to create; and unless the Spirit of God shares in it and blesses it, all our creating is useless. The Spirit blows where it will (John 3:8). There are times of abundance and there are times of drought, in Christian speech as elsewhere in faith. Where our language fails, the Spirit will come to our support (Rom. 8:26). But we know that to a generation of faith living under grace, language will be given: W. H. Auden, Georges Bernanos, T. S. Eliot. The church has never prayed in vain for the Creator Spirit, even though at times it has had to pray in patience.

In its highest expressions, creativity in the language of faith is a charisma. When a church has a capable Christian musician who can write a new hymn, as Luther or Charles Wesley, or when theology finds expression as in *The Devil's Advocate,* this is a charisma of grace. Such charisma will have to be aware of the restrictions that all *charismata* in Christian life bear: it cannot demand exclusiveness or it destroys itself; there can be deep Christian faith where this charisma is not present in any sublime form; and this charisma in Christian faith serves with all other *charismata* the one purpose of proclaiming Christ the crucified (I Cor. 2:2) and of shouting the song of joy about the victory of Easter (15:57). What Paul writes to the Corinthians concerning speaking in tongues has value: the goal can never be self-edification (14:4) but is always the adoration of God (14:24), and in opposition to confusion (14:33) stands order (14:40). When the charisma of speech is authentic, the Holy Spirit will not destroy the center of faith but will move the bearer of the charisma to subordinate himself to it. However, creativity in the language of faith is not merely one charisma beside others. It is vital that the word of God reach the world, not as a boring, but as a vivid word; and whenever theology has been creative, it has created a new semantic frontier, from Origen and Tertullian to Schleiermacher and Karl Barth. Theological creativity frequently lacks the liveliness it should possess (as in the lamentable form of Irenaeus' work) and preaching often needs desperately theological keenness. Between these two, many variations are possible, yet where both are absent, or practically absent, theology and preaching, instruction and response, fail. Christian faith cannot exist without a vital speech, and vital speech certainly means, among other things, a lively speech. Of course, ultimately, here again the Spirit can intercede where man fails, and God can have children among bare rocks. But this is not up to us to accept or to determine. At the outset of the ministry stands the command to preach (Matt. 10:7), since this preaching leads to hearing and hearing leads to faith (Rom. 10:17). We are aware that God can reach the world with poor language, but woe to us when we are happy with this. The man who speaks about the foolishness of his language (I Cor. 1:21) is the man with the most powerful, lively, and original speech of the early church.

This leads us to the last crucial limitation of Christian language. All speech is language in front of the Holy God who comes to man in order to act. This is what we have called the "Hebraic roots" of New Testament language. It is the language of Isaiah before, during, and after the vision in the temple (Isa. 6). As is the case already in the Bible itself, the Christian will use all kinds of language by which to express his faith and his response. He cannot help doing so; otherwise, he would have to speak in tongues. We have said that the language of response must always ask if it is destroying the main pole in biblical relational speech. If the language of man is speech in front of a living God, then it cannot replace this God. There is no metaphysic, i.e., there is no inherent principle in any language to which God must submit. This is the key characteristic of biblical speech. The metaphor of "flesh-body" in Paul is not purely Hebraic but is partly Hellenistic with dualistic connotations; but this ontological metaphor does not create an ontology of flesh versus pneuma in which God is set ontologically on the side of the pneuma. "God is Spirit" (John 4:24) is not an axiomatic statement which is ontologically coherent—otherwise, the result would have to be a monism of the mind and a denial of the biblical God in his alien character. Such consequences, even if they seem justified by the occasional use of such language, would represent a profound misunderstanding of Johannine speech. The Christian seeks to understand his language. When Paul places the Spirit above "plausible words" (I Cor. 2:4), he does not advocate irresponsible irrationalism, but he knows that understanding of our speech depends upon our faith. This does not lead to Dadaism. But it represents a warning to all analysis of language. When Christian speech is uttered in front of a living God who sends his Spirit in ever new creativity, then I cannot force God into speech that is mine since he gave me the freedom to create this speech.

The language of faith is language between the event of Christ and the end of the times. It is meant to subordinate itself to the canonical uniqueness and it is meant to be new in the conflict with the world. In this tension lies our existence as Christians. Every time the meaning of Christ is rediscovered, a new language is born out of the clash of two worlds, the gospel and the present; every time this birth takes place, the church must wait for the judgment concerning this new language. Here lies a final double meaning of the Holy Spirit for the speech of our faith. We wait for the Spirit to challenge us to creativity, and we wait for the Spirit to point toward the failure. Is not creativity a step beyond judgment, in Athanasius, in William of Ockham, in John Wesley? By accepting the freedom to create in the newness of the Spirit we put ourselves under the judgment of this Spirit. The language of faith is never ultimate, either in the past or in the present. In the final adoration of history, a hymn of praise will fill the spaces of heaven; but until then the church is driven into hearing ever again and creating ever again the imagery by which it can understand, communicate, and praise the biblical miracle of God's love for man. The church must always wait for the end, ready to have its language challenged and renewed. Christian language is the speech of the believer who is rooted in the gospel, who speaks to the present, and who waits for the end:

Lingua semper reformanda.

When God came to man he touched the soil of his creation
and made it his own once more, Nazareth
the fish of the lake and the ram of the lea
A hand groping for a hand
lepers, a prostitute, the rotten priests
In a tavern of the town he drinks with the crooks.

Hate spits at the face that came to restore
what was made to reflect its glory
You crazy brother get home
They beg him to leave their hamlet
Lynch him, lynch him, lynch him
God is broken by the wood he formed.

Has life ever meaning?—of course not
only the dreamer hopes for sense in aimless beauty
But from the Body that stepped on the soil
cipher and ikon, a word
reaches the ear that long ago
ceased to vibrate to the wave of grace.

He speaks—and the earth breathes his speech
a turbulent and effervescent symphony of
an act that a millenium cannot describe
Wheat and tare, reaped when the clouds close for a last time
I am the door
Language ringing with the chime of redemption.

Life regained in the lightning of a dawn
meaninglessness turned into glory
A heavenly madrigal spans the sphere of
aeons dead with the agony of God
Two men
walking to the rhythm of a third.

Stones pierce the flesh of a youth
a planet shaken by a tale
that the mouths of babes commence to stammer
and the mind of a rabbi
tumbling in the light of a blazing desert
lives again.

Glossary

AEON—"Time," "World," "Age"; in Gnosticism the concept becomes personified. "Heavenly aeons" are metaphysical cosmic entities of the heavenly reality.

APOCRYPHAL ACTS—The extensive legendary literature about the lives of the apostles (Paul, Peter, Thomas, John, Andrew, etc.), dating from the second and third centuries and sometimes using pagan novels for background material. Its theology is frequently dualistic and Docetic. Because of the spectacular content, these Acts were extremely popular in the early church.

APOCRYPHON JOHANNIS—The second treatise in *Papyrus Beroliniensis 8502,* also contained in three manuscripts of Chenoboskion, an important Coptic document of second-century Gnosticism.

APOLOGISTS—The literature of Christian authors who addressed the pagan world in the second century, beginning with Quadratus and Aristides, leading to the philosophers Justin and Athenagoras, and ending with Theophilus and Melito. Tertullian and Origen really belong to another type of theological literature, although they have, like many others in this period, written "apologies."

BARNABAS—A theological essay, written perhaps after the last Jewish revolt of Bar-Cochba (135-138), which has an extensive christological typology of the Old Testament.

BASILIDES—An Egyptian Gnostic who wrote in the second quarter of the second century.

CHENOBOSKION—An early Christian town in the neighborhood of

251

which the Gnostic documents, first called the Library of Nag Hammadi, were discovered in 1945.

CLEMENT OF ROME—One of the presbyters in the collegiate government of the Roman congregation who wrote, in the last years of the first century, a letter called *First Clement* to the Christian community of Corinth.

CLEMENTINE LITERATURE—Pseudepigraphic literature under the name of Clement. *II Clement* is a sermon by an unknown, perhaps Egyptian, theologian from the middle of the second century. The Clementine *Homilies* and *Recognitions* are a novel about the lives of Peter and Clement of Rome, probably not written before the beginning of the third century.

DIDACHE—A church manual from a church in Syria, probably from the early second century, which uses archaic material of primitive Christianity.

DOCETISM—The consequent spiritualization of the historical Christ which denies his physical reality on earth; he only "seemed" to have a body.

DUALISM—The ontological separation of the world into two opposing principles. Dualism can have countless variations of the two basic types: an ultimate Iranian dualism which never solves the antithesis between light and darkness, or a limited dualism which exists under an ultimate monism. In Gnosticism both types exist, although the second type is characteristic of the great Gnostic systems.

EKKLESIA—The church, the assembly, the congregation. In the second century *ekklesia* is personified in the revelations of Hermas and in Gnosticism; in the latter it has become an aeon.

GNOSIS—"Knowledge" of the revealed truth. The Gnostic *gnosis,* a revealed and redeeming heavenly mystery, allows man to rise to the pneumatic world and thereby saves him.

GNOSTICISM—The movement with which Christian faith comes in contact during the second century and which is frequently found within Christianity with varying degrees of Christian substance, from the Johannine *Evangelium Veritatis* to extreme syncretism such as we find in the Naassene sect. The extent and roots of Gnosticism are difficult to determine. Pre-Christian Gnostic elements are visible as far back as the Qumran texts and the *Psalms of Thomas.* For historical research the distinction between pregnosis and Gnosticism is absolutely necessary. Old Testament language must have played a role in the rise of Gnosticism but of equal importance were the pseudo-philosophical forces of Hellenistic syncretism which created, with or without Christian support, the various Gnostic movements.

GOSPEL OF MARY *(Evang. Mar.)* —An apocryphal gospel of second-century Gnosticism, extant in Coptic at the beginning of *Pap. Ber. 8502.*

GOSPEL OF THOMAS *(Evang. Thom.)* —A collection of 114 Logia of Jesus under the name of a gospel, discovered in 1945 in Chenoboskion.

GOSPEL OF TRUTH *(Evang. Ver.)* —The important discovery of Chenoboskion, containing a meditation about the Christian revelation from an early Gnostic viewpoint. It dates back to the early phases of Valentinianism and may, or may not, have been the product of the young Valentinus himself.

HERMAS—A Roman layman who wrote a number of pamphlets *(Visions, Mandates, Similitudes)* concerning the problem of discipline and repentance in the church of Rome, in which he used one or more Jewish documents.

HERMETIC WRITINGS—A group of Egyptian writings from the second and third centuries, non- or semi-Christian, full of the philosophic and religious mixture that produced the Gnostic movements.

HIPPOLYTUS—A Roman theologian from the beginning of the third century who wrote a large work against the Gnostics in which he quotes them extensively.

IGNATIUS—A bishop of Antioch, condemned to die in the Roman arena, who wrote seven letters on his death voyage to Rome.

INFANCY-GOSPEL OF THOMAS—An apocryphal legend about the youth of Jesus, not to be confused with the *Gospel of Thomas.*

IRENAEUS—Born in Asia Minor, he went to Lyons where he became bishop after the cruel persecution of 177. We possess his attack against Gnosticism *(Adversus Haereses)* which, unfortunately, is only partly extant in its Greek original, and a demonstration of Apostolic faith *(Epideixis)* .

MELITO OF SARDES—A bishop of Sardes in Asia Minor in the second half of the second century. His extensive work, among which there was an "Apology" (around 170) is lost, but a small "Paschal Homily" was discovered about 25 years ago.

MURATORIAN FRAGMENT—The oldest list of canonical books extant, from the second part of the second century.

MYSTERION—The secret; in Gnosticism a technical term for the secret truth that is revealed to the Gnostic, the formula of salvation accessible only to the Gnostic.

MYSTERION OF THE GREAT LOGOS *(Myst. Log.)* —A Coptic document of late Gnosticism, closely related to the two *books of Jeû.*

PISTIS SOPHIA—A Gnostic treatise of the third century, a product of later Gnosticism, containing numerous details concerning the revelation of the great mysterion.

PLEROMA—The "fullness"; in Gnostic literature the "totality" of the metaphysical and the heavenly world.

PROTEVANGELION OF JAMES—An apocryphal legend about the childhood of Jesus, edited 1958 in the first ancient manuscript *(Papyrus Bodmer V)* .

PTOLEMY—An Italian representatve of the Valentinian school, he is one of the most Christian thinkers of Gnosticism. He wrote a letter to Flora concerning the Old Testament.

SOPHIA JESU CHRISTI—A second-century treatise of Gnosticism contained in the last part of *Papyrus Berol. 8502.*

Chronology

100-110

Didache; perhaps the *Pastoral epistles.* Cerinthus the Gnostic. Trajan Roman emperor 98-117.

110-20

Letters and martyrdom of Ignatius, bishop of Antioch. Correspondence between the younger Pliny, governor of Bithynia, and Trajan (112). Death of the Roman historian Tacitus. Letter of Polycarp, bishop of Smyrna, to the church in Philippi.

120-30

Gospel of Truth; rise of Valentinianism. Hadrian Roman emperor 117-38. Death of the Roman historian Plutarch.

130-40

Epistle of Barnabas; revolt of the Jews under Bar-Cochba (132-35). Apology of Quadratus. Papias, bishop of Hieropolis. Valentinus and Basilides.

140-50

Hermas in Rome. Marcion. The Roman emperor Antoninus Pius (138-61).

150-60

Martyrdom of Polycarp (156). Apologies of Justin and Aristides. Rise of Montanism.

160-70

Martyrdom of Justin the philosopher (165). Marcus Aurelius Roman emperor (161-80).

170-80

Martyrdom of Lyons and Vienne (177). Irenaeus becomes bishop of Lyons. The apologies of Tatian and Athenagoras. Melito, bishop of Sardes.

180-90

Martyrdom of Scili (185). Birth of Origen (184). Theophilus of Antioch. Commodus Roman Emperor (180-92).

190-200

Clement of Alexandria head of the Catechetical School. Septimius Severus Roman emperor (193-211).

Subject Index

Scripture Index